In praise of
the Backyard Berry Book
A hands-on guide to growing berries, brambles, &
vine fruit in the home garden
by Stella Otto

"written in plain hands-on language, clear and purposeful drawings,
the definitive how-to guide to small fruit gardening."
BackHome

"...enjoyable to read, easy to refer to."
Fruit Gardener

"Stella Otto has done it again! When we reviewed her first book, *the
Backyard Orchardist*, we wrote "What we like most about this book
is that it isn't intimidating. Stella Otto doesn't act like some expert-
from-on high; she gently and convincingly enables us to realize that,
yes, we can grow fruit successfully." Ditto for *the Backyard Berry
Book*.....you should by all means read this book."
HortIdeas

"likely to be much-thumbed as a reference by the green-thumbed
crowd."
Small Press

"one of the best books on growing berries I've seen in a long time."
Newark (NJ) Star-Ledger

♦ By Benjamin Franklin Award-winning author
♦ Garden Book Club Alternate Selection
♦ Rodale Organic Gardening Book Club Alternate Selection
♦ Feature excerpt in *Country Journal* magazine
♦ Reviews in newspapers, magazines and trade publications
including American Homestyle & Garden, Booklist, and Bloomsbury
Review

the Backyard Orchardist:
A complete guide to growing fruit trees in the home garden

Stella Otto's first book is:
   * Winner - 1994 Benjamin Franklin Award for Best First Book
   * Finalist for Best Garden Book 1994 Benjamin Franklin Award
   * Garden Book Club Alternate Selection

Here's what reviewers have to say:

"*The Backyard Orchardist* is a first rate effort and will fill a conspicuous void on the bookshelf."
   Horticulture

"This little gem is the finest single source of fruit growing information published to date....very comprehensive..."
   Pomona, newsletter of the North American Fruit Explorers

"....packed with down-to-earth information that the home gardener and master gardener crave."
   Journal of Small Fruit and Viticulture

"What we like most about this book is it isn't intimidating....she gently and convincingly enables us to realize that, yes, *we can grow fruit successfully.*
....bulging with facts which can be put to work by both novice and experienced amateur fruit growers."
   HortIdeas

"...the finest reference (by far) for the beginner!"
   Ed Fackler, Rocky Meadow Orchard & Nursery

"...a <u>fantastic</u> book. It will really fill an informational void on this topic."
   Julie Francke, Master Gardener Coordinator
   Leelanau County (Michigan) Cooperative Extension

the
BackYard
Berry Book

A hands-on guide to growing berries,
brambles, and vine fruit
in the home garden

the BackYard Berry Book

A hands-on guide to growing berries, brambles, and vine fruit in the home garden

by Stella Otto

OttoGraphics • *Maple City, Michigan*

Publisher's Cataloging-in-Publication Data

Otto, Stella B.
    the Backyard Berry Book: A hands-on guide to growing berries, brambles, &
    vine fruit in the home garden/by Stella Otto.
        p. cm.
    Includes index.
1. Fruit-culture. 2. Fruit-berries. 3. Viticulture 4.Fruit-varieties. I. Title
SB355.O78   1995   634-dc20   94-093935
ISBN 0-9634520-6-1

Foreign rights and specialty sales please contact publisher:
OttoGraphics. 8082 Maple City Rd., Maple City, MI 49664.
Phone: 616-228-7513.

Trade distribution by:
Chelsea Green Publishing Co.
P.O. Box 428, White River Junction, VT 05001.
Phone: 802-295-6300, Fax: 802-295-6444
TO ORDER Phone: 1-800-639-4099, Fax: 603-448-2576.

Manufactured in the United States of America

10 9 8 7 6 5 4 3 2

Contents

Section VI. Resources

List of Illustrations

Acknowledgements

When I started writing my first book several years ago, I enjoyed the support of many people who shared the excitement of my new venture. Now, as I complete this book, I continue to value the support of the many individuals who have helped me as this publishing venture becomes more complex.

Special thanks go to Karen Couture and Ellen van Gemeren for their critiques and faithful proof-reading, often under pressure of tight deadlines, and to Jan Riggenbach and Gene Logsdon for taking time from their busy writing schedules to honor me with cover quotes.

To Jim Nugent, Duke Elsner, and Gary Thornton for generous and extended loan of many reference materials I express great gratitude. Their generosity saved me many trips to the library.

Larry Mawby receives my great appreciation for sharing much of his experience in grape growing, and use of his picturesque vineyard for photo sessions. Dan Hartman receives my sincere thanks for sharing his knowledge on blueberries and lingonberries and his generous donation of plant material to use in promotion of this book.

Also, thank-you to the many others - Edward Bottoms, Kathy Buhler, Alexander Eppler, Bob Glanzman, Barbara Gorrill, Bob Gough, Barbara Goulart, William Ison, Dr. Jim Johnson, Dr. Gerard Krewer, David Kuchta, Ed Mashburn, Sucile Mellor, Paul Otten, Lon Rombough, Jack Ruttle, and Dr. Harold Willis - who shared their experience growing various small fruits and berries, reviewed manuscript chapters, helped with publishing technicalities, or offered their thoughts on how to make this book both comprehensive and easily used.

To Kate Bandos, for keeping watch on the many critical deadlines and prepublication submissions; to Peggy Robinson for her enthusiastic support and patience as we coordinate many aspects of producing and marketing this book; and to Laurie Davis for exceptional efforts on cover design and illustration, I express deep appreciation. I could not have made my deadlines without your considerable help.

Finally to my family - Eric, my books' best salesman; Karyn who waited patiently to arrive the day after our cover photo session and who has been my cooperative companion in the final months of putting this book together; and Francis who has made my job easier by picking up many loose ends as deadline day loomed - thank you!

Preface

Like most people....

........do you eagerly await the first ripe fruit of summer?

........do you find that somehow those picture perfect berries that appear on the grocery store shelf leave something to be desired?

........would you enjoy tickling your palate with a new culinary adventure?

Wait no longer!

You *can* enjoy the true sweetness of ripe strawberries or raspberries. Even in the smallest space of a condominium terrace, you can try out your green thumb and experience the divine pleasure that backyard berry growing has to offer.

First among its rewards is, of course, a ready supply of the very freshest fruit - yours for the picking. Coming straight from your garden to your kitchen, the delicate berries can be harvested at their peak flavor. Enjoy a yellow raspberry as it engulfs your palate in sweetness or the subtle hint of pineapple flavor offered by an alpine strawberry. Would a piquant syrup or chutney enhance your favorite buttermilk pancake or a roast goose? Lingonberries or currants will provide just the right touch.

In a hurry to get growing? Many berries will start producing within a year or two of planting and they can easily be incorporated into the landscape as borders, hedges, or arbors. Berry bushes will do double duty offering a colorful addition to the landscape with their display of fall color.

For bird lovers, berries offer tempting nesting grounds to provide you with close up viewing of your feathered friends, who, although they will likely snitch a few ripe berries, will also repay you with some insect control around the yard and garden.

Happily, starting a berry garden does not have to be expensive. Berry plants are reasonably priced, usually comparable to other small landscape shrubs. In most cases a small number of plants will provide all the berries needed by a household. If you are already a gardener, you probably even have the few basic tools necessary for berry gardening: a spade for planting, some pruning shears or clippers, and something to water the garden with.

Isn't it time you dig in? Plant that berry garden, and prepare to enjoy the fruitful harvest!

1. Success with Backyard Berries

Gardeners and non-gardeners alike are often lured to growing food crops out of a desire for self sufficiency and control of the family budget. While many grow the typical vegetable garden of tomatoes, corn, and beans, they also dream of the meal's finishing touch - dessert. Thus the fruit garden takes root. For both the novice and the adventuresome, the fruit garden can yield many delights for the palate. With today's "nouvelle" cuisine, the enjoyment of small fruit is not limited to the dessert course alone!

The Backyard Berry Book will concentrate on a portion of the fruit garden, namely the small fruit. Just what are the small fruit? Certainly some kiwifruit grow larger than cherries and mulberries are smaller than strawberries. The small fruit we will be talking about will be fruit that do not grow on trees. Also excluded is fruit that primarily grows wild as an uncultivated crop. So, for the sake of definition, small fruit will be those grown as a cultivated, perennial crop, on small plants, canes, bushes, or vines - strawberries, rhubarb, brambles, blueberries, lingonberries, currants, gooseberries, grapes, and kiwifruit.

At the Root of It All

As with many skills, learning the basics first will lead to greater success and satisfaction. Many novice fruit growers, in their haste to enjoy the "fruit of their labor", overlook the most essential ingredient to a successful fruit garden - preparation. As a horticulturist, I receive many questions from people who have already planted their fruit garden and now don't understand why an abundant harvest is not forthcoming. In talking with them further, I learn that little thought was given to the plant's requirements, and in many cases the chosen fruit is mismatched with the conditions in which it is planted.

So that you may avoid the frustration of a meager harvest, *the Backyard Berry Book* will begin, if you will, at the roots. By understanding some basic botany, soil science, and horticulture your chances of enjoying many fruitful harvests will be greatly increased.

Should you have any doubts and think these subjects too complex, have faith and read on. First, I think you will find delight in several points to which you will say "Ah-ha!, so that's it". Second, knowing and understanding the fundamentals behind small fruit growing will also help you with other gardens you may grow - vegetables, herbs, flowers and more. So, before you buy a single fruit plant, do your homework. Learn the fundamentals. Your effort will be repaid many times over.

Section I.

Getting to the Roots - Fundamentals of Small Fruit Growing

2. Site Selection & Preparation

To help any fruiting plant or vine grow and produce to its potential, there are several things that can and should be done.First, you will need to determine whether your geographic region of the country is suitable for fruit growing. Most regions fortunately are, but you will have the most satisfactory results if you choose those fruit most suited to your climate. The map in Figure 1 will give you a general idea of which fruit are suited to various regions of the country.

Second, you will need to consider the length of the growing season in your area. This is often the biggest limiting factor in raising fruit producing plants. Fortunately, most berries have a short enough season requirement that this does not pose a problem. Some grape varieties, as well as fall bearing raspberries, may not ripen sufficiently in the shortest growing season areas, however. The map in Figure 2 indicates typical growing season lengths around the United States.

The third factor to consider, depending on the area of the country you live in, is temperature extremes. In the north this may mean winter cold. In some areas of the south, extreme heat and humidity or very dry weather may require specifically adapted varieties and types of fruit. Your local extension service can point out considerations that may be necessary in your specific area.

After assessing the general suitability of your area for fruit growing, one of the first and most important, but often neglected, activities to attend to is the selection and thorough preparation of a specific planting site.

Selecting the Site

Naturally one of the first questions you will ask yourself as you look around your yard is "Where am I going to plant my fruit garden?". Often the most apparent location is alongside the vegetable garden.

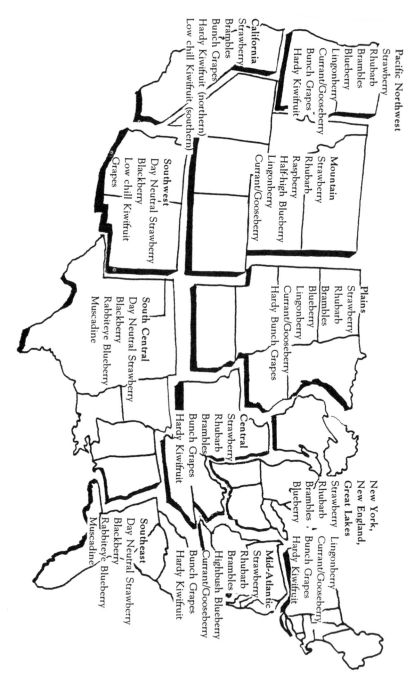

Figure 1. Fruit Best Suited to Different Regions of the United States

18 the Backyard Berry Book

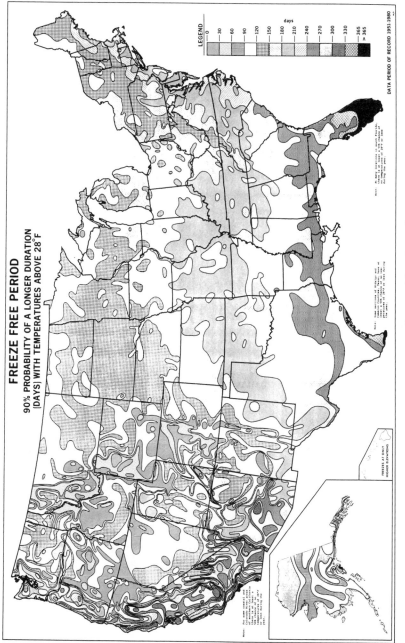

FREEZE FREE PERIOD

90% PROBABILITY OF A LONGER DURATION (DAYS) WITH TEMPERATURES ABOVE 28°F

LEGEND

days

0
30
60
90
120
150
180
210
240
270
300
330
365
> 365

DATA PERIOD OF RECORD 1951-1980

Reprinted from U.S. Climatic Data Center Report Climatology No. 20

Figure 2. Growing Season Length

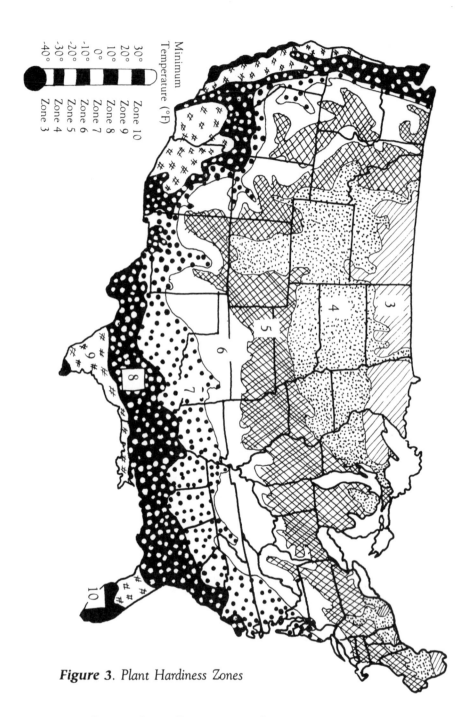

Minimum Temperature (°F)

30° Zone 10
20° Zone 9
10° Zone 8
0° Zone 7
-10° Zone 6
-20° Zone 5
-30° Zone 4
-40° Zone 3

Figure 3. *Plant Hardiness Zones*

20 the Backyard Berry Book

This is fine if the conditions are suitable, but often it is wise to look a bit further. To determine the best site for a fruit garden, it is important to understand the needs of the fruit to be grown. Some fruit, such as strawberries, are more prone to diseases in heavy, wet soils. Other fruit, such as grapes, may grow best on gravelly soils that are ordinarily considered rather poor, while fruit such as blueberries require well drained soils that are high in organic matter. If a number of different types of fruit are to be grown, it may be best to plant them in various locations around the yard. The chapters on the individual fruit will discuss their requirements in detail. Soil types and structure are examined further in this chapter.

Once you have considered the soil needs of the plant, you will also need to consider the elevation of the planting site in some cases. Early blooming fruit, such as strawberries, are often damaged by late spring frosts. This, however, may not be a big concern with later blooming fruit such as raspberries, so you may be able to plant them in the lower lying areas of your garden. Locations of higher elevation will be slightly less prone to frost problems, whereas low lying areas of the garden often become "frost pockets" that are the first to accumulate and hold cold air. If you have ever looked out over an area with low lying valleys on a cool evening, you may have noticed this phenomenon. The heavier, cold air settles in the valley as a fog cloud, while a clear layer of lighter warm air sits above it. When a small geographic area is affected in this manner it is often known as a microclimate. The same thing can happen in your garden (even if on a small scale). Regional microclimates are often found where large bodies of water temper the air for several miles inland. Smaller microclimates may be found near house walls that radiate a small amount of heat to the plants located nearby or provide them with cool shade in warm climates. Assuming the soil is acceptable, you would be wise to opt for planting your earliest blooming fruit in the most elevated areas of your property.

With certain plants, particularly in harsher climates, some protection from strong prevailing winds is helpful. Locating the plants near a building or hedgerow can often reduce windburn. Be careful, at the same time, not to plant in too shaded a location. Most fruit plants need six or more hours of sunlight daily to consistently produce a high quality crop.

Conversely, in some very warm areas of intense sun, partial protection from sunburn may be necessary. This can be accomplished by using shade cloth or planting in a location that is shaded by trees, buildings, or a fence during the warmest hours of the day.

Finally, to make caring for your fruit garden easy and most enjoyable, consider how close to your garden a faucet or other clean water source is. Also consider how close the garden is to the kitchen door. You will find that having quick, ready access from the kitchen to the garden makes fixing a last minute fruit salad or dessert much more convenient. As a result you will be much more likely to use your fruit garden to full advantage.

To summarize, first, it is wise to know the needs of the particular type of fruit you intend to grow when locating a small fruit planting. Then consider general climate, length of growing season, microclimate, soil type and drainage, elevation, sun exposure, proximity to water, and convenience before choosing a final location.

Soil

Once a general assessment of the planting site has been made, the first vital element to consider in depth is the soil. There are several factors to observe when studying the soil's productive capacity.

First, a good look at your soil texture is in order. If your planting area is flat and small, a few hundred square feet, very likely your soil type and texture will be fairly uniform throughout. If, however, your area possesses some obvious changes in elevation or covers several acres, you may encounter variations in soil types. Each one may be suitable to growing different things. The major soil types can be generally defined as sand, loam, and clay.

Sand, as most of us are familiar with it, is made up of large particles, relatively speaking. These are weathered pieces of minerals that are fairly coarse in texture. Large pore spaces for water and oxygen are found between sand particles. Little or no organic matter is present in very sandy soil. Water tends to run through sand quite quickly, providing rapid drainage, but also making sand subject to excessive erosion by rain. One place where you are likely to find sand is right around the foundation of your home. The sand builders use as backfill to provide good foundation drainage is typically lacking in plant nutrients and not particularly suitable for growing fruit. On the other hand, sandy soils that are well supplemented with organic matter and nutrients are often suitable for berries and vine fruit, which grow best when provided with adequate soil drainage.

Loam soils are composed of medium size particles. They are a combination of about 50% sand, up to 25% clay, and silt as the remaining soil particles. These soils are commonly found in areas of woodland or pasture where there have been many years of ongoing decay of old leaves, grass and other plant matter through natural processes. Well aged compost is another source of loamy soil. The individual soil particles of a loam are generally smaller than those of sand, giving it a finer texture than sand. Loam soil holds together as a more cohesive mass and has a substantially greater capacity to hold water and nutrients than sand does. Well drained loam soils are also very suitable for small fruit crops.

Sand   Loam   Clay

Figure 4. *Magnified View of Sand, Loam, and Clay*

Clay soils are made up of very small, fine textured, highly weathered particles. Clay tends to have very high moisture holding capacity which can sometimes become a problem by waterlogging root areas. Clay particles have strong ionic charges and are chemically attracted to each other. As a result clay soil can hold a considerable amount of nutrients but also has a tendency to become very hard, almost like cement, if allowed to dry out completely. This "cementing" happens because the very small particles fit together so closely. Figure 4 compares the relative soil particle size of sand, loam and clay. Most small fruit do not grow particularly well in clay soil.

In between these three main soil types are "combination soils": the sandy loams and the clay loams. As their names imply, they are a mixture of a varying percentage of sand and loam or loam and clay. These are often the best soils for fruit growing, as they normally have a better balance of desirable characteristics. For example, a sandy loam may have good soil drainage, thanks to the sand portion. Yet it will also have the ability to hold adequate moisture due to the organic component of the loam. Clay loams may have high water holding capacity, but will not cement as badly when they dry out because of the air space that is present between the larger particles of organic matter that make up the loam portion. These air spaces will also help prevent the soil from becoming badly waterlogged.

All other factors being equal, a sandy loam will be the most versatile soil for growing a selection of different fruit. As you will see in upcoming chapters, there are also a number of soil modifying techniques that will allow you to grow fruit if your particular garden soil appears at first not to be ideal. With some work it is possible to modify the soil pH, improve soil drainage, and increase the soil's ability to provide nutrients.

Site Preparation

Whether you are fortunate to have ideal soil for fruit growing in your garden or not - and few gardeners are - careful site preparation is necessary to produce a thriving crop. The most effective plan of site preparation is best started a year or two ahead or at the very least during the fall prior to planting. Site preparation basically involves four steps:

1. Controlling weeds & nematodes
2. Adjusting pH and nutrient levels where necessary
3. Adding organic matter to the soil
4. Correcting internal and surface drainage problems

Controlling Weeds and Nematodes

Most berry plants and fruiting vines have relatively small, shallow root systems, so they do not compete well with weeds for soil moisture and nutrients. It cannot be stressed enough that controlling weeds in the berry planting is very important. The easiest time to control weeds effectively is before any fruit has been planted. There are several ways to do this.

Many people today shy away from using chemical materials on their food gardens. Fortunately, several non-chemical weed control options exist, especially for the smaller garden. Rototilling, plowing, or cultivating the site several times during the growing season prior to planting will help control weeds to a large extent. Since weed seeds germinate differently depending on temperature, moisture and the time of the season, it will probably be necessary to till every three to four weeks during the growing season. Each tilling will bring a certain amount of new seed to the surface to germinate, so you will have to be the judge of how often tilling is necessary under your conditions and when major weed growth has been controlled. Once the weeds seem well under control, a cover crop can be planted to enhance the soil and keep the weed population in check.

Another method of weed control that is feasible for the small garden is soil solarization. Under this system, the soil is heated by the sun and maintained at a temperature high enough to kill most germinating weed seed. Any weeds that do emerge are smothered by a plastic covering. This method needs to be applied a full growing season in advance, as follows:

In early spring, preferably before too many weeds have emerged, rototill the soil to a depth of about twelve inches. Rake the area smooth, breaking up any large soil clods. Dig a four inch deep furrow around the tilled area and water the area until it is well soaked. Cover the planting area tightly with a large sheet of clear plastic. (Clear plastic will encourage germination of existing weed seeds which black or colored plastics will not.) The plastic should be touching the soil surface. The edges of the plastic are then sealed in place by covering them with ridges of dirt in the previously dug furrow. The plastic is left in place for a month to month and a half or more. This method is most effective in areas with hot, bright sunny weather and warm nights because these areas have both enough sunlight to encourage the weed seeds to germinate and enough heat to sufficiently heat the area under the plastic to killing temperatures. Although it works successfully in some years in northern climates, soil solarization can't be counted on to give consistent weed control every year in areas with short growing seasons, since the area under the plastic may not remain hot enough at all times to completely kill the weed population.

In areas with thick, vigorous grass, using chemical weed killers - herbicides - probably involves the least amount of work and is also the most effective. The planting site can be sprayed with a translocated growth inhibitor type weed killer such as Roundup™. When applied at the proper time, this type of product is quite good at controlling grasses and other emerged weeds without leaving a resi-

Site Selection & Preparation 25

Figure 5. Grass at the four leaf stage

due in the soil to damage berries that may be planted later. Roundup is best applied when the grass is actively growing and four "leaves" have emerged.

If you start preparing your site at any time other than early spring, if may be helpful to mow and then water your planting area to encourage weed growth. When the grass is at the proper stage, apply Roundup™ to the foliage at the rates indicated on the package. About two weeks after the planting area has been sprayed, you should see the weeds and grass turning whitish-yellow or brown and dying. At this point, you can rototill in the dead plant material and proceed with the other steps in soil preparation.

Note that Roundup™ will only control weeds that have already emerged and are actively growing. It will not control ungerminated weed seeds still in the soil. Since this material works by killing the active growing point in the plant and is quite nonspecific, it can damage or kill neighboring plants, trees, and shrubs if it is allowed to make contact with their leaves or other green tissue. So, it is important to apply this material carefully and only on a wind-free day. Chemical herbicides that have a long residual effect in the soil are not recommended for berries and fruit vines as many of them also act as herbicides on the plants you desire to grow.

Another soil borne problem that is best controlled before planting is nematodes. Nematodes are frequently found in soils where fruit has grown previously and in weedy fields, especially those with high numbers of dandelions. Nematodes are microscopic soil organisms. They feed on plant roots and often contribute to plant illness by wounding plant roots. Weak roots are not able to take up nutrients as effectively as healthy ones. Tissue wounds can also become a site for diseases to enter the plant.

Often, signs of nematodes are not readily apparent, but the trained horticulturist may suspect nematodes if plants are stunted or producing poorly for no obvious reason. It is best to test for nematodes before planting any fruit since control remedies are best taken before a permanent planting is established. Nematodes can be

26 the Backyard Berry Book

identified by submitting a soil sample to the local extension office or a similar testing laboratory. This can be done at the same time that your soil test for nutrients is submitted. Commercial fruit growers commonly control nematodes with chemical fumigants, but this is quite expensive, potentially dangerous and not warranted for the backyard gardener. The soil solarization technique described above will help reduce nematode populations. Another reasonable way for the home gardener to control nematodes, or at least reduce their populations to nondamaging levels, is in selecting specific non-host cover crops. Sorghum-sudan grass (Sudax) is one cover crop that does a particularly good job of reducing nematode numbers and is discussed on the following pages.

Adjusting Soil pH and Nutrients

Once the weeds and nematodes in the future planting site have been tamed, it is time to insure that the fruit plants will have sufficient and proper nutrients available when they are planted. Adding fertilizers to the soil or minerals to adjust the soil pH is commonly done at the same time that one would plant a cover crop. If it has not already been done, now is the time to send in a soil sample for testing. (How to take the sample is discussed further in Chapter 5.) In several weeks, you should receive the test results back with recommendations for materials and amounts to apply tailored to your site. To better understand the recommendations, you may want to skip ahead at this point, and read Chapter 5 that discusses plant nutrition and soil pH in detail.

Adding Organic Matter to the Soil

Planting cover crops, or "green manures", in preparation for your garden has a number of benefits. As mentioned earlier, nematode control is one. Of even greater benefit is the fact that as cover crops are plowed or rototilled into the soil, they add considerable organic matter to the soil. Organic matter is an important component of a productive soil for several reasons. It helps build a soil structure that retains needed moisture, but drains excess moisture well. Organic matter also provides more sites for mineral and nutrient exchange, thereby adding to the fertility of the soil. Some cover crops will add a certain amount of nutrients to the soil as they are broken down by soil microorganisms. This is particularly true for nitrogen fixing legumes. Nutrients of course, are needed for proper plant growth.

A number of cover crops release natural weed killing chemicals as they decompose. This effect is called allelopathy. Most of these chemicals work to kill germinating seeds as they emerge. You can often control weeds in your fruit garden site by choosing and growing a succession of allelopathic cover crops for two or three years prior to planting your fruit. Rototilling between cover crops will provide additional weed control.

Most cover crops are annuals. Some are hardy enough to survive cold winter temperatures and will continue to grow in the spring, dying in summer after they have produced their seed heads. These cover crops are often referred to as "winter annuals". In northern climates, you will want to plant your winter annual cover crops around late August. In southern climates winter annuals can be planted as late as November.

Cover crops that are killed by hard frosts are known as "summer annuals" and typically need to be planted early enough in the growing season to become established before the end of the season.

In different areas of the country, different cover crops have become customary. They include legumes such as:

Alsike, Ladino, and White Clover - These various clovers all perform similarly. They grow best when seeded in early spring and are useful for their nitrogen fixing ability.

Red Clover - Red clover is a short lived perennial that becomes established quickly. It too grows best when seeded in early spring. It is adapted to a wider range of soils than alfalfa.

Hairy vetch - A winter annual, hairy vetch, is typically seeded in late summer or early fall. It competes well with weeds and has some allelopathic qualities.

Crimson clover - Another clover, crimson clover competes well with weeds and is a good choice of cover crop where initial weed competition is expected to be strong.

Sweet clover - Sweet clover is a biennial cover crop that is a good organic matter contributor. Its taproot system is helpful in situations where it is needed to break-up a hardpan.

Alfalfa - This perennial, best planted in April, May, or late July to mid-August, needs well drained soil and high soil pH to grow well. Its deep taproot is useful for breaking a hard-pan, but can be hard to deal with unless you have strong tillage equipment.

Popular non-legume cover crops include:

Buckwheat - This annual grain establishes quickly when seeded in late May-early June. It will go to seed in mid summer if allowed to do so. Do not allow that to occur, unless you want it to naturally self-seed. Buckwheat tolerates low pH and smothers weeds well. It is not the best cover crop in dry areas as it has a low drought tolerance. It is also beneficial as a host for parasitic wasps that play a part in biological insect control.

Oats - This easy to grow grain is commonly used as a summer annual cover crop. Plant it in late summer and allow to it to winter kill naturally. It is relatively easy to incorporate into the garden in the spring. Residue can also be left on the soil surface and planted into directly to take advantage of oat straw's allelopathic qualities.

Rye - Rye, the grain, not the grass, is normally seeded in late summer for use in home gardens. It will overwinter and continue growth in the spring if not tilled under. For home gardens it is best to incorporate it into the soil in early spring since it may require larger farm equipment to do the job if left to grow for a full season. Rye straw is also allelopathic.

Sudan grass (and Sorghum-Sudan grass) - Typically seeded in late June-early July, this summer cover crop needs heat for good growth. To keep it manageable in the home garden it can be mowed and allowed to regrow several times during the season. It is a quick soil builder, adding large amounts of organic matter in one season. It is also a non-host crop that is useful in reducing nematode populations.

Several other grain type cover crops can be used, but they are difficult to incorporate without the benefit of typical farm equipment. Only those easiest to use in the home garden have been discussed here. Consulting with your local extension office will help you determine which ones will be most effective for your particular needs. A single cover crop, or often a rotation of a summer and a fall cover crop, are grown for at least one season prior to planting. Then, in the spring, prior to planting, the soil is tilled a final time and should be ready for your fruit plants.

Correcting Soil Drainage Problems

For most home gardens the job of soil preparation will now be basically complete. For a few unlucky but persistent souls whose soils are very heavy and poorly drained, some steps may still need to be taken to minimize problems brought on by excess soil moisture. The simplest solution to poor drainage, assuming your fruit garden doesn't cover acres, is to plant on a raised bed (or raised mound if you are considering random fruit bushes). To create a raised bed, simply build up a bed of well drained soil that is six to eight inches higher than the surrounding ground. The size length and width of the bed can be built to suit the space requirements of your chosen fruit. If you like, you can surround the bed with a wood frame, preferably of rot resistant wood such as cedar or redwood. Do not use chemically treated deck lumber as the chemicals can easily leach into your soil. Be sure the soil in the bed is well supplemented with organic matter. Some sand can also be added to improve drainage, but be aware that if you need to go to this extent to modify your soil, you may face a continuous challenge in fruit growing.

Initially, building raised beds does entail a certain amount of work that may tempt some gardeners to try to avoid this chore. The effort is worth the payoff, however. If small fruit plants are planted in poorly drained, heavy soils, most will soon succumb to a variety of root diseases that thrive in wet, oxygen poor conditions. The one-time effort of creating raised beds should eliminate the futile effort of regularly replanting an unsuitable site.

Windbreaks

Before this chapter on site preparation is closed, a short word about windbreaks is in order. In most cases, the fruit garden should be located so as to receive some air circulation but still avoid strong winds that can damage the fruit or plants. In some situations this may not be possible - the best soil or other site attributes may occur on the windiest location. In such a case a windbreak can help solve the problem. Windbreaks can also function like a snow fence in harsh northern climates.

Typical windbreaks are created by planting a row of closely spaced, fast growing trees. Poplar is often used. For more permanent year round protection, a row of poplar is planted behind a slower growing row of evergreens. If you are establishing a new hedgerow, a general rule of thumb is that a windbreak can be expected to offer protection to a distance of seven to eight times its height.

3. Plant Selection & Propagation

One of the keys to a productive fruit garden is the selection of healthy, vigorous plants. What you will want to look for as desirable qualities in your plants will be similar, whether it's a blueberry, strawberry, bramble or any other small fruit plant you are purchasing.

Selecting a Healthy Plant

Nursery catalogs and local garden centers are both handy places to find fruit plants for your garden. Most mail order catalogs have the advantage of offering a wide selection, including many of the newest varieties. Indeed, with so many varieties that sound absolutely wonderful, it can be hard to make the final choice. Mail order catalogs also often have a selection of the less common or specialty types of fruit that may be difficult to find at local garden centers.

Local garden centers tend to have a smaller array to choose from, but offer the advantage of varieties that have probably grown and produced well locally for a long time. At a local garden center you can also inspect your selection directly, while you will have to trust that the mail order plant will arrive in healthy condition. Whether you decide to purchase your plants locally or by mail order, there are a few points you should look for or expect of a high quality plant.

1. Look for plants that are certified virus free. For many small fruit plants, viruses shorten their life, reduce their productivity, and decrease the quality of the crop. Although you will not be able to tell by appearance whether a plant is virus free, that information is often on the package or advertised in the catalog. In most states the Department of Agriculture inspects nursery fields regularly and issues a certificate to those growers whose plants appear free of viruses. Since there are no cures once a virus is introduced into your berry patch, the best prevention is buying *certified* virus free stock.

2. The plant should appear to be in good health overall. In some cases this may be difficult to determine if the plant is dormant. Dormant strawberry plants often look like nothing more than a bunch of roots with a few scrawny leaves attached and a dormant rhubarb root looks about as alive as a gnarled up chunk of old, dead wood. Several of the points below should help you evaluate the plant's health in spite of its initial appearance.

3. The roots should be strong and vigorous. Brittle, small roots indicate that they have dried out and will grow poorly when planted.

4. Plants should be free of mold and rot. Sometimes a little bit of white, cottony mold may appear on plants that have been held at high humidity in cold storage. This would really not pose a problem. A plant that is covered with lots of mold or dark, rotten, water soaked areas may have been held in conditions that were too moist and is not a good buy.

5. If you are purchasing a bush, the dormant branches should appear healthy and with a good diameter. (An eighth of an inch or better.) Branches that are brittle and needle-thin indicate a weak or dried out plant. Buds should be plump, not dry and falling off.

6. If the plant is potted, it is best to choose one early in the season that is relatively dormant; not too far leafed out. Fully leafed out plants or those planted during the summer will have more difficulty adjusting to transplanting and will require much closer attention to avoid drying out.

Types of Nursery Stock

When buying plants you will find that they are likely to be available in one of the following forms:

1. Bareroot, dormant plants. This is what you are most likely to receive from a mail order catalog. Often the roots are wrapped in damp moss or other packaging to keep them from drying out. These plants should be kept cool to retain dormancy and planted as soon as possible after danger of severe frost

Figure 6. Bareroot plant

is past. (A light frost isn't usually a concern with dormant plants.)

32 the Backyard Berry Book

Dormant, bareroot plants are easy and inexpensive to ship. Also dormant plants usually make a fast start in growth once planted in proper conditions.

2. Tissue cultured plugs. Relatively new on the nursery scene, these plants have been propagated from a small piece of growing shoot tip and raised in a nutrient medium or potting soil plug in a controlled laboratory or greenhouse environment. This has allowed for better selection of virus free stock than with field grown plants. Since these plants have been raised in a controlled environment, they should be planted only after all danger of frost is past and watered very carefully for several weeks after planting to avoid drying out. To help some of these plants to better withstand the change from greenhouse to outdoors, a few nurseries are now offering what is known as "nursery mature" stock. These plants have

Figure 7. Tissue cultured plug

been acclimated for several months by growing outdoors in a nursery.

Although more costly than other types of nursery stock, once established, tissue cultured plants appear to grow more vigorously and to be slightly more productive. Fruit plants most likely to be tissue cultured are strawberries, raspberries, and blueberries.

3. Balled and burlapped. These may be dormant or starting to grow in the spring. Try to select the more dormant specimens. Typically, these plants have been dug from the ground in early spring while still dormant. A ball of dirt has been retained around the roots, and the root ball has been wrapped in a piece of burlap. This protects the roots somewhat from excessive transplant shock and is especially useful when transplanting large, older plants. Most balled and burlapped plants will be found at local nurseries and are bushes such as currant or blueberry.

Figure 8. Balled and Burlapped Plant

Plant Selection & Propagation 33

4. Potted. Basically similar to balled and burlapped, these plants may have grown in the pot for a season or two. Although summer planting is not highly recommended for fruit plants, if you must summer plant, a potted plant will suffer the least transplant shock. Blueberries and lingonberries are available as dormant potted stock.

After gaining some experience with fruit plants, you will find that it is usually preferable for the home gardener to purchase dormant bareroot stock for strawberries, rhubarb, and vine fruits. Planted early in the spring, they really take the least amount of fuss and adjust easily to transplanting. Tissue cultured plants, if you are willing to make the initial effort of helping them overcome the transplant shock in the first few months, will often out-grow and out-produce conventionally propagated plants within a few short growing seasons. Tissue cultured brambles are recommended for best results.

Dormant, potted plants that are two or three years old are the best choice for bush fruits. Plant them when they are dormant and avoid large older bushes. Older plants have often grown in the pot for years because they did not grow well when they were young and may grow poorly when planted if they have become rootbound.

Selecting Specific Varieties

Once you have decided what type of fruit to grow, you will still need to decide what specific varieties will best meet your needs and garden conditions. When choosing specific varieties, asking yourself the following questions may help you narrow the choices:

1. Is the berry tasty? Some varieties have stronger flavor than others or are sweeter. Some varieties are more consistent in their flavor from year to year than others, as well.

2. How is the fruit's overall quality? Is it soft or firm? Does it ripen quickly or will it hold on the plant for a day or two if I don't get it picked right away?

3. How will I use my berries; eat them fresh, freeze them, or make jam or wine? For fresh eating you will undoubtedly want a sweet juicy berry, while smaller, tarter berries often make better jam. For frozen berries, you will probably want ones that are fairly firm and don't just turn to mush when thawed.

4. How disease resistant is the variety I am considering? This is especially important if you want to grow your crop under strict organic methods. In some cases, disease or pest resistance is achieved

by grafting a desirable variety to a particular rootstock that is resistant to soil borne organisms for which there is no other cure.

5. Is the variety I am considering well suited to my climate and my garden conditions?

If you are still not sure what variety will be best for you, try a small planting of several varieties that seem initially suitable. After evaluating them for a few seasons, you can then plant more of the ones you liked best. Another way to get some variety suggestions is by talking to local extension agents, master gardeners, or a neighbor who has had success growing fruit.

Propagation

Most home gardeners who have had several seasons of success with a small planting of fruit often think of increasing the size of their berry patch. At that time, thoughts often turn to the idea of propagating their own plants rather than purchasing additional plants. For many small fruit plants, propagation can be an interesting and rewarding challenge. For certain other fruit, it is either not warranted or very difficult to do. Choosing the right propagation method will help make your endeavor successful. To ensure best results and prevent the spread of diseases and root borne pests, propagate only healthy pest and disease free plants. Propagating weak, diseased plants will prove to be a false economy. If you do not have good plant stock to work from, you would be well advised to purchase new stock. For those readers who would like to give propagation a try, the following methods hold the most promise.

Tip Layering

Tip layering is the method of propagation in which new plants are produced by encouraging the growing tips of existing plants to take root and eventually severing the newly rooted plant from the old,

Figure 9. *Tip Layering*

original plant. As you will see in the bramble chapters, black raspberries, purple raspberries, and blackberries readily tip layer. European gooseberries are also propagated by tip layering. To encourage these plants to tip layer, bend the canes over gently so that the tip of the canes make contact with the soil. This is often quite easy, as these brambles have a tendency to do just that naturally. In order to secure the cane tip, it can be held down loosely with a piece of bent wire and then covered with a mound of dirt. Remember to allow several inches of the cane tip to stick out on the other side of the dirt mound. By the end of the summer, the layered tip should have begun to root. You can check by gently scooping back the dirt a bit. At that time, clip the original cane near the mound so that you leave the roots attached to the new tip. If you would like to move the plants to a new location, such as to form a new row of canes, you can transplant it early the following spring.

Runners

A natural variation of layering is the production of runner plants. June bearing strawberries, and to a much lesser extent everbearing strawberries, send out runner plants after fruiting. Runner plants are new "daughter" plants that develop on a stalk attached to the original "mother" plant. When you renovate a strawberry patch, as discussed in

Figure 10. Runners

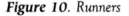

chapter 10, you are encouraging the growth and development of additional runner plants. In most cases, these runner plants will grow near the same location as the mother plants. If you would like to start a new strawberry patch, it is possible to transplant the rooted runner plants, or try rooting the runners in separate flower pots for relocation later. Once the runners have an established root system, simply clip the stalk that connects them to the mother plant and transplant them to your new, prepared bed. Usually the first and second daughter plants produced by each mother plant will be the strongest.

Rooted Cuttings

Rooted cuttings are clippings taken from existing plants, that have been grown to develop a root system of their own. Rooted cuttings can be used to increase your supply of most berry bushes - currants, gooseberries, and blueberries, as well as some grapes. In most cases, these plants are not grafted to another root system the way fruit trees are, so it is quite possible to take cuttings of healthy branches and encourage them to root. One exception to this is the European grapes varieties. Their root system is very susceptible to a plant louse (grape phylloxera - more details on this problem are in chapter 18) that is found in North America. They must therefore be grafted to a resistant rootstock. There are two types of rooted cuttings, softwood and hardwood. Softwood cuttings are generally taken from green, actively

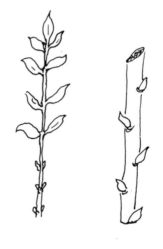

Figure 11. Softwood Cuttings

growing wood during the spring or summer. Softwood cuttings are often the most successful method for reproducing hard-to-propagate species. Hardwood cuttings are usually taken from mature, one year old wood during the dormant season, typically in late winter. They are often slower to start rooting than softwood cuttings, but do not have as exacting requirements for moisture.

To take a softwood cutting of the bush fruits, select healthy, actively growing one year old wood; preferably about 1/8 inch in diameter. Cut pieces that are about four inches long for blueberries, six to eight inches long for currants, and ten to twelve inches long for American gooseberry cuttings. Make your bottom cut just below a node. Remove the leaves from the lower half of the cutting. The end can be dipped in a rooting hormone powder, but studies have shown variable results in the effectiveness of this practice. It seems to work best for gooseberry and currant. Stick the cut end into sterile potting soil, sand, or other rooting medium, so that only one or two buds are exposed above the surface. If you grow your cuttings in planting flats (old wood cherry lugs work nicely), providing heat below the roots with a heating mat will help speed root development. A bottom temperature of 72°F. has been found to be most favorable for developing roots in most cases. Within four to six weeks, the cutting should have formed a callus and started to root. Once the roots are several inches long. The cuttings can be acclimated to the outdoors and transplanted.

Since grapes "bleed" sap heavily when cut during the growing season, grapes are often propagated as hardwood cuttings during the dormant season. Prunings in good condition can be used as long as they are treated soon after being removed from the vine. Be sure to select only one year old wood and be sure to keep the cuttings oriented with the proper end up, that is with the growing tip up and the root end down. One way to distinguish top and bottom is to make a slanted cut on one end and a flat cut on the other.Once the cutting pieces have been trimmed to size, they can be bundled and wrapped in newspaper or other material to protect them from drying out. Bury the whole bundle in sand in a marked spot and protect it from mice. Late in the winter or early spring, retrieve the bundle. Treat with rooting hormone and place them in a flat for rooting just as you would with the bush fruit.

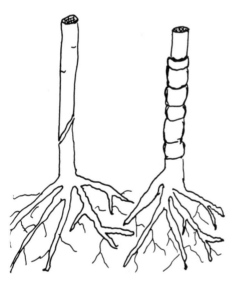

Figure 12. *Grape scion and rootstock being grafted in a bench graft*

Grafting

Grafting is a technique commonly used for propagation of fruit trees. It is also used to propagate grapes that are to be grown on pest and disease resistant rootstock (more on this is found in chapter 19). Typically, grafted grapes are produced by a method known as bench grafting. A dormant grape scion about eight inches long is cut with an angle at the bottom (or root end of the piece). This angle is matched to as similar a cut as possible at the top, or shoot end, of the dormant rootstock. The graft is secured in place by wrapping with a special budding wrap that may be a piece of 1/4 inch wide degradable elastic or stretchy wax material. The grafts are then held in cold storage until early spring, just before bud break. Once the ground is thawed in spring and danger of severe frost is past, the grafts are planted out in a nursery and grown for one or two seasons before transplanting to the vineyard.

Tissue Culture

Tissue culture is the newest form of propagation used for cloning small fruit plants. Since it requires completely sterile conditions, it is not usually performed by the home gardener. It requires expensive equipment and is commonly done in a laboratory setting, so we will not discuss it in detail here. Essentially, a small piece (or just a few cells) of the plant's growing tip are carefully removed and placed on a nutrient growing media in a test tube or petri dish. Once new rootlets develop, the plant is transferred to a soil plug to mature. This method is very useful in insuring that plant stock is virus free and is becoming quite commonly used today to propagate brambles.

Division

Rhubarb and red and yellow raspberries can all be propagated by division. The raspberries have a natural tendency to send suckers up along their entire root system. To transplant these suckers, merely cut through the roots with a sharp spade, leaving some root with the original plant and some with the new sucker. Plant the sucker in its new location, just as you would a newly purchased plant.

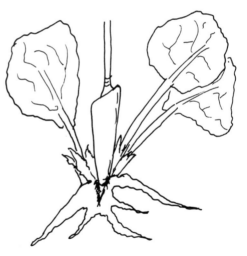

Figure 13. Division

To divide a rhubarb root, again with a sharp spade, cut the root piece of a large plant into one or more plants, each with several bud eyes. Plant it as you would any newly purchased plant.

Propagating Patented Varieties

Before you start propagating plants though, be aware that certain varieties are patented and propagation rights are legally protected just like other items holding a patent. Some people are under the misconception that as long as you are propagating for your own use and not for sale, propagating patented material is allowed. That is not the case, so be aware. Nurseries have indeed prosecuted some cases of patent infringement.

It is normally easy to tell if you have purchased a patented variety because this information is usually advertised in the catalog or on the plant tag. You can also obtain information on patented varieties from the patent office in Washington, D.C. or the nursery where you purchased the original plants. Several 1993-94 issues of *Pomona*, the journal of the North American Fruit Explorers, also contain listings of patented varieties, the patent holder, and when the patent will expire. You may want to write this organization to become a member and purchase back issues. (The address is listed in the resource section at the end of this book.)

4. Understanding Berry Botany

Most gardeners begin their hobby pursuit by literally digging in and getting their hands dirty. As hands-on experience is acquired, often a desire blossoms for a better understanding of how or why plants grow and produce in their particular way. To satisfy this desire for greater knowledge an increasing number of gardeners are turning to special interest garden clubs, courses such as the Master Gardener programs, or books on botany. To help you understand more about how berries and other small fruits grow, this chapter will discuss some basic botany.

Since the flower is the first visible sign, each spring, of a future crop, it is a good place to start. Without the flower, there would be no fruit and without the fruit there would, at some point in the larger scheme of things, be no preservation of the species. The flowers of most fruit contain all the structures, both male and female, necessary for reproduction. These include the female parts which are:

The stigma - the sticky receptive surface that pollen becomes attached to during the pollination process.

The style - the "stalk" that the stigma is located on and through which the germinated pollen grain grows until it reaches the embryo sac.

The ovary - the fleshy area that serves to protect the ovule and also eventually becomes the fleshy part of the fruit.

The ovule - the structure inside the flower that contains the female genetic material and that will eventually become the seed or pit of the fruit.

The pistil - the stigma, style and ovary together are collectively called the pistil.

The carpel - the portion of the pistil that contains the ovule. In some cases, the pistil will contain multiple carpels.

The male parts of the flower are:

The pollen grain - a small dust size particle that serves as the location of the male genetic material.

The anther - the structure that houses two sacs that contain the many pollen grains.

The filament - a stalk upon which the anther is held to elevate it and make the pollen more accessible.

Together the anther and filament are often called **the stamen.** Petals and sepals serve to protect the reproductive parts. The colorful petals may also serve as a visual way to attract bees to the flower.

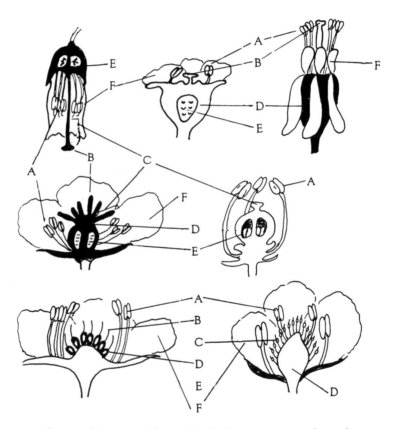

Flowers of (top row, left to right) blueberry, currant, and gooseberry. Second row: kiwifruit (female), grape. Third row: raspberry, strawberry. A-anther, B-stigma, C-pistil, D-receptacle, E-ovary, F-petal

Figure 14. Structure of various berry flowers

42 the Backyard Berry Book

Most flowers that have both male and female structures in the same blossom are known as complete flowers. In some fruit plants, notably kiwifruit and muscadine grape, the flowers may contain both male and female structures, but only one set of structures is functional. In these cases the plant is considered either a male plant or a female plant. This will be a point to be aware of when pollination is discussed later in this chapter. Figure 14 showed typical arrangements of a "small fruit" blossom.

What is a Berry?

Most of the fruits discussed in this book are popularly and collectively known as berries. In several cases, however this is actually a misnomer. True berries are by definition simple fruit, formed from one ovary. They have a fleshy ovary wall (or pericarp) and one or more carpels. In most cases the carpels will contain many seeds. To confuse matters, some of what we popularly consider vegetables, such as tomatoes or cucumbers, are actually berries. Fruit such as grapes, currants, and blueberries would also be examples of true berries.

Other fruit often called berries, such as the brambles and strawberries, are actually aggregate fruit made up of a number of unfused carpels which have developed from a single flower. In the case of the raspberry, the fruit is formed as an aggregate of drupelets surrounding a central stalk. To digress again, a drupe is a single fleshy fruit surrounding a stone. The drupelets adhere to a central receptacle, or stalk, to form a single fruit.

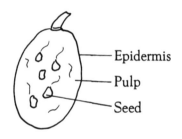

Figure 15. True Berry Structure shown in Grape

Aggregate fruit are typically made up of many individual drupelets. Each bramble flower, for example, may have from 100-125 pistils, each containing two ovules. One ovule develops into the seed, the other ovule into the fleshy drupe surrounding the seed. Seventy-five or more drupelets typically mature to form an individual "berry" found on the raspberry plant.

Drupe fruit grow with a steady increase in size until four or five days before maturity. During those last days, their size increases rapidly. To reach maximum size at harvest, it is very important that the fruit have adequate water during this growth stage.

Strawberries are similar to brambles in that they also are aggregate fruit. In their case, though, the aggregate is made up of numerous achenes. Achenes are single seeded fruit with a fairly thin pericarp. In the case of the strawberry, the dry seed is visible on the surface of the fruit rather than being surrounded by a fleshy layer.

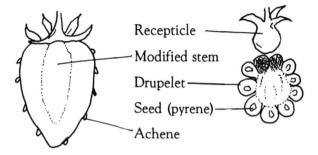

Recepticle
Modified stem
Drupelet
Seed (pyrene)
Achene

Figure 16. *Aggregate Fruit*

Although it is somewhat technical to understand the botanical differences between the various "berries", this may prove helpful when you are later trying to figure out why the fruit in your clusters of grapes are quite sparse or your raspberries have hard, dry areas.

Understanding Fruit Bud Development

Another fundamental concept to understand is how and when fruit buds are actually formed within the plant's tissue. Once a fruiting plant, bush or vine has reached a stage of maturity in which it will fruit, it has started on a regular path of developing flower buds annually that will eventually result in a fruit crop. (You may see the terms fruit bud or flower bud used. The two terms are synonymous and used interchangeably.) This shift from producing purely vegetative buds to producing both vegetative and fruiting buds is normally a sign that the plant's juvenile stage has ended. For most "small fruit" plants the juvenile stage lasts only a year or two. In the case of strawberries, they are mature enough to flower in the season of planting (although not really strong enough to bear a fruit crop).

Most people do not realize that the formation of the fruit bud is actually taking place the season before the flower becomes a visible

44 the Backyard Berry Book

bloom on the plant. In early summer, depending on the amount of sun exposure and temperature influences, the bud tissue begins to differentiate and form the beginning of a flower bud. Most of the fruit buds are formed before the plant goes into its winter dormant or rest stage.

Chilling

While the plant is dormant, internal growth processes continue at a very slow pace. During this time the fruit plant needs to be subjected to a certain amount of time below 45°F, or fruit and leaf buds may not develop and open normally. Although rarely a problem in northern climates, varieties with special low chilling requirements need to be selected in some regions of the south and the west coast.

Typical Chilling Requirements

Blackberry	1100-1400	Grape	$\leq$ 100
Blueberry	650-850	Kiwifruit	750-800
highbush	700-1200	Lingonberry	
rabbiteye	360-500	Raspberry	1100-1400
Currant		Rhubarb	
Gooseberry		Strawberry	100-300

Pollination

In order for successful development of the above mentioned fruit to occur, several processes must take place between the male and female parts of the flower. A beautifully blooming fruit plant or vine alone does not guarantee that there will be a crop to harvest.

The first step in the process from bloom to fruit is the transfer of pollen from the male anther to the female stigma. This process is known as pollination and is usually aided by a pollenizer, most often a bee. In plant breeding operations this process can be selectively carried out with a small paint brush. After pollination, assuming that the pollen had developed properly earlier, the pollen grain must germinate and grow down the stigma to the ovule where the male genetic material from the pollen tube is united with the female genetic material in the embryo sac. This uniting process is called fertilization. Most of this process will not be visible to the human eye, but shortly after bloom you will notice that the flower petals have fallen off and the fruit presumably begins to develop. Not all blossoms will have been fertilized, and shortly after bloom a number of flowers will drop from the plant never to develop. This is perfectly normal and occurs because no viable seed was formed in these fruit. Blossoms that have been damaged by late spring frosts may have damaged flower parts that prevent proper pollination and fruit growth. If weather conditions have been cold or damp and bees have not been active, these processes also may not take place properly.

In most cases, the blossom of a given type of berry can be properly pollinated by pollen from another blossom of the same variety. When this can occur, the plant is referred to as being self-fruitful. In some cases, pollination is more successful or even requires that a blossom from one variety be pollinated by pollen from a different variety than itself, (but still by the same type of fruit, that is kiwifruit by kiwifruit, etc.). In this case, the variety is said to be self-unfruitful. When you are growing a variety that is known to be self-unfruitful, it will be necessary to plant at least two compatible varieties with similar bloom times near each other. Most often these are planted in adjacent rows. Berries that are generally considered self-unfruitful include kiwifruit, many muscadine grape varieties, and rabbiteye blueberries.

Where the pollination and fertilization processes have been successful, the fruit will continue to grow and eventually produce a mature edible fruit. In fruit such as kiwifruit, where there are both male and female plants, you will need at least one of each sex for successful pollination.

Cold Hardiness

One final item of concern in understanding berry growth and survival is typically thought of as a "problem" of northern climates. That is cold hardiness. Even growers in more moderate climates would do well to consider this issue, however, since the occasional unexpected cold snap can do plenty of damage to the fruit planting if one is not prepared.

In considering cold hardiness, there are actually two points to address. The first is the hardiness of the plant itself - how well does the plant withstand cold. Second is hardiness of the actual flower bud. Often the plant may be quite hardy and have no problem surviving even the coldest of winter temperatures. If the plant tends to bloom early in the spring, it may still be subject to severe crop loss from frost damage unless the fruit bud is also very hardy.

Numerous factors affect cold hardiness. The plant's innate hardiness you, of course, have little influence over. How you apply certain cultural techniques (which are discussed in detail in later chapters) however, can have considerable influence over how well your berry plants tolerate cold stress. As one might assume, a strong healthy plant is usually the most able to withstand the cold. To keep your plants strong and healthy, seeing that they have adequate and balanced nutrition throughout the growing season is important. Keeping the berry patch free of weed competition, which robs water and nutrients, will help considerably. Plants weakened by insects or diseases will also have more difficulty in withstanding stress.

If you are in an area that normally experiences broad temperature swings in the fall or severe cold in winter, it is important that your berry plants be gradually and properly acclimated as they go into the winter dormant stage. Green, or actively growing, tissue is usually the most easily damaged by cold. In order to allow tissue to "harden down" or gradually slow its growth, avoid applying fertilizer or water late in the growing season. (No fertilizer after July 4, is a good rule of thumb. Pruning plants just as they are beginning to harden down may stimulate new growth which can be susceptible to sudden cold. So, it is best to avoid pruning in the late fall in cold climate areas.

Often cold injury occurs, not in the deep of winter but in early spring, as plants are emerging from dormancy. Selecting plants whose chilling requirements are matched to your growing climate will help plants stay dormant until major cold is past. If you select a plant with too low (i.e. short) a chill requirement for your area, it can be fooled into growing by those inevitable winter thaws that seem to occur around Ground Hog Day.

Actual fruit bud damage often occurs in spring, when developing blossoms are injured by a late, unexpected frost. Identifying an injured blossom is fairly simple.

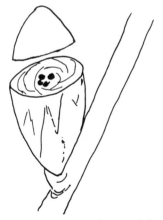

Figure 17. Frost damaged fruit bud

Understanding Berry Botany 47

Usually within a day following frost injury, blossom centers (actually the flower pistil) will appear black. Of course, these blossoms can no longer be properly pollinated and no fruit will result from them. The chart below shows the low temperatures that the fully dormant fruit plant can withstand. The plant is usually much more cold hardy than the developing blossom. As warm temperatures occur, the plant will break dormancy and unopened blossoms may be damaged even when temperatures are around 28°F.

Typical Cold Hardiness of Dormant Fruit Plants (°F)

Blackberry, erect	-10	Grape, Hybrid	-10 - -25
Blackberry, trailing	0	Grape, Muscadine	0
Blueberry, highbush	-15	Kiwifruit	10
Blueberry, lowbush	-20 - -25	Hardy Kiwifruit	-25 - -40
Blueberry, rabbiteye	-15	Lingonberry	-20
Currant	-30	Raspberry, Black	-20
Gooseberry	-35	Raspberry, Red	-30
Grape, American	-30 - -35	Rhubarb	-20
Grape, European	0 - -15	Strawberry	0

5. Soil Nutrition, pH, and Water

All living plants need certain nutrients and energy to grow and fruit properly. Green plants are uniquely adapted to provide for their needs through the cycle of photosynthesis. During photosynthesis, the plant takes in sunlight and uses sun energy to produce the sugars it requires. A closer look will explain the process.

Photosynthesis

For proper photosynthesis the plant needs sunlight, water, carbon dioxide, oxygen and certain minerals. The roots absorb water and minerals from the soil below. These ingredients are transported through vessels in the plant up to the green leaves. Chlorophyll, a green pigment in the leaf, absorbs sunlight and transforms it into usable energy. This energy is then used to process carbon dioxide absorbed from the air and other nutrients transported from the roots. The result is enzymes, sugar, and other carbohydrates.

Some of the sugars produced are converted to energy and used right away to maintain the plant's daily growth process. Some sugar is changed into starch, oils or protein. Unused sugar is stored for future use in various locations throughout the plant. Much of the sugar is stored in the fruit and accounts for its sweet taste. Figure 18 should help you visualize how this works.

Many factors affect the plant's ability to carry on efficient photosynthesis. The gardener's goal should be to care for the plant in ways that will encourage photosynthesis. After looking at Figure 18 it should be obvious why it is important to select a soil that is not so heavy and waterlogged that it holds insufficient oxygen or one that is so sandy that water drains away extremely quickly.

Since sunlight is so critical to photosynthesis, proper plant structure and healthy leaf surface also take on an important role in

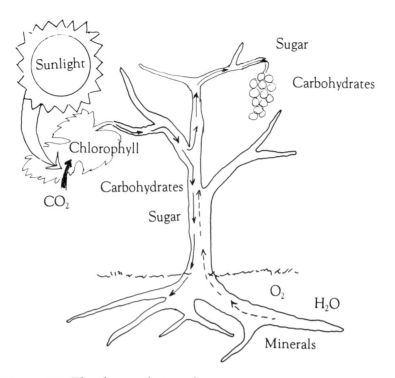

Figure 18. *The photosynthesis cycle*

the process. A major goal of pruning is to allow sunlight into the inside of the bush, vine, or plant row so that proper photosynthesis can occur. What the gardener does to establish an open plant structure will greatly affect the amount of sunlight available to the plant.

Healthy, disease free leaves are best able to carry on the photosynthesis process. It is interesting to note that each individual growing fruit needs the support of a certain minimal number of leaves to develop and ripen properly. Additional leaves are needed to support the growth of shoots and roots. One can see now why pest and disease control is advantageous even if the fruit is not being directly damaged. All of these aspects of plant care are important in helping the plant achieve maximum production and storage of sugar. Other chapters discuss soil selection, pruning, and control of diseases, all of which are important to efficient photosynthesis. This chapter will examine soil acidity, water, plant nutrients and their sources, and why they are important to the fruit plant.

50 the Backyard Berry Book

Soil pH - What is it?

Here it is - soil pH. Every gardening book talks about it, but most readers are still confused by soil pH. It always sounds like chemistry and quite frankly, it is. For the home gardener, it is not essential to understand all the chemistry involved with pH measurement, but a general understanding certainly is useful. To keep the explanation simple, we will stick to the basic ideas one needs to understand in growing fruit.

The term "pH" is a measure used to indicate the acidity or alkalinity (sometimes casually referred to as sweetness) of the soil. Knowing the acidity or alkalinity of a soil can be important because it affects the amount and form of nutrients available to the plant.

A logarithmic scale of 0 to 14 is used to express soil pH, with 0 being pure acid and 14 pure alkaline. ("pH" is the mathematical symbol used to indicate the negative exponent representing the concentration of hydrogen ions in a solution.) Water has a hydrogen ion concentration of 10^{-7}, also referred to as a pH of 7. This point (of 7) on the pH scale is considered neutral. Soil pH of less than 7 is considered acid while a soil pH greater than 7 is considered to be alkaline. Each increase (or decrease) of one point on the pH scale represents a tenfold difference in the concentration of hydrogen ions in the solution. Therefore a soil with a pH of 5.0 is ten times more acidic or has ten times more hydrogen ions than a soil with a pH of 6.0. It is one hundred times more acid or has one hundred times more hydrogen ions than a soil of pH 7.0. To be suitable for fruit growing, it is generally accepted that a soil should have a pH of 6.0 to 7.0, with 6.5 to 6.8 preferred. There are some exceptions though; at least two fruit crops discussed in this book, blueberries and lingonberries, prefer a pH of 4.5 to 5.5.

Preferred pH Ranges for Small Fruit

Blackberry	5.5 - 7.0	Kiwifruit	5.0 - 6.5
Blueberry	4.5 - 5.5	Lingonberry	4.5 - 5.5
Currant	6.2 - 6.5	Raspberry	6.0 - 6.8
Gooseberry	6.2 - 6.5	Rhubarb	5.5 - 6.5
Grape	6.0 - 7.5	Strawberry	6.5 - 6.8

Most garden centers sell small home pH measurement kits, that although not extremely accurate, can give you a "ball park" pH reading. Another resource for obtaining more accurate results is your local cooperative extension service which can, for a small fee, send your soil sample to a university lab for testing. The section on soil and tissue testing later in this chapter outlines the procedure for taking these samples. It is a good idea to take a complete soil sample *before* starting your backyard berry patch (or other permanent planting for that matter), so that you know what you are working with when you start. For a backyard planting it will be unlikely that you would need to repeat this test very often, assuming that your initial pH is in acceptable range and you don't encounter nutrition related problems with the growth of your fruit.

Modifying pH

As mentioned earlier, pH is used as a measure of soil acidity or alkalinity and represents a logarithmic scale of active hydrogen concentration in a solution. Hydrogen alone has no direct benefit nutritionally to plants. However, adjusting pH is important for the role it plays in loading available nutrients into the soil system. As an example, when lime is added to the soil the acid (H^+) moves from the soil to the lime. The lime, being calcium carbonate, breaks down to give calcium ions to the soil for plant use. At the same time, the carbonate combines with hydrogen and is released as carbon dioxide and water. Soil acidity is necessary to break minerals out of their native state and make the nutrients available for plant use; potassium out of feldspar, magnesium out of dolomite, and more.

Generally the nutrients required by fruit bearing plants are most readily available in a pH range from 6.0 to 6.8, as you can see from Figure 19. A few berry plants, such as blueberries, have unusual needs for a specific nutrient such as, in this case, iron. From Figure 19 it is obvious why they favor an acidic pH range where iron is more available to the plant.

Soil moisture also has an indirect effect on soil pH, since it contributes to the weathering of mineral particles and their concentration in the soil solution. Soils in wet regions tend to become acid over time due to acids produced by the breakdown of organic matter and fertilizers added to them. Alkaline soils are common in dry climates. If soil tests indicate a need to modify your pH, you can do

pH Range of Widest Nutrient Availability

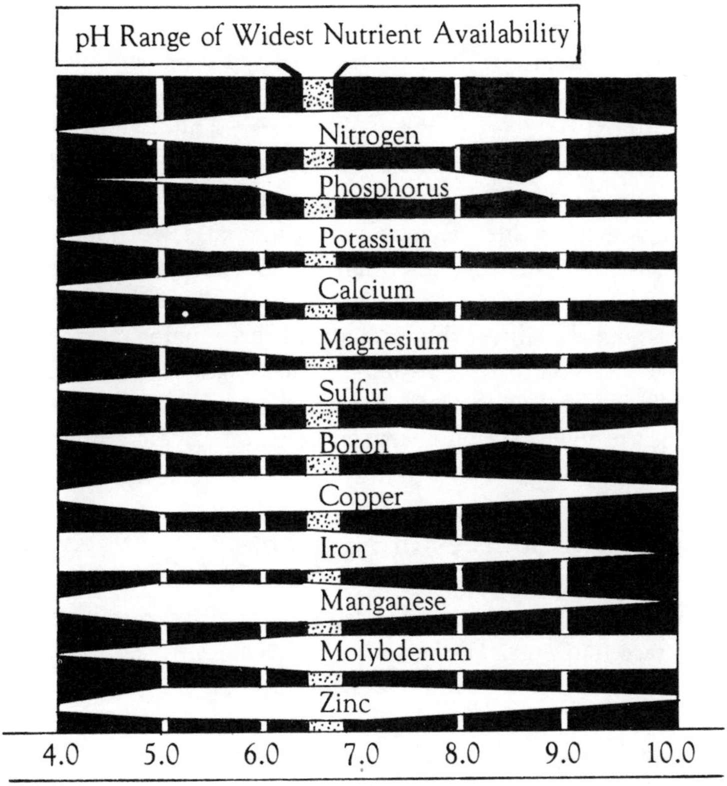

Nitrogen
Phosphorus
Potassium
Calcium
Magnesium
Sulfur
Boron
Copper
Iron
Manganese
Molybdenum
Zinc

| 4.0 | 5.0 | 6.0 | 7.0 | 8.0 | 9.0 | 10.0 |

Figure 19. Nutrient Availability at Different pHs

that by adding calcitic or dolomitic lime to make it more alkaline (raise the pH). Adding sulfur will make it more acid (lower the pH). Both materials are commonly available at garden centers. A general guide to modifying your soil is found below. Specific amounts for your situation can be obtained from your extension agent.

Amendment to add to 1000 ft.² of garden to change pH one point.

Soil type	Lime	Sulfur
Sand	50 lbs.	8 - 10 lbs.
Loam	60 - 70 lbs.	20 - 25 lbs.
Clay	80 lbs.	30 lbs.

Soil Nutrition, pH, and Water 53

Choosing a Fertilizer

Much like vitamins, fertilizers come in many shapes and kinds. To make choosing a fertilizer easier, first look at the label, which by law must be printed on every package of fertilizer. This label must give you the percentage of three major nutrients, nitrogen, phosphorus, and potassium. You will hear these referred to as N-P-K, in reference to their chemical element symbols. You may also see notations of numbers such as 15-5-10. These numbers indicate that the fertilizer is at least 15% nitrogen per pound of fertilizer, 5% phosphorus, and, 10% potassium. Fertilizers that include all three major nutrients are referred to as complete fertilizers. Percentages of other minor nutrients may also be indicated on the label. Later in this chapter, you will learn how these numbers can help you calculate how much actual fertilizer to apply.

Function and Sources of Nutrients

Plant nutrients are commonly divided into 3 groups: major, secondary and trace nutrients. The major nutrients are nitrogen, phosphorus, and potassium. All three are crucial for plant growth.

Major Nutrients

Nitrogen - Nitrogen, as a major nutrient, is primarily responsible for shoot growth and green color in the leaves. A plant uses nitrogen that is in the chemical form of nitrate nitrogen. Calcium nitrate (15-0-0), sodium nitrate (16-0-0), and potassium nitrate (13-0-44) are fertilizers that supply this immediately available form of nitrogen.

A less readily available form of nitrogen is ammonium nitrogen. It can be found in ammonium sulfate (21-0-0), monoammonium phosphate (11-52-0), or diammonium phosphate (18-46-0). Over a period of several months, ammonium nitrogen is converted by soil bacteria, to nitrate nitrogen. Another fertilizer, ammonium nitrate (33-0-0), provides both nitrate and ammonium nitrogen for combined quick and slow release of nitrogen.

A third form of nitrogen is organic nitrogen. In this case, the term organic is meant as its chemically primitive form - that carbon is included in its makeup - not the popular current connotation of "organic". Organic nitrogen must be converted first to ammonium nitrogen and then to nitrate nitrogen. This process takes time, sometimes up to several years to complete. Urea fertilizer (45-0-0) is a common form of organic nitrogen.

Nitrogen is normally in low supply and heavily used by fruit bearing plants. In most regions of the country it will be necessary to supplement the soil with a nitrogen source on a regular basis, usually every year. However, it is important to apply nitrogen judiciously. It can easily burn plant roots or cause excess shoot growth at the expense of producing fruit buds. If applied at the wrong time, it can also cause soft fruit. This is especially true with strawberries.

Phosphorus - Plants rely on phosphorus to help in the growth of roots, seeds, and early leaves. Phosphorus is not used directly, but rather converted to nucleic acids and other metabolic substances for use in growth processes. It is slow to work in the soil since it is not readily dissolved. Therefore it should be applied to the soil ahead of planting if the soil is shown to be lacking. Phosphorus can be found in rock phosphate and complete fertilizers such as superphosphate, monoammonium phosphate, and diammonium phosphate.

Potassium - Potassium, the third major nutrient, is used by the plant in producing fruit, growing roots and resisting disease. It works by helping to transport starch and sugar through the plant. It is found in potassium nitrate, potassium sulfate, and muriate of potash.

Secondary Nutrients

Calcium, magnesium, and sulfur are often called secondary nutrients. They are as important to plant growth as the major nutrients, but are generally needed in smaller quantities than nitrogen or potassium. They may need to be supplied on an occasional basis. Soil or tissue tests can be used to determine when these nutrients are deficient and give some idea of how much additional nutrient is needed.

Trace Nutrients

Trace nutrients are all necessary for plant growth functions but in very small, or "trace" amounts. An excess of trace nutrients can even cause a poisoning or toxicity to your fruit plant. The trace minerals are boron, copper, chlorine, iron, manganese, molybdenum, and zinc. Seaweed emulsion is sometimes used as a source of trace minerals and plant growth hormones. Deficiencies and excesses of these minerals vary considerably in different parts of the country. Tissue testing and consulting with a local extension agent will be the safest way to determine if and when additional trace nutrients are needed.

Soil Testing

Before applying fertilizers to your planting site it is wise to know what nutrients are already present in your soil or plant. By testing the soil you can avoid spending money on unneeded or incorrect fertilizers. Also, by avoiding over-application, you avoid mineral leaching that contributes to ground water pollution. Two forms of plant nutrient testing can be helpful to the fruit gardener. Soil testing, will tell you what nutrients are present in the soil, in a form that is available to the plant. Tissue testing, will tell you more definitely which of those nutrients has been taken up by the plant.

Soil testing is quite simple. Samples are taken with a probe that can be pushed into the soil. The probe is a metal cylinder about an inch and a half in diameter and about thirty inches long. One side is cut out along its length and a handle across the top allows you to push it into the soil and pull out a core. A soil probe is often available for loan through the county extension office. If not, samples for the home garden can also be taken with a garden trowel. In either case, be sure your sampling instrument is clean and free of rust, as contamination can effect the results, when testing for iron.

To take a soil sample, gather fifteen to twenty sample cores or trowels full, to a depth of around six inches, from the planting area. (For a homeowner with a small lot, this could include the whole backyard.) Mix them together well in a clean plastic bucket. Then bring a portion of this mixture (two cups is common) to your extension office in a plastic bag. The sample will be forwarded to a laboratory and you should have results back in a few weeks.

Tissue Testing

Knowing what nutrients are present in the soil does not necessarily indicate which nutrients have actually been taken up into the plant. This is where a tissue test can provide more accurate information. More commonly used with fruit trees, tissue samples are occasionally taken on small fruit as well. They are used most frequently on grapes. Grape tissue tests are taken by removing a sample of one hundred leaves from the actively growing vine. Take leaves from the middle of the current growing season's growth. Select randomly, but avoid leaves with very obvious insect damage or residue from spray applications. Once the leaves have been gathered, cut the leaf from the petiole (stalk that attached it to the vine). Typically only the petioles are sent in on grape tissue tests. The test is fairly expensive though, so consult the nutrient deficiency chart first to see if you can identify the problem. Your extension office can also help identify the problem or provide complete instructions on gathering the sample.

Nutrient Deficiency Symptoms

Nitrogen (N)	Visible on old leaves first. Uniform pale green color or turning yellow. Small leaves, weak growth. Small fruit.
Phosphorus (P)	New leaves small, bluish green. Purple leaf veins and margins. Stunted growth.
Potassium (K)	Visible on old leaves first. Small leaves with curled or rolled edges. Abundant flowers but poor fruit set. Small fruit with poor color.
Calcium (Ca)	Appears on new leaves first. Yellowed leaf margins. Shoot-tip dieback.
Magnesium (Mg)	Shows up on middle age and old leaves first. Yellowed margins and interveinal areas. Premature fruit maturity and fruit drop.
Sulfur (S)	Uniform yellowing of leaves. Leaves often take on an orange/red cast. Thin woody shoots.
Boron (B)	Small misshapen young leaves. Abnormal flower development. Bark or stem corking. Wilting & shoot dieback.
Copper (Cu)	Whitish color between leaf veins. Tip withering & leaf fall. Poor fruit set. Small, poor quality fruit.
Iron (Fe)	Seen in tip leaves first. Netted yellowing pattern. Leaf tips & margins die.
Manganese (Mn)	Occurs on older, mid shoot leaves first. Bands of yellow between veins. Paper-thin leaves. Poor fruit size & color.
Zinc (Zn)	Leaves on tip of branch stunted. Grow in tight rosette. Irregular, rolled leaf margins. Poor bud break. Reduced fruit set on some but not all shoots.

Soil Nutrition, pH, and Water 57

Understanding Soil Test Results

To insure proper nutrition for the garden, most gardeners at some point rely on a soil test to give them an accurate reading of what minerals and nutrients are present in the soil and in what relative proportions. Very often, once the test results arrive, the gardener is overwhelmed by what appears as a big sheet of technical terms and numbers. So, they rely on the accompanying recommendations of their extension agent to guide them in the amount and type of fertilizer to apply. For the weekend gardener, short on time, this method will suffice. For those green thumbs desiring to know more, the soil test holds a wealth of information that needn't be a mystery.

Although the printout format will vary from one soil test laboratory to the next, most include the following important information:

1) The levels of available major and secondary nutrients will be shown. It is important to look at these values not only as they stand alone, but in relation to the other nutrients. From the chart in Figure 20, the gardener should see how deficiencies or excesses of a given nutrient may influence the availability of other nutrients.

2) Soil management group. This is an indication of the soil texture of the sample - clay, clay loam, loam, sandy loam, or sand. The soil type will affect the nutrient or cation exchange capacity and the amount of leaching likely to occur.

3) Cation Exchange Capacity (CEC). Cation Exchange Capacity is an indicator of the soil's ability to attract and hold positively charged particles (cations). The exchange capacity is dependent on the soil type and amount of organic matter in the soil. It is a fairly constant value and not easily changed. It is usually expressed in milliequivalents per 100 grams of solution.

4) pH. As discussed earlier in this chapter, pH is a measure of active soil acidity or alkalinity.

5) Lime index. This is an indicator of the soil's potential or reserve acidity. It is used to calculate the amount of lime needed to raise the pH of an acid soil. Heavier soils have a greater ability to resist changes in pH due to greater reserve acidity. Since it is used to determine how much lime is needed to bring the soil pH to 6.5, lime index is only indicated on soil tests with low pH levels. Two different soil types with the same pH may have different lime indexes due to differences in reserve acidity. Soils with a lime index between

NUTRIENT INTERACTIONS

IF THE ELEMENT (OR SOIL CONDITION) AT THE LEFT IS TOO HIGH (H) OR TOO LOW (L), A DEFICIENCY OF THE ELEMENT AT THE TOP CAN RESULT.

(information compiled from many books and journals)

	N	P	K	Ca	Mg	S	Fe	Al	Cu	B	Zn	Mo	Mn	Na	Cl	Co
N (nitrogen)			H								H					
P (phosphorus)	L								very H	H	L	H				
K (potassium)		H		H	H					H	very H					
Ca (calcium)		H			H		H			H						
Mg (magnesium)	H	H	H	H												
S (sulfur)	L															
Fe (iron)		H + Al + low pH		H + Al,Mn + low pH	H + Al,Mn + low pH				H + Mn				L			
Al (aluminum)		H + Fe + low pH		H + Fe,Mn + low pH					H			H				
Cu (copper)																
B (boron)					H		H									
Zn (zinc)							H		H							
Mo (molybdenum)	L															
Mn (manganese)	H		H + Fe,Al + low pH	H + Fe,Mn + low pH			H + low pH		H + Fe							
Na (sodium)			H	H												
Cl (chlorine)			H													
Co (cobalt)																
Ni (nickel)							H									
pH		L + H Fe,Al		L + Al Fe,Mn	L + Al Fe,Mn	H or L + Mn	H or L + Mn		H	H or L	H	L	H + org. m			
organic matter									H	L	H		H + H pH			H

Figure 20 Reprinted from The Coming Revolution in Agriculture courtesy of Harold Willis

Soil Nutrition, pH, and Water 59

60 and 70 are generally considered not to need additional lime.

6)   Base saturation. Also sometimes referred to as the calcium:magnesium ratio (Ca:Mg), the base saturation is a measure of the balance between calcium, magnesium, potassium, and hydrogen in the soil and is used an indicator of magnesium deficiency. The soil test assumes that the percentages of these exchangeable bases equals 100%. Magnesium values higher than 3% and greater than the percentage of potassium indicate that adequate magnesium is available. A well balanced soil should have a Ca:Mg ratio between 4:1 and 7:1. At pH 6.2, base saturation should be 65-75% calcium, 10-15% magnesium, 2-5% potassium, 10-20% hydrogen and 3-5% other cations (sodium, iron, manganese, copper, and zinc).

Fertilizer - How Much?

How much fertilizer to apply is something that is difficult to address with one set formula. The answer can vary with the soil type, amount of soil organic matter, crop volume, and the type of fertilizer being applied. Recommendations based on soil test results can serve as a starting point when preparing a new planting. For established plants, the amount of shoot growth is a helpful guide. Productivity of the crop is also an indicator of plant health.

When using fertilizer recommendations, the gardener needs to be aware of whether the recommendation is given in terms of actual nutrient (i.e. nitrogen) to apply or overall amount of a given fertilizer (i.e. urea, which is only 46% actual nitrogen). Also be cognizant of the amount of area - per square foot, per 100 foot of row, or per acre - the recommended rate is given for. Extension bulletins are often used as a source of general information. Since they are primarily written with commercial fruit growers in mind, the recommendations are usually given on a per acre basis. For the home garden, some conversion may be necessary. The following formulas and tables should make this relatively easy.

pounds/acre ÷ 43,560 = pounds/square foot
30 lbs./acre = 1 oz./100 sq. ft.
450 lbs./acre = 1 lb./100 sq. ft.
1 ton/acre = 5 lbs./100 sq. ft.
1 lb. fertilizer = ± 6 medium handfuls

A one pound coffee can will hold approximately 2 1/2 pounds of commercial fertilizer.

Amount of fertilizer (pounds/1000 sq. ft.) to Supply Given Amounts of Actual Nitrogen

Actual Nitrogen (lbs/acre)	Ammonium sulfate 21% N	Ammonium nitrate 30% N	Urea 46% N	Mixed Fertilizer 10-10-10
30	3.25	2.0	1.5	6.9
40	4.33	2.75	2.0	9.1
50	5.50	3.50	2.5	11.5
60	6.50	4.0	3.0	13.75

(.7 lbs.\1000 sq. ft.=30 lbs.\acre, .9 lbs.\1000 sq. ft.=40 lbs.\acre, 1.15 lbs.\1000 sq. ft.=50 lbs.\acre, 1.33 lbs.\1000 sq. ft.=40 lbs.\acre)

Since each of the berry crops has quite different nutrient needs, rather than generalize in this chapter, specific needs are discussed in the respective fruit chapters. Nitrogen fertilizer is usually applied in late winter or early spring, except in the case of June bearing strawberries where it is applied directly following renovation. This way it is released as the plant starts its new growth for the season. During exceptionally cold or rainy springs a small additional application of quick release fertilizer such as calcium nitrate can be made in late June to supplement some of what may have leached out of the root zone. Avoid applying fertilizer, especially nitrogen, in late summer and autumn as this stimulates growth, and vigorously growing plants may not harden down sufficiently for winter.

Nutrient Sources

Plant nutrients can be found in numerous synthetically manufactured fertilizers as well as in "organic" fertilizers of natural origin. Often the type of fertilizer used will be dictated by how quickly the various nutrients need to be available to the plant. Some fertilizers are fairly soluble in water and are rapidly broken down into chemical forms that are easily used by the plant. These fertilizers are often referred to as quick release fertilizers. Fertilizers that require longer weathering to break down to usable forms are classified as moderate or slow release. In general, natural fertilizer materials that are popularly considered "organic" fall into the moderate or slow release categories. The following chart gives an idea of some of the more common fertilizers' comparative rates of release and their N-P-K percentages.

Nutrient Sources

Fertilizer Material	Actual % Nutrient By Weight			
	N	P_2O_5	K_2O	Other
Rapid Release Rate				
Ammonium sulfate	20			24 S
Ammonium nitrate	32.5			
Calcium nitrate	15.5			20 Ca
Diammonium phosphate	17-20	46		
Muriate of potash			60-62	
Potassium nitrate	13.4		44	
Potassium sulfate			45-52	
Seaweed emulsion (foliar)	1	1	4	numerous trace
Superphosphate		20		20 Ca
Triple superphosphate		46		
Urea	42-46			
Wood Ash		1-2	3-7	
Moderate Release Rate				
Animal Tankage	7	10		
Bat Guano	5-12	8-11	2	
Blood Meal	12	2	.5	
Manure (varies with type)	.25-6	.15-4	.25-3	
Kaolinite			12	
Milorganite	5	2-5	2	
Monoammonium phosphate	11	52		
Potassium magnesium sulfate (SulPoMag)			22	11 Mg 11 S
Slow Release Rate				
Basic slag		3.5-8		3.5Mg
Bone meal		18.5		22 Ca
Colloidal phosphate		14-28		26-33 Ca 4 Fe
Compost	1-2	1-6	1-3	
Greensand			5-7	
Potassium carbonate			56	
Rock phosphate		20-32		32 Ca

Water - How Much?

If you thought judging fertilizer amounts was tricky, water could give you a real challenge. Soil type and local conditions come into play so much that, again, it is hard to give specific water recommendations. A few guidelines should help you get started. From there you will have to experiment until you find what works for your garden.

When watering berry plants, bushes, and vines, two things are important to remember. One, absolutely avoid letting the plant become so dry that it wilts, and two, a deep watering once a week will do more good in developing deep roots than a little sprinkle every few days.

You can measure rainfall and evaporation by leaving a five gallon bucket out in an open spot and recording the water level weekly. A general rule of thumb is that fruit plants need at least one inch of water per week. During the final weeks of fruit ripening, two inches per week is needed for the best quality raspberries, blueberries, and kiwifruit. If you are in an area that has a water shortage, watering during the period of rapid fruit size expansion is the most critical. This is usually the three to four weeks prior to anticipated harvest.

Irrigation

Many areas of the United States experience dry periods during some portion of the fruit growing season. During these times, natural rainfall does not provide all the moisture needed to support both the growing plant and the developing fruit. Fortunately this problem can be overcome by providing some type of supplemental water for the berry garden.

In most home gardens, ordinary sprinkling is the method of choice. The necessary equipment - a sufficiently long hose and some type of sprinkler that will cover the desired area - is relatively inexpensive. It is very easy to acquire at any garden center or discount store and, being very "low-tech", it is easy to operate. The amount of water capacity required by this type of system will vary greatly, depending on the type of sprinkler used.

On a larger scale, some berry growers will invest in an overhead irrigation system. This system typically consists of a supply line of two to four inch diameter pipe and a series of raised sprinkler heads arising from the main feeder pipes. This system requires more water

Soil Nutrition, pH, and Water 63

capacity than most home water supplies provide. Typical water requirements are thirty to forty or more gallons per minute, so it is often necessary to drill a well or feed the system from a pond. If a large planting of strawberries needs to be protected from spring frosts, this type of system usually has the capacity to handle that job as well.

Both of these methods of overhead sprinkling will provide water fairly quickly to a given area, but also have several disadvantages. In areas where water is scarce or expensive, overhead sprinkling is expensive and not very water conserving. Also, overhead sprinkling exposes leaf and fruit tissue to extended periods of wetness that allow fungus diseases to develop.

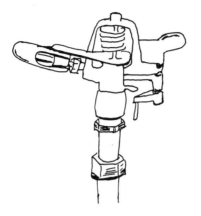

Figure 21. *Overhead irrigation sprinkler head*

A more moisture conserving method of providing water to fruit plantings is trickle irrigation. These systems often use as little as one to two gallons of water per hour for each emitter in the system.

Trickle irrigation systems are usually made up of a two to three-inch diameter main-line from the water source. This feeds a lightweight flexible tube that is perforated at regular intervals. The feeder lines may also have small water emitters releasing moisture at intervals that typically range from twelve inches to four feet. The trickle tubing usually runs the length of each plant row and is either placed on the soil surface near the plant or buried just below the surface in the root zone. Trickle systems are available in sizes for the small berry patch to the large acreage farm. Often the systems are easily expandable as the berry patch expands, provided sufficient water capacity is available.

Although this system is quite water conserving, it too has drawbacks. Due to the small size of the tube perforations or emitters, the water source needs to be free of debris to avoid clogging. Maintenance of the system is somewhat technical and needs to be done on

64 the Backyard Berry Book

a regular basis, otherwise mineral deposits or algae that build up over time can cause clogging problems. Broken trickle tubes are likely to occur when the tube is nicked by a mower, rototiller or hoe, but fortunately breaks are fairly easy to repair.

Relying on a trickle system to provide adequate water for a berry planting also requires a slightly different approach than using an overhead system. While an overhead system can provide a fairly substantial quantity of water quickly, should conditions become too dry, a trickle system cannot. In fact, extremely dry soils are very difficult to re-wet adequately with a trickle system. A trickle system works on the concept of supplying a regular steady supply of moisture that keeps the soil from reaching a moisture deficit. Consequently, a trickle system must be turned on early in the season and operated regularly, with the assumption that optimum rainfall may not be forthcoming. This takes a little bit of forethought, but is certainly not difficult to do.

Sustainable Soil Building

As gardeners are becoming more aware of the need to maintain the garden as a self sustaining entity, two "old-fashioned" practices are once again coming to the forefront - mulching and composting. Complete books are now being written on these subjects, so one can only begin to touch on the highlights of them within the following short sections. It is not the purpose of this section to outline all the fine points of mulching and composting but rather to make the gardener aware of the effects that these practices can have on maintaining a fertile soil. To learn more about these important aspects of building a healthy soil, the reader may want to consult the sources listed in the bibliography. As an introduction, the sections that follow will open the door to alternatives to synthetic herbicides and fertilizers and lead to long term soil building techniques.

Mulching

Using mulch in the garden has become a popular way of conserving soil moisture and controlling weeds. Straw, bark chips, gravel, and even specially manufactured plastic mulches suit the purpose well. Leaves and grass clippings work too, but have a tendency to mat down heavily.

Some materials such as gravel and plastic, contribute little or nothing to the soil, although they work well as mulches. Plastic mulches can even present disposal problems if they are not biodegradable. Today, more of the "plastic" mulches are being made of vegetable starches that do eventually break down when exposed to light and weathering (and this point is key - few manufactured degradable mulches decay properly without exposure to light).

Plant materials used as mulch will eventually be broken down by natural processes. Over time these materials, although they cannot be counted on to contribute substantial nutrients to the soil, will, unlike synthetic herbicides, add some organic matter. Materials such as sawdust or bark chips will, of course, take longer to decay than straw or grass clippings. One important point to remember when using any natural plant matter as mulch, is the need to provide extra nitrogen to the garden. Soil organisms that break down these mulches use considerable soil nitrogen in the process. If additional nitrogen is not supplied to them through supplemental feeding, they will compete with the fruit plants to use what is already in the soil. How much additional nitrogen is needed will depend in part on the amount and type of mulch, the amount of existing soil nitrogen, and the activity level of the soil microbes. Lacking a rule of thumb, the best gauge of the amount of nitrogen to add will be the fruit plants. If they start showing any symptoms of nitrogen deficiency - most notably the leaves taking on a lighter green color - start adding small quantities of a fast releasing form of nitrogen to the garden.

One other caution when using mulch: it provides a nice home for mice and other rodents. Be sure to rake the mulch back from your plant crowns each fall unless it is needed for winter cold protection. Otherwise, you may discover many gnawed and dead canes or vines in the spring. Once temperatures warm in the spring and rodents are active enough to search wider for preferred foods, the mulch can again be placed around the plants. At this time the gardener will probably also find that additional mulch needs to be added to replace that which decayed during the past growing season.

Compost - Garbage to Gold

As environmental awareness increases, more gardeners are discovering the alchemy of turning garden and kitchen "garbage" into "gold". Composting has become popular, and for good reason. Garden trimmings and kitchen scraps are quite easy to recycle into a healthy supplement for the garden. Compost provides slow release, readily available nutrients for plant growth. It also improves the soil structure, making the soil looser and better aerated.

Composting is a relatively easy process if a few fundamentals are understood. First a few key ingredients are necessary. These are primarily sources of carbon and nitrogen. Then, one needs a means of turning the carbon and nitrogen sources into forms usable by the plant. Finally energy is needed to fuel the decomposition process.

Sources of carbon and nitrogen are abundant in our environment, but how does the novice composter know what is what? Very unscientifically, one can think of plant and animal waste that is "brown" as generally being carbon sources and that which is "green" as providing nitrogen. Some of those materials include:

Brown		Green	
Straw	50	Fruit Pomace	25
Sawdust	100-500	Brewery Waste	
Grain hulls	100	Cottonseed meal	5
Coffee grounds	12	Blood meal	10-12
Paper	100	Fish & shellfish waste	6
Dead leaves	14-110+	Kitchen scraps	12
Woodchips	100	Lawn grass clippings	25

Most of these materials are available as by-products of our own homes and gardens or as refuse from various food processing operations. If your own supply is insufficient, you may be able to get more within your community simply for the asking and the effort of hauling it away. It is by no means important that all these materials be included in any given compost pile, only that a balance of carbon and nitrogen containing products be used to form the pile. Ideally one should strive for an eventual ratio of 25:1, carbon-to-nitrogen (C/N) in the compost pile. The numbers next to the "ingredients" in the chart above should provide some relative guidelines. Although they are expressed as a single number they should be read as a ratio relative to one part nitrogen. For example, straw has a ratio of fifty parts carbon to one part nitrogen (or 50:1).

So, how does the this heap of carbon and nitrogen become finished compost? In the presence of oxygen numerous decay causing bacteria and microorganisms will accomplish the job. This process will occur naturally without any help, although it will take time, sometimes years. The gardener who would like to have use of a regular supply of compost can speed the process along in several ways. First, how fast the raw materials are converted to compost is partly a function of the sheer numbers of microbes present. Adding farm animal manure will help boost the number of microbes in addition to supplying various other nutrients to the pile. Second, heat generated by the working microbes will speed the process, since the microbes work faster the warmer it is (up to about 150°F.). These microbes also need oxygen and a certain amount of water to function effectively. Building the pile from materials of varying particle size, some fine (such as bloodmeal) and some coarse (such as woodchips) will help aeration. If natural rainfall does not keep it moist, the pile should be watered occasionally. Avoid waterlogging the pile for extended periods though, or oxygen will be excluded and decomposition will turn to fermentation, resulting in wasted nutrients and toxic by-products. Finally, turning the pile occasionally, though not mandatory, will help expose the cool, less decomposed exterior to the larger population of microbes working in the warm interior.

Once it's compost, what do you do with it? Use it of course! Use it wherever you would use fertilizer. Although the nutrient content will vary depending on the original materials used, over time regular applications of compost will provide a wide range of nutrients to both the plant and the soil. Unlike synthetic fertilizers, it is hard to overdose with finished compost. Properly finished compost will not burn tender roots as some other nutrient sources do. (Damage can occur, however, with unfinished compost or compost in which fermentation has taken place.) Compost can also be forked into new planting sites during preparation, to add both nutrients and structure to the soil.

6. Pest Control Strategies

Typically when one mentions the word "pest" to a gardener, the first thought that comes to mind is an insect or perhaps a plant disease of one sort or another. However, pests in the small fruit planting can take numerous forms. Vertebrate pests such as birds, deer, rodents, and other wildlife can also raise the ire of many a gardener. Another type of garden pest that can cause considerable havoc in the small fruit planting is not thought about as often - the weed.

In most home garden small fruit plantings insects and diseases are, as one would expect, occasional problems. Frequently, these pests do not create problems of major magnitude and in many cases they can be tolerated without the need for eradication. Pests such as birds and deer can cause more serious problems for the home gardener, mostly due to the small overall size of the fruit garden and these pests' ability to feed quickly and voraciously. Yet, they too can be dealt with effectively in most cases. Finally, weeds, as any experienced gardener has come to realize, are a fact of life. Sometimes weeds may seem like an unending nemesis, and indeed they can cause considerable competition to the plants, as well as work for the gardener. Here too, however, there are ways to outwit the majority of the pests and reduce the gardener's work considerably. This chapter will discuss general approaches to dealing with pests and what is necessary for effective control. The following chapters will discuss more specific ways of controlling various pests.

Approaches to Pest Control

In the recent past most gardeners had the impression that pest control in the garden could only be accomplished by spraying some sort of chemical. Fortunately, this is usually not necessary in the backyard small fruit planting. In many cases pest outbreaks in the well-cared-for small fruit planting are not of major concern and only cause minimal damage to the crop. With increasing awareness of organic gardening and new developments in integrated pest management, alternatives to chemical controls are also becoming more available. Indeed, for the home gardener non-chemical pest controls are often the only feasible option as the number of allowable pesticides has dwindled. Which method you should use is a choice you will have to make.

To begin, one should be aware of the different categories of pest control methods available. Basically, approaches to pest control can be broken down into the following categories:

1) Cultural Practices
2) Chemical Controls
3) Organic Controls
4) Biological Controls
5) Integrated Pest Management Techniques

Cultural Practices

Many potential pest problems of the home fruit garden can be avoided or minimized by paying attention to the cultural practices that are applied to the garden. Cultural practices are those actions that the gardener takes in regular care of the garden - site preparation, cultivation, mulching, pruning, and more. In reading the preceding chapters, you have already come across an array of cultural practices. In this chapter, you will learn more about their importance and how they can be tied together to make gardening an even more enjoyable experience. Consideration of cultural practices for effective pest control often begins before the fruit garden is even planted. This is particularly true when dealing with weeds and plant diseases.

Weeds can pose a considerable problem in the small fruit garden due to their strong competition for water and nutrients needed by the relatively shallow rooted small fruit plants. Since small fruit plantings are often established to last many years, regular annual tillage, as one would perform on a vegetable garden, is not a feasible means of weed control for the fruit garden. This problem is often overcome with a combination of cultural practices: proper site preparation prior to planting, some sort of cultivation between plant rows, and annual mulching to deter further weed growth. All of these cultural practices have been discussed in previous chapters.

Selection of appropriate cultural techniques can also be very beneficial in the control of certain diseases and insects. Keeping plant rows narrow or properly pruned to allow ample air circulation will help minimize the development of numerous fungus diseases and allow proper pesticide penetration when necessary. Selection of disease resistant varieties can be used to avoid disease problems if local growing conditions normally foster certain diseases. Crop rotation for prevention of soil borne diseases is another important cultural practice to use when replanting a garden site. Also, attention to maintaining proper, balanced plant nutrition will help the healthy plant better withstand insect outbreaks that may occur.

Chemical Controls

Chemical control has been considered by many as the mainstream pest control method in recent decades. This method has assumed that all "bugs" and diseases are problems to be eliminated. In this book, chemical materials are considered to be those manufactured or extensively processed as opposed to those left in their fairly natural form. Advantages of chemical use include quick, effective control of insects and diseases with a minimal expenditure of labor. Chemical controls are also responsible for the attractive abundance of unblemished produce demanded by many consumers today. Undesirable consequences of chemical control methods include insects and diseases developing resistance to certain chemicals and ecological ramifications, such as ground water pollution. Accidental poisoning of the person applying chemicals and possible long term health problems are also risks of chemical control systems. Due to these concerns, the number of chemical materials legally available for use on home fruit gardens is extremely limited. In some cases the few remaining chemical materials may only be available for use by a licensed pesticide applicator.

Although chemical pest controls are often quick and easy, their environmental effects must be balanced with the effectiveness and cost of other nonchemical pest control means. Chemical controls do have a place in occasional control of pests in the small fruit garden. They can be particularly useful in preventing fungus diseases that spread quickly and have few nonchemical control means. In insect control, chemicals can be used selectively to allow natural predators to establish biological control of the insect pest. This will be discussed further in this chapter. Often however, it is more beneficial to the environment to pursue other nonchemical methods first.

This is especially true in the area of weed control. Many shallow rooted berry plants are even sensitive to damage by weed control chemicals (herbicides), so these materials need to be applied by a trained, experienced applicator to avoid injury to the planting. Herbicides often remain in the soil for extended time periods and can affect future plantings on the site. In contrast to these disadvantages of chemical control, cultivating and mulching are effective weed control options that also help build the soil.

Organic Controls

With present day ecological awareness, organic pest control is much talked about. Just what exactly is organic gardening? Justifiably there is some confusion as individuals and various groups each have their own definitions. As someone once defined their understanding to the author, "unsprayed and unfertilized", is a simplistic definition. On the other end of the spectrum are organic grower groups that do allow selective use of certain "chemical" pesticides in their certification programs. For purposes of this book, organic strategies will be defined as those that use primarily naturally occurring materials in relatively unprocessed form. These materials include ground rock mineral fertilizers, manure, compost, dormant oils, and many plant-derived insecticides. This is not to say that all these materials are good or safe and that man-made ones are all bad or dangerous. Excessive manure applications can cause just as much water pollution as manufactured fertilizers. Some organic pesticides, such as nicotine sulfate, are more poisonous than manufactured ones, such as Imidan. Most of the cultural practices discussed throughout this book are also often incorporated into an organic pest control regimen.

Growing fruit organically can be somewhat more complex than relying primarily on chemicals. It requires that you have a thorough understanding of the growth processes of the plant, the fruit, the pests, and the related beneficial organisms; and how they are all part of an interrelated cycle. Organic gardening practices normally entail more than just pest control. When gardening organically, more emphasis is placed on soil building and fertility management than is typically done with chemical systems. The major advantage of an organic system is that it works in harmony with the natural system and takes advantage of many renewable natural resources. Disadvantages are that it can be labor intensive and fruit may not be as picture perfect and blemish free as many people have become used to. Although most pest control materials deemed acceptable in organic gardens have very short residual life in the environment, some of these materials are still highly toxic. They need to be used with equal care and respect as chemical pest controls are. In some cases, organic pest control methods may not be as quick or effective as chemical control methods. However, partially due to the lack of available chemical pest control materials for the small fruit gardener, many of the practices that will be used in pest control for berries and fruiting vines will fall into the broad scope of organic practices.

Biological Controls

Biological pest control is best defined as a situation in which a "beneficial" organism is used to control a pest organism by predation, parasitism, or competition. Biological control can also be achieved by disrupting the mating patterns of certain pest organisms. Biological pest control is most commonly thought of as applying to insect control, but certain biological controls can also be applied to nematodes and weeds in small fruit plantings.

In biological insect control, the pest insect is often controlled by other insects that are its natural predators. Biological techniques are most commonly used to control mites, aphids, and the plant-feeding caterpillar stages of many moths or butterflies. The control organisms for these pests include predatory mites, lacewings, ladybugs, and praying mantises. Insecticidal bacteria, such as *Bacillus thuringiensis* (Bt), microbial insecticides (such as granulosis virus), and parasitic wasps and nematodes are also common biological insect controls. These various biological controls may be referred to as "predators" or as "beneficials". Although they may technically function in somewhat different manners, they are, in practical terms, similar in their end result. Therefore, the terms "predator" and "beneficial" are often used interchangeably and synonymously when discussing pest control.

For several years now, commercial fruit growers have been using pheromones to monitor the presence of certain insects in their fruit plantings. Typically these pheromones are synthetic reproductions of specific insects' sex attractant or mating hormones. More recently these same pheromones have been used to actually confuse mating patterns of certain small fruit insect pests, most notably grape berry moth. By confusing the mating patterns of the pest, the males are attracted to the pheromone trap rather than to the female insect. Consequently no breeding with the female occurs. As a result, she produces sterile eggs that do not hatch. Since no larvae emerge from the eggs to feed, little damage is done to the fruit and pest populations eventually decline.

The use of biological methods may sound like the perfect answer to the pest control dilemma. It makes use of organisms already present in the ecosystem without detrimental environmental effects. Like all control methods, however, biological techniques do have some limitations. First, most predator insects are quite host specific. That is, they are likely to feed only on one or two very targeted pest species. This is why it often does not pay to purchase "beneficials" that were raised in an area of the country far from your location; their prey is apt to be totally different than the pest in your garden.

Second, sufficient numbers of the pest need to be present in your garden throughout the season to keep the predators adequately fed, lest they die from lack of food just before a new, major outbreak of pests. Maintaining this balance requires a reasonable understanding of entomology as well as the effect of pesticides on your beneficial insect population.

Third, most pheromone disruptants are effective only over a fairly sizeable area, typically two acres or more. In smaller areas, pheromones can still be used for monitoring purposes, but they are not likely to be effective as mating disruptants. Previously mated females will travel considerable distance and can easily fly into your garden from surrounding areas.

As already mentioned, biological methods of weed control have some application in the small scale fruit planting, although they are not frequently talked about. Most research regarding biological weed control has been done with "weeder geese". These geese prefer to feed on young emerging grasses and other weed seedlings. By enclosing the geese in a moveable pen with small amounts of food at one end and water at the other, the geese can be encouraged to graze on the weeds as they move about the pen. As weeds are controlled in one spot, the pen and geese can be moved to a new location. Although somewhat cumbersome for larger scale berry growers, this method of weed control may be quite feasible for the home gardener who enjoys animal raising as well as fruit growing.

Integrated Pest Management

Integrated Pest Management (IPM) is a strategy that is rapidly gaining acceptance in both commercial farm operations and home gardens. In practical terms, it can be defined as a blending of all of the pest control strategies already outlined. The philosophy of IPM can be considered holistic since it takes the total ecosystem into consideration - plant, soil, pest, and growing conditions - and looks at how these aspects interrelate and how each is impacted by the chosen control method. Yet, it does not espouse one method to be "good" while another is "bad". Instead, IPM borrows the best aspects of biological, cultural, chemical, and organic control methods, weighs them against the disadvantages, and applies them in the context of an interdependent system to manage the fruit garden as a constantly changing, living system. In many ways, it is a middle ground between chemical control and pure organic control methods.

An integrated pest management system allows you to decide what trade-offs you are willing to make. To limit the amount or type of pesticides you use, you may be willing to accept more blemished fruit or a few worms. Perhaps you would rather use a less toxic "chemical" pesticide than a highly toxic "natural" one. Maybe you will choose to allow a few weeds to grow near your garden to serve as habitat and breeding ground for beneficial insects rather than maintaining the perfectly manicured showcase garden. The choices are yours when you have sufficient information. Most of the pest control strategies discussed in this book have a focus toward IPM. If your personal philosophy leans heavily toward other methods, by all means follow your chosen path. Consider, though, that IPM will have much to offer you that is of value.

Effective Pest Control

One of the main concepts behind the integrated pest management, organic gardening and biological control approaches is that not every occurrence of a pest or disease demands instant control. Some pests can be tolerated and some diseases prevented. Only when pest conditions become excessive, are controls needed. All effective pest control programs share certain basic principles. They include:
1) Planning for problem prevention
2) Proper identification of the pest or problem

3) Selection of an effective control agent - be it a biological control organism, organic pesticide, or chemical material

4) Proper timing in application of the control method

5) Proper coverage of the plant surface

As already mentioned, certain pest problems can be prevented with a bit of forethought. Preventing disease problems by planting disease resistant varieties is the most obvious. Site preparation to reduce weed competition is also worthwhile. Very often, if the proper habitat exists, predator insects will be at work, controlling pests without the gardener even noticing their presence. Care should be taken not to disrupt them.

If you come to a point where you feel pest control is needed, the next step is to properly identify the pest or problem. Remember that not all problems will be caused by the typical insect pests. Often nutrient deficiency symptoms may look like a possible disease to the inexperienced gardener, so be sure to consider these too when searching for the source of a problem. Many common insect and disease problems should be identifiable after reading chapters 7 and 8. The local extension agent can identify more unusual problems.

Once the pest has been identified, the magnitude of damage being done needs to be assessed and, when warranted, a control method will need to be chosen. In many cases, this will be some type of pesticide, but it could also be some type of predator insect. Pesticide, (-cide meaning "to kill"), is the term generally used to define a material that kills pests - be it an insect, disease, or weed. The materials can generally be broken down into the categories of insecticide, fungicide (to kill fungi responsible for many diseases), bactericide or herbicide (to kill weeds or "herbs").

Choosing a material targeted specifically for the purpose of controlling the given problem is preferred in integrated pest management. It is often the most effective and, if chosen properly, is least injurious to beneficial insects that also inhabit the garden.

The next requirement of an effective pest or disease control program is applying the selected material at a time when it will be most effective. The importance of proper timing cannot be understated! Even the most effective material will not work well if it is applied at the wrong time. In chapter 7 you will become aware that most insects are likely to be vulnerable to controls when they are immature or unprotected, such as when they are molting. Diseases are usually easiest to control before the bacteria or fungal spores have increased to great numbers. Weeds are easiest to control when they are still small.

Since each growing season is different, it is impossible to say that a given spray applied on a given date will always work. The development of most insects can be correlated to certain growth phases in the plant. Since they are both influenced by the accumulation of degree units brought on by warming weather, in most years these developmental and growth phases will coincide with each other even though they do not always occur on the same calendar dates from year to year. As you keep records and gain experience, you will be able to fine tune your control timing by watching the development of your plants and pests.

Finally, if pesticides are used, they must be applied so that they are deposited to reach their target. Care must be taken that plant leaves are well covered on both top and bottom side and that only minimal pesticide blows away in the wind. This usually can be done be applying materials at a wind-still time such as early morning or late evening. When beneficial insects are used as controls, sufficient numbers of feeding beneficials must be present to do the job.

Safe Handling of Pesticides

All too often, safety in handling and application of pesticides is something that is glanced over or left out entirely in gardening books. It may not be something glamorous to think about, but do remember that a poison by any other name is still a poison. Whether it is a manmade chemical or an organic material, it requires respect and a dose of responsible common sense. Most unintentional pesticide poisonings happen when material is used without proper knowledge or protection. In many states it is now necessary to be licensed to buy and apply the more toxic pesticides. If you choose to use these materials, pass the licensing exam. If you are using the less toxic materials handle them with care and respect. As minimum common sense safety precautions:

1) Read the label carefully and know what you are using. Use only the recommended rate of material. **Follow the label directions carefully.**

2) Do not mix two pesticide materials together unless they are known to be compatible.

3) Whenever possible, mix up only as much spray as you will

need for your current application. If you have a small amount of material left after spraying, it is better to give your fruit garden a bit heavier spray application. Through exposure to the weather, spray materials are most easily broken down naturally. **Do not dump leftover spray in a concentrated spot on the ground or down a sewer,** where it is harder for it to break down properly.

4) Store unused pesticides out of reach of children, in a well marked, locked cabinet.

5) **Never** save left over spray materials in something other than its properly marked, original container.

6) Spray only under calm conditions when spray will not drift onto neighboring property, pets, or yourself.

7) Dress properly. Wear long sleeves, pants and work shoes; **NO** bare feet, sandals, shorts or bathing suits.

8) Use protective clothing (rubber gloves, boots, respirator, face shield) when called for.

9) Do not eat, drink, or smoke while using pesticides. Wash carefully when finished.

10) Dispose of containers properly according to accepted local recommendations. This usually will mean rinsing the containers three times with clean water and disposing of them at a properly licensed landfill.

11) Follow the recommended interval from last spray to harvest.

Handy Equivalent Measures

1 pint/100 gallons = 1 tsp./gal.
3 tsp. = 1 Tbsp.
16 Tbsp. = 1 cup
2 cups = 1 pint

1 oz.	=	2 Tbsp.	=	360 drops
1/2 oz.		1 Tbsp.		180
1/4 oz.		1 1/2 tsp.		90
1/6 oz.		1 tsp.		60
1/8 oz.		3/4 tsp.		45
1/12 oz.		1/2 tsp.		30
1/24 oz.		1/4 tsp.		15

7. Insect - Friend or Foe

No doubt, one of the questions asked most frequently by backyard fruit growers is, "what is this insect feeding on my fruit plant's leaves or chewing on my fruit?" Because of their easy visibility, these effects of insect presence are usually first to be noticed. Chewing on fruit or leaves can certainly do serious damage to your crop, and as a result the adversarial relationship between gardener and insect often begins here. One needs to realize, though, that not all insects are bad. Many are actually very beneficial; and some exist in the garden with little or no consequence.

In this chapter you will learn to identify the insects, both good and bad, most common to small fruit plantings as well as how to control or encourage these insects. Since many insects change form during different stages of development, they are sometimes difficult for the novice gardener to identify. Consequently, it is helpful to understand insect life cycles. This understanding may also help you to identify an unfamiliar insect.

Understanding Insect Life Cycles

All insects and mites go through similar and predictable stages as they mature from the egg to the adult. Basically this cycle can be diagrammed as follows (Figure 22):

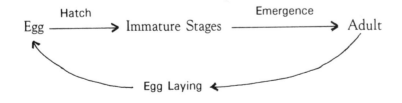

Figure 22. General insect life cycle

All insects start as eggs, laid by the adult female. She may lay a single egg or a mass of eggs. Under favorable conditions, the egg hatches and goes through several immature stages. At the end of this growth phase the insect emerges as an adult. Mating takes place and the cycle is repeated. For some insects, it may take a full growing season, from spring to fall, to go through one complete cycle. Others may complete the cycle in a matter of days and produce several generations within a single growing season. At certain times during this cycle, the insect is more vulnerable to predators and pesticides than at other times. An understanding of the different growth periods will show the gardener how one might take advantage of this vulnerability to control unwanted pests. Of course, beneficial insects also go through these same stages and one needs to be cautious not to damage the beneficial insect population during these times.

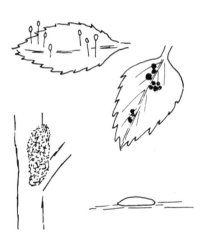

The insect eggs can take many forms. Some are flattened ovals, some are set up on stalks and some may be barrel shaped. They may be laid individually (such as aphid, mite, or fruit fly eggs) or they may be found in compact groups surrounded by protective coverings (such as tent caterpillars or leaf rollers). Eggs are laid in numerous locations, such as the underside of a leaf; inside the developing fruit flesh; in the growing shoot, crown or cane; and in the soil. Most eggs are fairly resilient and therefore not easy to control at this stage. Some have a hard exterior for protection. Others are protected because they are laid within the plant tissue where predators or pesticides are less likely to reach them. A few eggs, such as those of mites, are easier to control. They are fairly soft and permeable which makes them easy to smother with a dormant oil. Also, they are typically laid on the undersides of leaves and are accessible to predators.

Figure 23. *Insect eggs*

Once the egg hatches, it goes through a number of growth stages called instars. Each instar is separated by a molting phase. Since insects have no skeletons to support their bodies, they are supported and protected by a hard, rigid exoskeleton or outer skin. Unlike vertebrates' skin, the exoskeleton does not expand as the insect develops. To grow, the insect must shed its exoskeleton and develop a new, larger one. This process is called molting. For a short time, while the insect is shedding its old skin and before the new skin is fully developed, the insect's soft body is exposed and quite vulnerable to injury. This is often the stage at which it is easiest to control the unwanted insect. This is also the stage at which many beneficial insects, too, are most susceptible to pesticides or predators.

When the insect molts, it not only grows larger, its body may change form too. This process of changing form is called metamorphosis. In some insects the adult form closely resembles the immature form, known as the nymph or larva. The only differences may be that the adult has wings and reproductive organs and is larger in size. This type of minor change in form is known as gradual metamorphosis. Insects that undergo gradual metamorphosis include plant bugs, aphids, mites, leafhoppers and scale.

Gradual Metamorphosis

Egg ⟶ Several Larval Stages ⟶ Adult
             (instars)

Complete Metamorphosis

Egg ⟶ Larval Stages ⟶ Pupa ⟶ Adult
             (instars)

Figure 24. *Gradual and complete metamorphosis compared*

Other insects undergo a process of complete metamorphosis. The change from the immature form to the adult is obvious and dramatic.

In complete metamorphosis, the insect develops from an egg through one or more larval stages. Many of the larvae appear as some sort of worm. The larva then undergoes a resting stage known as the pupa. When it emerges from the pupal stage it is completely transformed as an adult. Beetles, flies and moths exhibit complete metamorphosis.

Insects that undergo gradual metamorphosis, not only appear similar in form, but tend to spend their whole life cycle on the same host plant as well. Those that undergo complete metamorphosis, however, may inhabit very different locations and exhibit different feeding habits with different life stages.

Insect Damage

Damage caused by insects can be of two kinds, direct and indirect. Direct damage to the fruit usually occurs from chewing on the fruit, laying eggs in the fruit, burrowing within the fruit flesh or in some other way visibly disfiguring the fruit. Most often this is the damage the home gardener notices first and seeks to control. An occasional damaged fruit is not cause for alarm. Control is usually justified, however, if large numbers of fruit are being damaged.

Indirect damage is more subtle and involves damage to the plant. Insects will suck nutrients from the plant, bore into the crown or canes, or reduce the plant's food producing leaf surface by injuring the leaves. The damage weakens the plant and makes it more difficult for the plant to properly photosynthesize. Indirectly, your harvest is diminished by smaller or fewer fruit. Decisions on controlling indirect damage are hard to make. In most cases, a healthy plant can tolerate a limited amount of indirect damage, but often by the time less experienced gardeners notice indirect plant damage, it is already at fairly high levels. A conservative approach would be to watch the planting for a week or two. Observe whether the number of pests appears to be increasing, holding steady, or being reduced by indigenous biological controls. If conditions appear to be getting worse, control of the pest will likely be necessary.

General Insect Identification

Body color and shape are commonly used traits for identifying insects. It helps to be able to identify the basic body parts too. Both immature and adult insects' bodies are made up of three basic areas:

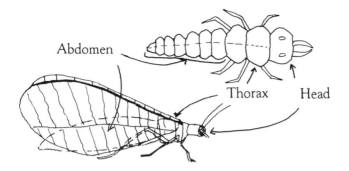

Figure 25. *Basic insect body parts*

the head, the thorax and the abdomen. Figure 25 shows various insects' stages and their body part arrangements. Basically, the head has the sensing organs (eyes, antennae, mouth). The legs and wings are attached to the thorax, and the abdomen carries the sex organs. In the immature stages some body parts, such as sex organs or legs, may be absent and in some cases the abdomen may have leg-like appendages. Some immature forms may also have very small heads. To identify your insect, observe carefully and ask yourself these questions:

    1) What color is its head and body?
    2) How many legs does it have?
    3) Does it appear to be adult or immature?
    4) Are its wings and body hairy or hairless?
    5) Does it have visible antennae?

By answering these questions and comparing your specimen insect to the illustrations in this book, you should be able to identify the primary group to which it belongs. In many cases, you may also be able to identify it more specifically by name.

    The illustrations on the following pages show the most common insect pests that the backyard fruit grower is likely to encounter. This chapter illustrates those insects commonly afflicting several of the small fruits. Those insects that are more specific to just one or two fruit will be found in the chapter devoted to that particular fruit. Common beneficial insects are also illustrated in this chapter. Certainly there are other insects which appear only occasionally or only in certain regions of the country. Your local cooperative extension service should be able to help in their identification.

Figure 26. Aphid

Aphids feed on most all small fruit. Their color varies by species from red, green, black, gray, to yellow. Less than ¼" long, this insect sucks sap from leaves causing them to appear mottled and eventually curl. Aphids can severely weaken the plant. Sticky "honeydew" excreted by the aphid can be come a substrate for sooty mold growth. Aphid populations can multiply quickly and should be controlled when they are first noticed. A strong spray of water will dislodge a portion of these pests. Ladybug larvae, lacewings and, parasitic wasps provide biological controls. Insecticidal soap will smother the eggs.

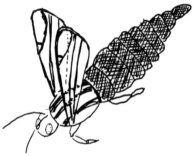

Figure 27. Borers

Borers of various types cause plant injury by boring into the cane, crown, or trunk and weakening fruit plants. These include grape root borer, and raspberry crown borers, which, as adult insects are ½" to 1" long wasp-like, clear winged moths. Body and wing patterns are black and yellow. The larvae are typically white or pale cream color with dark heads. strawberry crown borers are snout-nosed beetles and raspberry cane borers are in the sawfly family. Practical controls in the home garden require removing and destroying any canes or branches containing the larvae as soon as they are noticed.

Several **leafrollers** found on fruit trees are common on bush fruit and brambles. Adults vary in description from white with reddish bands on the wings, to reddish brown or brownish tan mottled wings often with characteristic V-shaped bands. They range in size from ½" to 1" long. The larvae vary in color, depending on the species. Damage is done by the larvae chewing on the fruit surface, buds, or leaves and spinning webs around leaves to form tightly curled feeding shelter. Small young larvae can be controlled with *B. thuringiensis* when they first appear. Rotenone and pyrethrin also provide control. Parasitic wasps are natural predators of leafroller larvae.

Figure 28. Leafrollers

84 the Backyard Berry Book

Mites suck sap from the leaves of strawberry, raspberry, blueberry, and grape causing yellowing or bronzing as symptoms. Other species burrow into currant leaves causing galls. Pinpoint in size, their color varies from red to translucent light yellow to cream. They are usually found on the underside of the leaf. Various predator mite species provide natural controls. Dormant oils smoother gall mite eggs when applied just before bud break. Insecticidal soap or pyre-

Figure 29. Mites

thrin can be used during the season when mite numbers reach damaging levels or symptoms are observed.

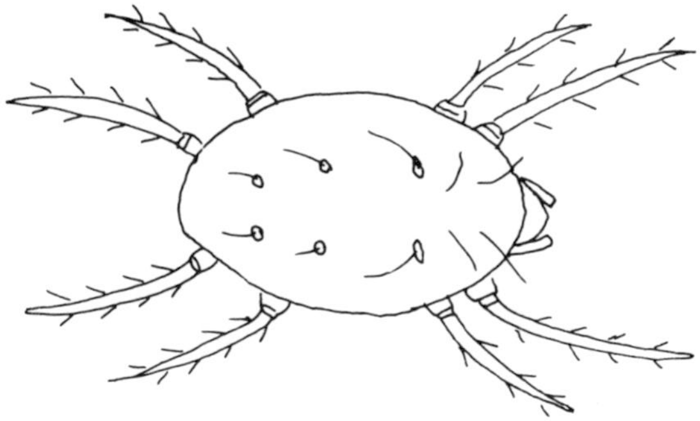

Rose Chafers are typically present in large numbers during June and July. They are worst on sandy sites adjacent to grassy areas. Damage is done to many small fruit when they skeletonize the leaves and flowers. Grapes are a preferred host, but this very motile winged beetle feeds on many plants. One half inch long, with tan red-

Figure 30. Rose Chafer

dish brown edged wings and black underbody, rose chafer has long, thin, hairy legs. Pyrethrin or Sevin controls this beetle, which can also be picked off by hand and drowned in a jar of water.

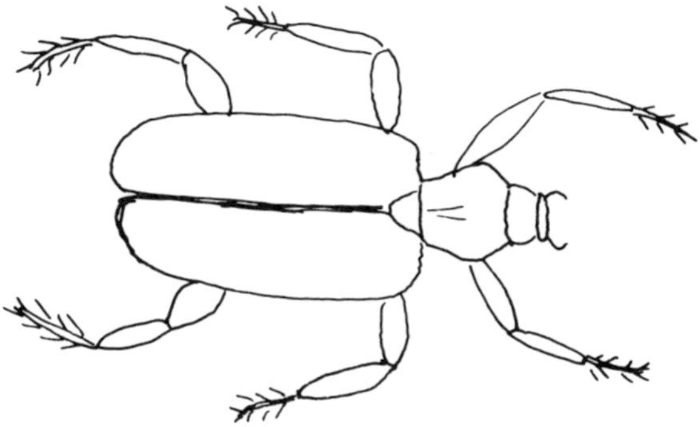

Cutworms are common where old sod has recently been turned into vineyard or berry patch. Found on all small fruit, cutworms feed on developing buds and shoots at the base of newly set plants. Climbing cutworms are especially fond of grapes and can quickly decimate a newly planted vineyard. Cutworms emerge early in the

Figure 31. *Cutworm*

Figure 32. *Tarnished Plant Bug*

spring as the ground warms and buds are just beginning to break. Although they feed primarily at night, cutworms can be located during the day by digging in the soil at the base of the plants. One to two inches long, the gray-brown to black caterpillar has a shiny head and greasy appearance. New plants can be partly protected with cardboard or plastic collars set several inches deep in the soil.

Tarnished plant bug is 1/4" long, with yellowish-brown mottled wings. Its body may have black spots or reddish stripes. It damages numerous fruit, including strawberry and raspberry, by injecting toxins into the fruit, causing hard, deformed, sunken areas on the fruit. Injured strawberries will show nubby, distorted tips. Tarnished plant bug overwinters in ground litter. One of the key controls is sanitation by removal of overwintering sites. Predators of tarnished plant bug include big-eyed bug which can be encouraged by planting subterranean clover or berseem.

Japanese Beetles, well known by most gardeners in the regions where they are a problem, are one half inch long and green bronze in color. The adult beetles find raspberry and grape preferred foods. Adult feeding skeletonizes leaves, weakening plants. The white grubs feed on the roots of new plants. Milky spore applied to the soil for several years eventually kills enough grubs to keep populations low. For more immediate results pick beetles off plants by hand and drown in a jar of water.

Figure 33. *Japanese Beetle*

86 the Backyard Berry Book

Many insects will produce more than one generation of offspring over the course of each fruit growing season. How many generations are produced is somewhat dependent on the length of the growing season in a geographic area. The listing below indicates what you can typically expect to observe.

Insect Generations per Growing Season

Insect Pest	Generations	Insect Pest	Generations
Aphids	3 - 4	Mites	6 - 8
Borers	1	Rose Chafer	1
Leafrollers	1 - 2	Tarnished Plant Bug	2 - 5

Development of the pests closely parallels the development of the fruit plants. Figure 34 shows the time during which major outbreaks of the more common insect pests are likely to occur in the northern United States. These are also the times during which control will be most important. In the south, the sequence of events will still be the same, but may occur several weeks earlier due to the earlier arrival of warm weather. Use the charts as a guide when observing the fruit planting and apply control measures only when actually necessary.

Beneficial Insects

Beneficial insects can contribute considerably to maintaining control of pest insects in the small fruit garden. Indeed, their efforts often go unnoticed merely because no major pest outbreak occurs to alert the backyard grower. Most gardeners are familiar with the appearance of the adult stage of numerous beneficials such as ladybug beetles, praying mantises, lacewings, and others. However, much of the job of controlling pests is actually done by the beneficial insects' immature stages. They are often the most voracious feeders while the mature adults have settled down to concentrate on mating and egg laying. The inexperienced gardener may even accidentally mistake these immature insects for something they are not, simply because they are not familiar with their appearance.

	APRIL	MAY	JUNE
			Bloom · Harvest
Strawberry			
Rhubarb			
Rapsberry-red			
Raspberry-black			
Blackberry			
Blueberry			
Lingonberry			
Currant			
Gooseberry			
Black currant			
Table grape			
Muscadine			
Kiwifruit			
Cutworm			
Aphids			
Leafrollers			
Mites			
Rose chafer			
Japanese beetle			
Strawberry crown borer			
Strawberry clipper			
Tarnished plant bug			
Strawberry sap beetle			
Rhubarb curculio			
Raspberry cane borer			
Raspberry crown borer			
Blueberry maggot			
Currant fruit fly			
Gooseberry fruitworm			
Imported currant worm			
Grape phylloxera			
Grape flea beetle			
Grape berry moth			

Figure 34. Pest development correlated to fruit plant development

88 the Backyard Berry Book

JULY   AUGUST   SEPTEMBER   OCTOBER

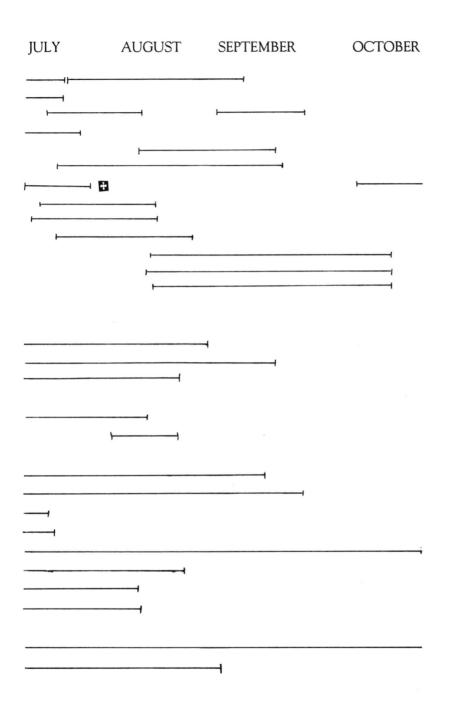

Insect - Friend or Foe 89

Using and Encouraging Beneficial Organisms for Pest Control

Using beneficial organisms for pest control requires a somewhat different mind-set than the traditional "spray 'em and kill 'em" approach to pest control. Although more is being learned daily, the use of beneficials is still in its early stages and much remains unknown about working with beneficials for optimum results.

One of the key points in the use of beneficials is, of course, acceptance of the idea that not all bugs are "bad" bugs. Many are indeed helpful and others are basically of no concern - neither helpful nor harmful. The gardener needs to realize that whatever pesticides, and in some cases fertilizers as well, are used in the garden may have an effect on the health of the beneficial population. In some cases beneficials may be more susceptible to a given pesticide than the insect for which the pesticide is intended. In other cases a pesticide used for another purpose, such as a disease control fungicide, may have a detrimental effect on the beneficial. So, the use of pesticides must be done very judiciously. This applies to both chemical and organic materials.

Using beneficials to best advantage also requires patience at times. Unlike most pesticides, which show results fairly quickly, beneficial populations may take time to build to a level where the effects of their efforts become visible. Often it is difficult for the impatient gardener to wait and watch while the crop is apparently poised for decimation. It helps to remember, however, that most fruit plants have a certain level of tolerance for pest damage and can indeed withstand some pest damage.

Another point to remember when counting on beneficial organisms for pest control is the fact that most beneficials are quite host specific. That is, they typically have one or two pests that they prey on, leaving other pests untouched. For example, a predator mite may do a wonderful job controlling your pest mite population, but will not feed at all on a strawberry clipper. Predator insects are often so specific that species vary from one geographic location to another, in many cases with much more variation in species than is found in pest populations. Often, when one purchases beneficial insects through a distant mail order catalog, they do not seem to be as effective as expected. This host specificity is one reason. The predators raised are likely to be those indigenous to the local area of the insectiary from which they are coming, and not necessarily the predator that is right for controlling your local pest population. In reality, little cataloging has been done to identify all the small local and regional populations of beneficial insects. So, in many cases it is hard to say accurately what predator species live where and exactly what pest species they control. Hopefully this information will become more available in the future. For now, the best approach to using beneficial insects in your small fruit planting may be to encourage those already living in your garden. The likelihood that they will feed on your pests is high because they certainly would not have survived for more than a generation without some native food source. They also have passed the test of being able to survive whatever climate conditions are typical in your area, be they dry, cold, hot, or fluctuating.

One of the easiest ways to encourage the growth of beneficial insect populations is by providing favorable habitats. This includes several factors. Proper food, water, shelter, and climatic environment are needed for beneficial populations to thrive. The most obvious food, of course, is the pest insect in the fruit garden. Simple as that sounds, keep in mind that a continuous minimal level of some sort of food source must be present so that the beneficial insect does not starve. Development of the pest and predator must coincide sufficiently so that peaks in predator populations are met with corresponding peaks in pest populations. Along with preying on garden pests, most beneficials spend part of their life feeding on alternate food sources. Very often these are flowering plants. Plants in the carrot, daisy, and mint families provide both food and moisture sources in their nectar and pollen.

Most beneficial insects find protection or overwinter in some sort of vegetative growth in or near the fruit garden. In some cases, predators may require a certain type of plant on which to complete certain stages of their life cycle. Often these are plants that are commonly classified as weeds or wildflowers. To encourage beneficial insect populations, it is often helpful to allow a border strip of weeds to grow near the fruit garden. These plants may also protect susceptible stages of the insect from environmental factors such as wind, dust, and excess sun. Over time the gardener can learn much about beneficial insects by observing and studying the insects found in and around the garden. This will be the best way to find out which insects are "friends" worth cultivating.

Effective Use of Beneficial Organisms

Under the right circumstances, some gardeners may still choose to purchase predator insects to introduce into the garden. When doing so, it helps to remember a few points that will make the introduction most successful:

1.) Make sure there is a proper match of predator and target insect. You will need to introduce a predator species that typically feeds on your given pest species. As an example, a predator that functions mainly as an egg parasite will not control adult insect stages.

2.) Proper timing of the predator release is very important. The feeding stage of the predator (which is often an immature stage) must be released when the susceptible stage of the pest is present, otherwise predators may die from lack of sufficient food.

3.) Predators must be released at the correct density or release rate. That is, enough (but not too many) predators must be released in order to achieve proper pest control. The proper release rate varies from one insect to the next and is often calculated by using the amount of planted area. For specific recommendations, consult the insectiary from which the beneficials are being purchased.

4.) Proper habitat to support adult as well as immature predators should be present. This includes water, nectar, and in some cases an alternate food source. Since beneficials are often released shortly before anticipated pest outbreaks, this is especially important. Otherwise beneficials may leave the area or die before major emergence and control of the pest has occurred.

To many gardeners' surprise, beneficial insects species often outnumber pest species in the fruit garden. Some of the following beneficial insects will surely be familiar while others do their work largely unnoticed. Some of them are similar in appearance to the pest insects so it is useful to learn their identifying characteristics.

Bigeyed Bugs name points out their most identifying characteristic. These 1/8 to 1/4 inch long black bugs are easily mistaken for the pest tarnished plant bug. On closer inspection their large protruding eyes distinguish them. Bigeyed bug feeds on numerous pests of the fruit garden including aphids, leafhoppers, mites, and plant bugs. Bigeyed bugs lay their eggs on goldenrod, pigweed, or soybeans and overwinter in garden litter.

Ground Beetles are voracious predators of numerous garden pests including cutworms, gypsy moths, slugs, and tent caterpillars. There are many species of this 3/4 to one inch long iridescent blue-black or brown beetles. Larvae have ten tapered segments and are black or brown. The adult beetle lives for two or three years and prefer white clover or sod to hide in.

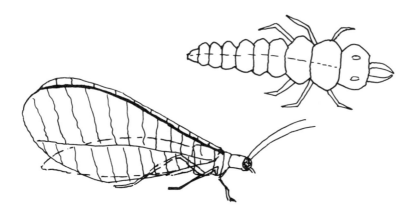

Figure 35. *Lacewing adult and larva*

Lacewing adults are 1/2 to 3/4 inch long, translucent whitish green insects with copper eyes. The larvae, also know as "aphid lions" for their terrific appetite for this pest, are light tan with long moth parts. Lacewing tend to be general predators and feed on garden pests including aphids, leafhoppers, mites, scale, and certain moth eggs. They can be encouraged by planting pollen and nectar bearing flowers.

Ladybug Beetle adults are easily recognized by most people. The adults are shiny black, red, or orange and about 1/16" long. Some have spots, others do not. The larva are less frequently recognized. Usually blue/black or reddish gray in color and 1/8" long, they are voracious feeders. Their primary prey is aphids, scale, and mites.

Praying Mantis has long been

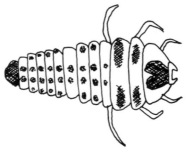

Figure 36. *Ladybug larva*

Insect - Friend or Foe 93

regarded as a beneficial insect in the garden due to its omnivorous appetite for other insects. Although, they are excellent predators of pests, they are unfortunately also voracious predators of other beneficial insects. Whether you truly want to encourage them, is a decision you will have.

Predator Mites are translucent tan to light red in color and similar in size and appearance to pest mites, which are their primary prey. **Syrphid Flies** are a "hovering" fly that looks much like a bee or yellow jacket wasp. The larvae are pale green to tan and "slug-like" in appearance. They feed on aphids and scale insects.

Other Beneficial Organisms

So far most discussion of biological controls has focussed on the use of beneficial or predator insects. Several other beneficial organisms exist that can also be a great help to the fruit gardener. One is the group of bacteria that have helpful properties. These bacteria work by invading a pest insect and weakening or killing it. Most of them act by upsetting the digestive functions of the pest. The bacteria have no effect on humans however. *Bacillus thuringiensis* (also known as Bt), is the most common bacteria used as an insecticide. This bacteria is used primarily to control the caterpillar stage of leaf feeding lepidoptera type (moth and butterfly) pests. These include such insects as grape leaf skeletonizer, tent caterpillar, and leaf rollers. To be effective, it must be ingested by the pest. It is less effective on caterpillars that feed inside the plant crowns, canes, and stems. These would include various borers. Another bacteria, *Bacillus popilliae* (milky spore) is used to control Japanese beetle grubs. *Agrobacterium radiobacter* works as a competitor to the bacteria that causes the disease crown gall. Since this disease primarily affects brambles, it is discussed in detail in chapter 12.

The bacteria that function as beneficial pest controls are typically short lived in the environment, often surviving only hours after having been sprayed. When using beneficial bacteria to control major pest outbreaks it may be necessary to spray numerous times, often only days apart until the majority of new emerging pests have been controlled.

8. Disease Identification

Diseases of small fruit fall into three major classifications based on what causes them. There are diseases caused by fungi, bacteria, and viruses. In all three cases, the actual organism causing the disease is hard to view with the naked eye, but the disease symptoms become readily apparent if allowed to progress. For most diseases, prevention is a more successful means of control than after the fact eradication. Therefore it is helpful to understand the conditions that bring on the various diseases and the conditions under which they flourish.

Fungus Diseases

Let us look first at those diseases caused by fungi. All the fungus organisms share a characteristic cycle of growth and reproduction. The general cycle is illustrated in Figure 37.

Most of the major fungus diseases common to small fruit have both a primary and a secondary infection period during which they may cause problems for your fruit or fruit plant. Overwintering leaves or fruit that have fallen to the ground often serve as host sites for fungal reproductive structures. During the primary infection phase, primary spores, or ascospores, are released from the reproductive structure. Under proper conditions the spores germinate and infect young developing flowers, fruit, or leaves. Secondary fungal fruiting structures are soon produced. If effective disease control measures are not applied during the primary infection phase, secondary fungal spores are released from the fruiting bodies and additional secondary disease infection of the fruit and leaves is likely throughout the growing season. Following secondary infection, diseased leaves and fruit often fall to the ground and overwinter. The following growing season new primary and secondary disease cycles are repeated.

In order to grow and continue reproducing, all fungi need certain favorable conditions. These include moisture, temperature, and a host (in this case, your fruit plant). In general, fungus diseases are most active in the temperature range present during the spring and

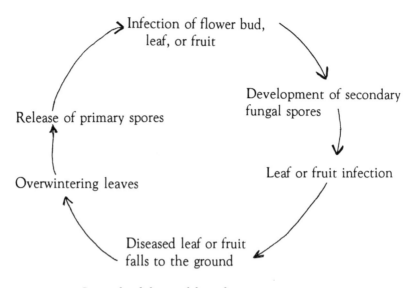

Infection of flower bud,
leaf, or fruit

Development of secondary
fungal spores

Release of primary spores

Leaf or fruit infection

Overwintering leaves

Diseased leaf or fruit
falls to the ground

Figure 37. *Generalized fungus life cycle*

summer growing seasons. When adequate moisture (from rain or high humidity) is present, the fungus will grow and infect either the plant or the developing fruit (and in some cases both). Different fungus diseases can cause mold and rot of the fruit, reduce the plant's leaf area and photosynthetic ability, or cause distorted growth of the leaves or fruit.

Identifying fungus diseases on small fruit can sometimes cause confusion for the novice gardener. Several small fruit species are host to certain fungus diseases that share the same name (such as anthracnose) while the symptoms, causal organism, and life cycle of the disease varies with the host plant. Small fruit are most commonly affected by the following fungus diseases:

Anthracnose infects brambles, strawberries and blueberries. On strawberry and blueberry the symptoms look like a slimy pink spore layer on the fruit. On stems and leaves, it appears as 1/4-3/4 inch dark sunken areas. It is a particular problem on day neutral strawberries, especially those grown on plastic mulch. On brambles, anthracnose appears as purple spots enlarging to 1/4 inch sunken gray circles with raised purple borders on canes, leaves, and occasionally on fruit. Severely diseased tissue drops out of the leaves, giving a "shot hole" appearance. It thrives in wet conditions above 60°F. Heavy rain in late spring and early summer presents prime disease conditions, as does overhead sprinkler irrigation. It is most serious on black and purple raspberries, but also occurs on red varieties. Control involves a combination of sanitation, removal of infected canes and branches right after fruiting, and lime-sulfur sprays in early spring.

Gray mold affects raspberries, strawberries, blueberries, and grapes. Also known as *Botrytis* Fruit Rot, this disease shows up on most fruit as a dusty gray mold on soft, ripe fruit. On blueberries, it primarily infects twigs and blossoms. It flourishes in cool temperatures with high humidity and is particularly problematic in the Pacific northwest. The best control for gray mold is to provide good air circulation and careful sanitation by removing decayed fruit and old infected canes and branches.

***Phytophthora* root rot** primarily affects brambles, blueberries, lingonberries, and rhubarb grown on poorly drained sites. Symptoms include wilting of bramble canes. Blueberries show yellowing or reddish coloration of the leaves. Eventually all affected plants exhibit stunted growth and dead feeder roots. There are no known chemical controls for root rot, but really the best control for this disease is prevention. Plants should be grown on properly drained sites or raised beds and excessive irrigation should be avoided.

Powdery Mildew infects a wide range of small fruit including brambles and blueberries. Gooseberries and European wine grape varieties are especially susceptible. Powdery mildew develops rapidly in high humidity and temperatures between 60 and 80°F. Unlike most other fungus diseases, it does not require free water for the spread of disease spores. Symptoms appear as white powdery patches of fungal mycelium on the upper or lower leaf surfaces. Later, leaves turn brown and dry and curl at the edges. As the disease advances, branches and fruit may become infected. Powdery mildew decreases the plant's photosynthetic ability and reduces cold hardiness of severely infected buds. Early season control of this disease is important to keep it from getting firmly established. Bordeaux sprays (a mixture of two pounds copper sulfate and six pounds hydrated lime per 100 gallons of water) prior to bud break or sulfur sprays during the season are effective controls. Caution needs to be used when applying sulfur sprays to certain grape varieties, however, as they are sensitive to leaf burn. Less susceptible varieties may show sulfur damage when temperatures exceed 85°F. shortly after application.

Verticillium wilt occurs most often under cool, humid conditions. It is a soil borne disease that effects a wide range of plants in the family Solanaceae, as well as strawberries and brambles. On strawberries, symptoms most commonly appear in the first year, when outer leaves turn brown and collapse. Brambles show symptoms when leaves yellow and canes turn blue and die by mid-season. The disease first appears on the lower part of the cane, progressing upward. Black raspberries are most susceptible, red raspberries less so, and blackberries are least susceptible. Verticillium wilt can live in the soil for ten years or more. There is no effective cure, so prevention is the best mechanism for control. Do not plant susceptible small fruit where tomatoes, peppers, potatoes, or eggplant been have grown recently. Sites previously planted to cotton, okra, mint, apricot, cherry, almond, and pecan can also carry verticillium wilt. Several broadleaf weeds, notably lamb's quarter, red root pigweed, and those in the nightshade family, such as horse nettle also harbor the disease.

Bacterial Diseases

Only a small number of diseases of small fruit are caused by bacteria. The most common of these is crown gall. Crown gall bacteria infect the roots of many fruit as well as other landscape trees. It is most common on raspberries and is also found in soil that has grown grapes for many years, although it appears to cause few symptoms on the grape root. The disease develops as small, tan colored rounded tumors on the root system. Eventually crown gall tumors become several inches in size, hard, and woody. Most often they end up girdling the crown or large main roots.

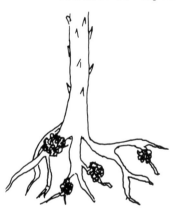

Figure 38. Crown gall

The best control method is to purchase disease free nursery plants. Roots can also be dipped in a solution of a noninfecting, competitive bacterium called *Agrobacterium radiobacter* if planting on a larger scale. This biological control works as a competitor to the detrimental gall causing bacteria. Uninfected plant roots are dipped in a solution containing the A. *radiobacter*, which then penetrates into the roots. When the soil borne pathogen bacteria A. *tumefaciens* later tries to enter the roots, it is unable to

98 the Backyard Berry Book

find suitable sites to colonize and thus the disease does not develop. The competitive bacteria itself causes no symptoms in the plant.

Virus and Miscellaneous Disorders

Virus diseases tend to develop more slowly than bacterial diseases, sometimes taking several years before noticeable symptoms occur. Often, virus disease symptoms may mimic other problems such as poor plant nutrition, fungus diseases, or general weakness of the plant, which makes viruses harder to identify. Several small fruit species are susceptible to virus diseases, but unfortunately few cures are available at this time. Much research is still being done on virus diseases and hopefully, in time, identification and control will become easier. For now, the best approach to controlling virus diseases in the small fruit planting is prevention. Be sure to always purchase virus free plant stock from a reputable nursery, as many viruses are first transmitted in the propagation process. Isolate new plantings from old or wild plantings that may have become infected. Keeping aphids, nematodes and other virus vectors under control will help restrict the spread of viruses, as these insects often transmit viruses from one plant to another when they feed. Specific viruses are discussed in the chapters on the individual fruit they affect.

Mycoplasma are also a source of diseases with symptoms similar to virus diseases. Unfortunately little is known about this source of disease other than that leafhoppers often transmit the mycoplasma. Approaches to control would be the same as for viruses.

Nematodes

Nematodes are not a fruit disease, nor are they an insect. They are microscopic round worms that live in the soil. Since nematode problems often mimic fruit disease symptoms, they will be discussed in this chapter.

Nematodes are primitive worms that feed as parasites on plant roots. Sometimes their feeding will weaken the roots sufficiently to allow secondary diseases to enter the tissue. If your fruit planting is growing poorly and you have ruled out other disease and nutrition causes, consider testing the soil for nematodes. Samples are taken just like the soil nutrient samples and can often be done at the same time. Your county extension office can advise on the proper procedure and timing for your area.

If you are able to examine the roots of your fruit plant, you may see nematode feeding symptoms. They include root galls, dead areas of root tissue, injured root tips, excessive branching of roots or generally stunted growth of the roots or plant.

Several methods of nematode control exist. Choosing resistant plant varieties, when possible, is the most feasible for the backyard fruit grower. Starving the nematode population for two or three seasons during site preparation with a cover crop they don't normally feed on can provide effective control. Suitable cover crops were mentioned in chapter 2. Parasitic nematodes also provide feasible small scale control of plant damaging nematodes. Although they attack other nematodes, beneficial parasitic nematode species do not damage plants. Clandosan, a material made primarily of crushed crab shell protein, offers yet another control means for nematodes in the home garden. It functions by stimulating naturally occurring soil microbes that attack pest nematodes. Normal application rates range from fifty to eighty pounds per thousand square feet and should be made annually. Clandosan must be incorporated into the soil, preferably by tilling, but irrigation may be used in perennial plantings. Soil fumigation is used in commercial fruit plantings, but is not very practical in the small space of the home garden and can be detrimental to beneficial soil microorganisms.

9. Wildlife Pests

Along with controlling insects and diseases, the backyard berry grower has to contend with other garden visitors as well. Fortunately, these pests are easy to identify and in some cases pose more of a nuisance in the backyard than a serious problem.

Birds

Birds in the home garden can be a mixed blessing. Often they make a substantial contribution to controlling insects and are valued as a nonchemical pest control. At the same time, birds enjoy feeding on fruit. This is particularly true with berries, and in some gardens birds prove to be the major pest.

Several deterrents are available. Most work for short periods. Experience has shown, though, that birds do learn which ones pose a real threat and soon ignore any single deterrent, if used for an extended period. The best strategy is to rotate erratically between methods.

For the fruit garden that is not too large, the only reliable bird deterrent method is to cover the garden completely with netting several weeks before harvest so that birds cannot reach the fruit. In order for this to be effective, care must be taken that the netting is

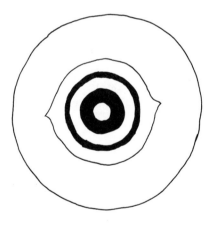

Figure 39. Bird "Scare Eye"

placed far enough away from the fruit that birds can not peck through it. One easy way to assure this is by building a lightweight frame of plastic pipe or wood that the netting can be draped over. If the frame is built in such a way that it can be easily disassembled it can be moved from one crop to another as needed throughout the growing season. When in use be sure that the netting is secured at ground level so that the birds cannot get in underneath it. When care is taken in applying the netting, this method is probably the most effective bird deterrent and, although the material requires some initial investment, it can be reused for many seasons if treated carefully. The major disadvantage of netting is that it needs to be removed each time the garden is to be picked.

Aluminum pie plates or strips of foil hung from string to wave in the breeze are an old trick used to scare away birds. Although initially useful, this method does not remain effective over a long time period. A more effective deterrent of the same vein is a metallic tape that is strung tightly along the rows of fruit in the berry patch or vineyard. When the wind blows, the tape moves and emits low frequency sounds that mimic the call of a bird in distress. This signals other birds to stay out of the area. This method is effective provided at least a slight breeze is present. The tape is quick and easy to apply and the sounds are outside those audible by humans.

A recent technique in bird scaring comes from Japan and appears to be working quite effectively in both berry patches and orchards. Here a large inflated beach ball sized balloon is suspended from a pole six to ten feet high. The balloon has been imprinted with a colored pattern that appears to the birds as the eye of a hawk. Most birds, except robins, will stay away from this apparent predator. If necessary, several balloons can be hung around the berry patch where bird populations are high. The balloons are readily available from many mail order garden suppliers.

Deer

Deer are more of a problem for the weekend farmer with country acreage than for the suburban gardener. They can, however, cause considerable damage to any garden, and do so in a hurry.

Various deer deterrents have proven themselves useful. Like bird deterrents, they need to be rotated, lest the deer become too familiar with one and ignore it. One popular and easy option is to drill a hole through a hotel size bar of scented soap and attach it with a "twist tie" to stakes placed every eight to ten feet in the garden.

Little cloth bags filled with human hair or animal blood and bone meal, known as tankage, can be tied to stakes. The scent keeps the deer wary and will deter them in areas where they have not become too domesticated from being fed by animal lovers. Tankage or hair bags will need to be changed every few weeks as the scent dissipates.

A commercially prepared spray of ammonia soap (Hinder™) or putrefied eggs (Deer Away™), is another possibility. This is not as foul as it sounds. Although the odor is quite strong

Figure 40. Hotel soap bars & tankage bags ready to hang as deer deterrent

to the deer, we humans have an inferior sense of smell in comparison and rarely detect any odor unless we purposely stick our noses in the plant. Even then the odor is mild. A word of caution on this type of product: it can burn tender young foliage and should be applied by soaking a sponge in the material and attaching it to stakes placed around the berry patch. Stakes at deer nose height do an effective job. The sponge will need to be resaturated periodically, especially after heavy rains. Hinder™ can also be applied to dormant berry bushes, although it is less effective in cold temperatures.

Fencing may be a deer deterrent of last resort. Although expensive on a large scale, it is often possible to enclose the small garden for a reasonable cost. If you do resort to fencing, remember that a deer is perfectly capable of jumping a nine foot fence or slithering under a wire as low as only two feet high.

Rodents

Mice, voles, and rabbits can play real havoc with fruit bushes and vines. Most of their damage is done in the winter and is a problem on woody canes, branches, and trunks of fruit plants. Under cover of snow, they will gnaw on the branches and trunks, often chewing away a wide ring of bark all the way around them. Rabbits will go so far as to actually cut the branches right off. The girdled area can be difficult to repair when discovered several months later. The best cure for rodent damage is prevention.

Many backyard gardeners mulch their fruit plants and in so doing create a potentially perfect habitat for mice. One easy preventive step is to keep all mulch back away from the trunk six to twelve inches. (This is good strategy for disease prevention too.) In the fall of the year, rake the mulch back even further to discourage rodents from setting up their winter home near your berry plants. Do not worry about strawberries, however. Mice usually leave them alone even if they are covered by mulch. The cold protection provided by the mulch far outweighs any slight rodent damage.

Gophers, Raccoons and Porcupines

Gophers will occasionally burrow in the garden but are primarily a problem only in kiwifruit, where they have a strong affinity for feeding on the roots. Raccoons sometimes cause damage by breaking vines and branches in addition to having voracious appetites and cleaning out your fruit supply. Wayward porcupines can be a sporadic pest in fruit plantings, gnawing off branches and giving bushes the appearance of a bad pruning job. Except in the case of gophers, which are discussed in depth in chapter 21, deterrents are of little help with these pests. Control consists of trapping the animal in a live trap and removing it to more hospitable territory. Shooting it is also an option, but is not well received in a suburban environment.

Section II.

Early Spring Fruit

10. Strawberries

Strawberries are one of the most widely grown fruit in the United States, second only to apples. With such widespread distribution, they are often the backyard gardener's first exposure to growing berries. One of the earliest spring crops, strawberries require only a small amount of space and are easily planted alongside the vegetable garden or in a patio container. As few as two dozen plants can supply the needs of a family of four.

Selecting and Preparing the Planting Site

As with most perennial plantings, proper site selection and site preparation pave the way to better production. When selecting a strawberry planting site, consider that June bearing and everbearing strawberry varieties need a minimum of six hours of sun daily to produce a crop, and ten or more hours of sunlight is highly beneficial in increasing yield. Day neutral varieties are less demanding in their need for sun and will easily tolerate being shaded during the hotter afternoon. (The different types of strawberries are discussed in detail later, so don't despair if you are confused about them at this point.)

Try to choose a location with sufficient elevation and air drainage. Early blooming strawberries are easily damaged by spring frost, especially if planted in low lying cold pockets. In areas where late spring frosts are typical, even late blooming varieties may be damaged from time to time. Strawberries prefer a moist, well drained soil with a high organic matter content. Although they will tolerate a soil pH range from 5.5 to 7.5, they will be most productive at a pH around 6.0.

As pointed out in an earlier chapter, unfortunately, few planting sites offer ideal conditions. Most, however, can be enhanced with a bit of preparation in the season prior to planting. Since strawberries are relatively shallow rooted, they do not compete well with weeds and are also quickly damaged by heavy handed hoeing. It is easiest and best to remove weeds from the planting site the summer prior to planting. Most gardeners prefer to do this by cultivating to a depth of six to eight inches. Use chemical weed killers with great caution, as strawberries are quite sensitive to herbicide residues carried over in the soil.

Following cultivation and the removal of as many weeds as possible, you can enhance the soil organic matter in one of two ways: If you are preparing the site the summer prior to planting, a green manure cover crop can be planted. Soil testing and the addition of any nutrients or pH modifiers is also best done at this time. If you do not have sufficient time to grow a green manure or your site requires additional organic matter supplementation, spade a two inch layer of peat, leaf mold, compost, or well rotted manure into the soil. If your soil is poorly drained, and you have your heart set on growing strawberries, you may want to grow your berries on raised beds. Beds two feet wide and six inches deep, supplemented with organic matter to improve drainage, often work well.

Growth Habits and Varieties

As with so many things today, a strawberry is no longer just a strawberry. The traditional varieties have normally borne fruit in June or early July and are called June bearers. More recently, new varieties have been introduced to extend the fruiting season. The first of these were called "everbearing" because they tended to produce a crop during the normal June harvest period but also produced another, smaller crop in late summer or early fall. The newest group of strawberries introduced are the "day neutral" berries. These strawberries will produce as long as temperatures are moderate. This will typically be from June to October in northern areas and January to August in mild coastal or southern climates. By choosing varieties from several groups, you can now have fresh strawberries continuously throughout the growing season. Let's look more closely at why each of these groups grow the way they do.

June Bearing

June bearing strawberries normally initiate fruit buds for the coming season during the shorter days and cooler temperatures of autumn. As days lengthen and become warmer, typically in June, they produce one major harvest that lasts for two to three weeks. After the harvest is over, the plants soon begin producing runners or daughter plants that will also bear fruit the following season. As shorter days and cooler temperatures return in late summer - early autumn, runner production ceases and fruit bud initiation occurs again. With proper renovation (more on this later), new runner plants allow a planting of June bearing strawberries to produce a sizeable harvest for three to four seasons.

Everbearing

The name everbearing is somewhat of a misnomer. As plant breeders searched for varieties to extend the strawberry harvest season, several varieties were discovered that produced more than just the typical, single early summer crop. Everbearing strawberries typically initiate fruit buds under the longer day length found in summer. Like the June bearer, they will produce a spring crop. Additionally, ever-bearing varieties will produce a smaller late summer crop of berries. The combined harvests from everbearing varieties typically is almost equal in quantity to the single harvest from June bearing varieties. The overall berry size however tends to be somewhat smaller. With the introduction of the day neutral strawberries discussed below, the old everbearing varieties are quickly falling by the wayside and are often no longer listed in nursery catalogs.

Day Neutral

Day neutral varieties are so named because, unlike June bearing or everbearing strawberries, they initiate their fruit buds without regard for day length. Since they continue to initiate fruit buds throughout the season, they continue to produce a berry crop all season long and could justifiably be called "true" everbearers. This can cause some confusion for the novice looking through nursery catalogs, as the older everbearing and the newer day neutral varieties are often still lumped together and sold under the heading of everbearing. If the distinction is unclear from the catalog, don't be afraid to ask. Your nursery professional should be able to clarify them for you. Also, unlike the previous two groups, the day neutral varieties produce very few runner plants, and so a few aspects of their culture are slightly different, as is explained later in this chapter.

Alpine

The alpine strawberry, frais de bois or wood strawberry as it is also known, is an unfortunately lesser known berry than the modern strawberry types just mentioned. Once favored by European nobility, their popularity probably waned because of their small size. Normally only one half to one inch long, the alpine strawberry has an intense flavor and produces a crop from June until frost. Both red and white (pale cream) colored varieties are available. The white varieties have a taste that resembles pineapple and are said to be less attractive to birds. The culture of the alpine strawberry is somewhat different from today's modern berry in that it does not typically set runner plants. It reproduces easily from seed and is a perfect plant for edgings, containers, or the kitchen-side herb garden.

Selecting Varieties

Strawberries are probably the most popularly planted fruit in home gardens. From a horticulturist's perspective, this is sometimes surprising. One would expect that with their widespread popularity strawberries would be very adaptable and show consistent production characteristics from one location to the next. This is not always the case, however. A variety that grows well in your well drained soil may produce poorly in your neighbor's heavy soil. Varieties that grow well on the west coast don't usually perform well on the East coast and vice versa. Some varieties even perform quite differently when grown in different regions within a state. Consequently, when you first start growing strawberries, you may need to try a number of varieties until you find several that are truly best suited to your conditions. Start your first season by choosing three or four varieties that appear suitable. When the time comes to replace the old bed with new plants, continue growing the one or two best selections and replace the other varieties with something new. Continue this type of elimination until you have found those varieties that are the most successful for you. These test trials can be lots of fun and with so many strawberry varieties available, you should have little problem finding several that will be particularly well suited to your individual garden conditions.

Once you have answered the basic questions on what you most want for qualities in your berries, you will still need to decide whether you prefer to have just one crop in early summer or whether you would like to extend the fruit supply throughout the season. This is purely a matter of personal preference, as present day varieties will offer either option.

By now you may be wondering how many plants to order. Under normal growing conditions, you can expect each original mother plant to produce an average of one quart of berries per season. Based on how many berries you expect to use, you can figure accordingly.

Let us now look at the specific types and varieties of strawberries best suited to the home garden. Strawberries are self-fruitful, so you will not need to worry about choosing varieties based on pollination requirements. However, planting several varieties will provide you with a longer harvest season. You will also be able to select varieties that are well suited to the uses favored by your family. Varieties selected for the chart that follows were chosen for resistance to the major strawberry diseases, flavor, and suitability for growing in the home garden. The chart is coded as follows, Primary Uses: E=eating, F=freezing, J=jam. Disease Resistance: RS=Red stele, V=Verticillium wilt, LSc=Leaf Scorch, LSp=Leaf Spot. Level of resistance: HR=Highly, R=Fairly, IR=Some, S=Notably susceptible.

Variety	Best Use	Disease Resistance				Comments
		RS	V	LSc	LSp	
June Bearing						
Early Season						
Earliglow	E,F	R	IR	IR	R	Excellent flavor
Annapolis	E,F	R		S	S	Hardy. Large berry.
Sunrise	E	R	R	R	VS	
Earlibelle	E,F	S		R	R	
Veestar						Hardy. Excellent flavor, firm berry.
Early Midseason						
Cavendish	E,F	HR	S	R	R	
Lester		R	S	R	R	Firm skin.
Surecrop	E,F	R	VR	R	R	Widely adapted, high yielding.

Variety	Best Use	Disease Resistance				Comments
		RS	V	LSc	LSp	
Midseason						
Redchief	E,F	R	R	R	IR	
Cardinal	E,F	S	S	R	R	For S. central & S. east. Inconsistent in the north.
Catskill	F	S	HR	R	S	Easy to grow. Top home garden variety. Hardy. Soft fruit.
Allstar	E,F	HR	IR	R	R	Productive. Firm, large fruit. N. east/MidAtlantic
Glooscap	J	S	IR			Very hardy. For Upper midwest.
Guardian		R	HR	R	R	
Scott	E,F	R	IR	R	R	Mild flavor.
Jewel	E,F	S	S	R	R	Top quality. Needs careful renovation. Hardy.
Late Season						
Midway	E,F,J	R	IR	S	S	Best on heavy soil.
Sparkle	E,F,J	R	S	IR	S	Tops for jam & freezing. Good in northern areas.
Delite		R	HR	IR	R	Hardy.
Lateglow	E,F	HR	IR	IR	IR	
Everbearing						
Fort Laramie	E,F,J					Very hardy (-30°F). Productive.
Gem (Superfection)	F,J					Dependable.
Ogallala	J					Very hardy. Wild berry flavor.
Ozark Beauty	E,F,J	S	S	R	R	Very productive. Hardy.
Puget Beauty	E			R	R	
Quinalt	E,J	R		R	R	High yields. California & Pacific northwest.
Oso Grande	E					Productive. Soft, medium size fruit.

Variety	Best Use	Disease Resistance RS V LSc LSp	Comments
Day Neutral			
Aptos		R	Hardy.
Brighton	E		Large fruit. Good for California.
Burlington			Widely adapted.
Fern	E		Very productive. California & midwest.
Hecker			Early. Similar to but hardier than Brighton. Good for California.
Selva			
Tribute	E	R R R S	Hardy. Productive, large fruit
Tristar	F	R R S	Hardy. Excellent flavor. Widely adapted. Productive.

Alpine Varieties

Alpine varieties are generally disease free and easily grown throughout the United States. The most readily available and popular varieties include:

Alexandria, which grows well from seed.

Baron Solemacher has fruit that is almost twice the size of wild strawberries. It grows well in partial shade.

Mignonette is noted for being one of the best flavored varieties. It is very productive, bearing many one inch fruit.

Pineapple Crush is a creamy yellow fruited variety. The pineapple flavored fruit are considered superb.

Rugen Improved is hardy in zones 5 - 10. Upright runners make it easy to manage in a home garden.

Planting Systems for the Garden

Today, modern strawberry varieties are typically grown using one of three systems: the matted row, the spaced matted row, or the hill system. On average, each strawberry plant requires one square foot of space, so choose your spacing and planting system according to the plant vigor and runner production of the varieties you have selected. Remember that June bearers produce more runners and are often more vigorous than everbearers and that day neutral plants produce almost no runners.

Of the three systems, the matted row requires the least effort to establish and maintain. In this system, plants are initially spaced eighteen to twenty-four inches apart in the row, with three to four feet between rows. The (original) "mother" plant is then permitted to set runners at will.

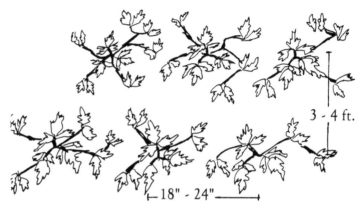

Figure 41. *Matted row system*

With the spaced matted row system, the distance between "mother" plants and between rows is similar to the matted row. The difference is that only a limited number of runners are allowed to

Figure 42. *Spaced matted row*

114 the Backyard Berry Book

grow. The selected runners are then manually positioned to take root at a specific spacing, typically six to twelve inches apart, and pinned into place with a small, inverted U-shaped piece of wire or hairpin. The remaining runners are removed as they appear. Although more labor intensive, the spaced matted row is also more productive since plant competition is reduced. Better air circulation between plants helps reduce fungus disease growth as well.

In the hill system plants are spaced at twelve inches apart, often in a staggered double row arrangement. All runners are removed. Most commonly used with day neutral or everbearing varieties that don't produce abundant runners, initial yields from this system can be quite high, but production decreases rapidly within one to three years of planting as the plants "play themselves out". The hill system is often used in conjunction with raised planting beds.

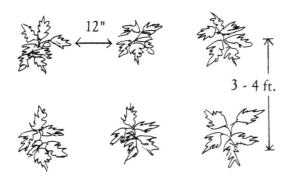

Figure 43. Hill system

The alpine strawberry, due to its nonrunner producing habit, is not usually grown using any of the above mentioned systems, although it could be easily planted in a hill system. Smaller in size than the modern varieties, alpine strawberry plants are typically grown from seed or by dividing older plants. When growing alpine strawberries from seed, you can start them indoors, much the way you do vegetable seeds. They also grow readily when direct seeded in the garden. Temperatures between 60 and 75°F are most favorable for fast germination. You will very likely find them reseeding readily enough so that an occasional thinning of extra plants is helpful to reduce competition and maintain top yields.

Planting in Small Spaces

Due to their small size, strawberries can be easily adapted to planting in very limited spaces. One of the most popular ways of planting strawberries in close quarters is in a crockery "strawberry jar". Readily available at most garden centers, these jars are typically made of terra cotta and have a dozen or more planting pockets or holes spaced around their sides. Strawberry jars are ideal for planting day neutral varieties or alpine strawberries as an annual crop. June bearing straw-berries will certainly grow in them as well, but will need to be replaced every two to three years.

Figure 44. Crockery strawberry jar

To use a strawberry jar, first soak the jar thoroughly by hosing it down or by setting it in a bucket of water. This will keep the crockery jar from drawing moisture out of the soil right after all the plants have been planted. Next put a shallow layer (about an inch) of coarse gravel in the bottom of the jar. Begin filling the jar with potting soil or one of the other container planting mixes available at most garden centers. When the soil reaches the level just below the first planting pocket, insert one strawberry plant into the pocket, spreading the roots out into the jar. Cover the roots with soil and water lightly. Continue planting in this manner until all the pockets are full. Top off the jar with soil, a few last plants, and water well. Place the jar on your patio or other favorite spot, water regularly, and enjoy!

If you have planted June bearing berries, you may need to protect the jar with a covering of mulch or bring it into a cool (less than 45°F) basement during the winter, since the soil in the exposed jar will freeze much more easily than garden ground. Otherwise, just discard old plants and replant in the spring.

Another method of planting in fairly limited space is by using a strawberry pyramid. This device consists of three concentric rings filled with dirt and stacked on top of each other pyramid style. You can fabricate your own pyramid from aluminum lawn edging or purchase prepackaged kits that include a central sprinkler and greenhouse dome.

A pyramid built to be six foot in diameter at the base will typically hold fifty strawberry plants, plenty for a family of four. Plants are usually situated nine to twelve

Figure 45. *Strawberry pyramid*

inches apart around the circles and are cared for in much the same way as any row planted berry.

Planting

It is best to plant strawberries as early in the spring as the soil is workable. Cold temperatures are unlikely to damage the dormant plants and will also give the roots a chance to adjust before they have to support a demanding, actively growing plant. Typical planting periods are February through early April in the south, March and April in the middle regions of the United States, and April to early May in the northern states. If you have ordered plants by mail and they arrive before you are ready to plant they can be held for a short time, preferably only a few days, in a cool place (between 33 and 40°F). For small quantities, your refrigerator will work fine. (Do not store the plants with ripening fruit, however. The ethylene gas given off by the fruit can severely damage the plants.) Since most mail order plants are shipped bare-root or wrapped in a small amount of sphagnum moss, inspect the roots upon their arrival. If necessary, moisten them slightly and wrap them in a plastic bag to keep the roots from drying out. Avoid letting them get soggy though, as this can encourage growth of fungus diseases.

If you have done some preliminary site preparation, your actual work at planting time will be relatively simple. Loosen the soil with a spade or fork one final time to break up any hard clods. Mark out your rows or raised beds, taking into account the row and plant spacing you have chosen. Just before you are ready to plant, open the bundles. Remove any flowers and runners. All but two or three old leaves should also be removed (if there are many old leaves on the plant). Damaged or extremely long roots should be trimmed back to four or five inches. Soak the plant roots in water for fifteen to thirty minutes. While planting, keep extra plants in a shallow pan of water covered with a damp cloth. If you are setting out many plants, work with a small quantity at a time and of course keep bundles of different varieties separate so they don't get mixed up.

Planting depth is extremely important for strawberries. With a trowel make a hole deep and wide enough to allow the roots to fan out comfortably when the crown's midpoint is planted level with the soil surface. Then, firm the soil around the roots with your hands and water thoroughly (two cups per plant is sufficient). After the watered-in plants have settled, recheck the planting depth and adjust as necessary. Finally, spreading a two inch layer of straw mulch around the plants will help keep the soil cool and moist.

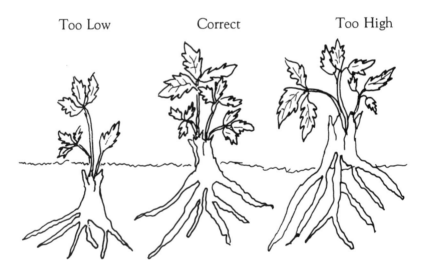

| Too Low | Correct | Too High |

Figure 46. Proper planting depth

A cool, cloudy day is ideal for setting out strawberry transplants. Direct sun and drying winds during planting can be very stressful to the plants, so be sure to protect them.

Care of the Berry Planting

The First Season

Caring for your berry plants, once they are in the ground, is relatively simple the first year. Following planting, a light mulch of straw or compost can be spread around the new plants to preserve moisture, keep roots cool, and control weeds. Water is important to strawberry plant growth. You should see that they receive about an inch of water per week, supplementing with irrigation or a soaker hose if natural rainfall is insufficient. One good soaking is much more beneficial than several light sprinklings. Watering in the morning will allow plant leaves to dry quickly and help prevent diseases. Pull any weeds that appear and do not fertilize the plants right after planting, since the tender new roots are easily burned. When the first runners appear, it is time to apply a complete fertilizer at the rate of 3/4 pound to 1 pound per 100 square feet.

On June bearing varieties, during the first growing season, all blossom buds need to be removed as they begin to appear, usually around five to six weeks after planting. Simply pinch the blossoms off by snapping the stems. This is often an agonizing task for the impatient gardener who wants to enjoy "the fruit of his or her labor" soon. However, it will have a lifelong effect on the productivity of the strawberry patch. The plant that has had the blossoms removed will produce stronger, healthier roots and runners in the first season, which will result in a stronger, more abundant berry set in the following season. As runner plants are produced, allow them to fill in according to the planting bed system you have chosen.

If you are growing everbearing or day neutral varieties, remove all the blossoms that appear during the first six weeks of growth (until about July 1 in northern climates). Allow the plants to set fruit from then on for a fall crop the first season. Remove runner plants that are produced, especially if you have chosen to use the hill planting system.

Mulching for winter protection is important with all strawberries grown in northern climates. After two or three good frosts the plants should have naturally hardened down. Apply a four to six inch layer of straw or other coarse plant material that holds plenty of insulating air space. Natural snow cover is an excellent mulch. However, keep in mind that the strawberry crown is easily damaged and may be killed at temperatures below 15°F. If your area is not guaranteed a good natural snowfall that remains throughout the winter, it is safer to apply a mulch.

When new growth begins in the spring, remove the mulch covering the plants. It can be kept in the garden as a moisture conserving measure during the rest of the season. If a severe frost is predicted during bloom, the mulch can also be used to re-cover the plants in order to protect the tender blossoms.

The Second Year and Beyond

In this second growing season you should be able to harvest the first crop from your June bearing varieties. If you live in an area with late spring frosts, you may need to provide frost protection for your strawberry blossoms during the early spring. This can be done by one of two methods. The planting can be covered with a spun bonded, synthetic row cover after the winter mulch has been removed. (So far it has been assumed that straw or similar material is being used as your mulch because it is relatively inexpensive and easy to obtain. The heavier weight synthetic covers also work well as winter protection, but are considerably more expensive than straw and must be replaced every few years as they suffer wear and tear.)

Although somewhat expensive, the row cover will provide several degrees of cold protection that can mean the difference between a minimal or sizeable crop in some years. The row cover, in acting like a greenhouse, will also speed up plant development, usually providing a crop of fruit about a week to ten days earlier than would be expected for uncovered plants. Yields on some varieties may be as much as 20 to 30% higher as well. In late spring when frost is still possible, simply remove the cover (you can pull it back and leave it in an outside row) during the day and re-cover at night. Once all danger of frost is past, you can remove the cover and store it for use in another season.

Overhead sprinkler irrigation can also provide frost protection. In general this method is more feasible for larger plantings than for small ones. It has several advantages as well as several disadvantages compared to using a row cover. First, the cost is high. The initial equipment is more costly than a row cover. Yet, once the equipment has been purchased, it lasts much longer than the row cover before needing repair or replacement. The water and electric charges for running the system can also be expensive, while covering a row costs nothing more than the few minutes of time involved. Second, a reliable high capacity water source is needed, which may necessitate drilling a special well. Third, the system needs to be turned on as danger of frost approaches, but not too far ahead of time in order to avoid excess watering of plants. This may require getting out of bed several times in the middle of the night to check the thermometer or hooking the sprinkler system into an automated, temperature sensitive timer. Finally, of course the sprinkler can be used for watering the planting throughout the season, which the row cover cannot. Whether frost protection is needed and worth the expense and effort, is a judgement that each gardener will have to make individually.

As the growing season continues, water and weed as you did during the first season, but do not fertilize yet. The fertilizer will be applied at renovation. If you are in a southern area and did not use a mulch for cold protection, it is still a good idea to spread mulch around the plants in early spring, prior to bloom. This will help keep the berries clean and free of diseases.

It is best to hand pull weeds in a small berry patch, as the strawberry's shallow roots are quite close to the surface and are easily damaged by hoeing. Mulch can be spread between the rows each spring as needed to keep weeds under control. Remember to remove diseased or damaged berries as they appear. This will help prevent the further spread of diseases. Also, regularly inspect your berry patch for pests and control them as warranted. If birds become a problem as berries ripen, you may need to cover your patch with netting sold for this purpose.

Care of everbearing and day neutral varieties during this second year is very similar to the care given June bearers. Frost protection, mulch, water, weed and pest control are all the same. If you want both a June fruit crop and a later summer crop from your everbearers and day neutrals, allow them to bloom and fruit at will. At this point day neutral varieties will benefit from a steady supply of nitrogen and potassium. Apply a slow release fertilizer monthly at the rate of 7 pounds per 1000 square feet total, split over three months. Do not apply a quick release nitrogen, as this will result in soft berries. If you also have June bearers and plan to rely on them for the majority of your early season crop, again remove the blossoms from your day neutral varieties for the first six weeks of the season. This will allow them to put most of their energy into the late summer and fall crops. You will find that these varieties remain productive for no more than three years or so. At that point, they should be totally replaced.

Renovating the June Bearing Planting

For best plant health and yield, June bearing strawberries require an annual renovation. After harvest is finished, mow off the foliage. This can be done with a standard lawn mower with the blade set at its highest setting. Check to be sure that the mowing is not damaging the plant crown. A week or two later, narrow the rows back to about eight to twelve inches. Using a rototiller is easiest, but the job can also be done with a hoe.

Fertilizing at this time of the year is best for encouraging large, firm berries, while spring fertilizer application causes soft fruit. The average berry patch will require about 1 1/4 to 1 1/2 pounds of a complete fertilizer per 100 square feet. In practical terms this is approximately two cups worth. Be sure to apply the fertilizer under dry conditions and brush it off the plant to avoid burning the foliage. Water the newly renovated planting and see that it is receives adequate moisture for the remainder of the season. Runner production will be stimulated by the renovation and fertilization and within several weeks the rows will again be filled-in twelve to eighteen inches wide with plants.

In the uncommon situation that renovation is delayed several weeks due to bad weather, omit mowing the leaves from the plant. Just rototill to narrow the row width and proceed with the other renovation steps as normal.

Along with encouraging strong plant growth, renovation also helps control leaf diseases. Maintained in this manner, the planting will produce well for four to five years. Most strawberry growers like to plant a new patch of June bearers every third or fourth spring. This avoids any interruption of harvestable fruit when the old planting is removed.

Pests and Diseases

Berry quality and yield can be greatly affected by several insects and diseases that plague strawberries. In order to most effectively control them, it helps to be able to identify the symptoms they cause and understand their life cycle. Some insects, such as Crown borers, June beetle larvae, leafrollers, and mites feed on more than just strawberries and have already been discussed and illustrated in chapter 7. Pests and diseases that are specific to strawberries will be discussed in the sections that follow.

Insects

Those pests causing the most obvious problem on strawberries are typically fruit damaging insects. Three are of primary concern to the home gardener.

Strawberry clipper, also called bud weevil, is the first insect of the season to bother strawberries. Only 1/10 of an inch long, these brownish beetles overwinter in woodland or garden leaf litter. Becoming active when temperatures exceed 65°F, the females emerge in the spring and look for strawberry flower buds in which to lay their eggs. They then clip or girdle the stem, leaving the bud barely hanging from the plant. The young larvae develop inside the bud, causing malformed fruit in any buds that do continue developing. Adults also

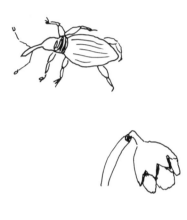
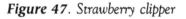

Figure 47. Strawberry clipper

feed on petals and other blossoms, but this does not normally injure the fruit. Just picking the insects off by hand in early spring is the simplest means of control. If you must resort to chemical controls, malathion and Sevin are most effective for the home garden.

Shortly after bloom, the **tarnished plant bug (or lygus bug)** becomes active and widespread. This 1/4 inch long, brown bug with black and yellow markings, finds strawberry blossoms one of its preferred food. It overwinters on herbaceous plants that are protected from the weather and can even overwinter in the strawberry patch, particularly if it is weedy. This insect feeds on the developing flower. Twenty to thirty days after infestation, damaged areas of the fruit become hard, dry, and gnarled. Berries with minor damage will be misshapen, while those with more severe damage often stop growing and

Figure 48. Tarnished Plant Bug Damage

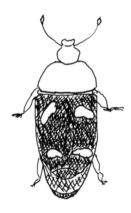

Figure 49. Strawberry Sap Beetle

form a hard green button or "nubbin" at the end. Since tarnished plant bug is not controlled by any chemicals available to the home gardener, keeping the strawberry patch weed free and isolated from overwintering sites is the best control means. A low level of plant bug injury may have to be tolerated.

Strawberry sap beetles pose a problem in the garden, once the fruit starts to develop. These small 1/8 inch long, brown beetles overwinter in leaf litter. By mid-June (in Michigan), they move to the strawberry plants to feed on the nearly ripe fruit. The feeding sites also become entry points for the hatching larvae, which feed inside the fruit. Damaged areas are soft and subject to invasion by fungus diseases. The sap beetle tends to seek out fruit that is resting on the ground, so keeping fruit mulched helps to control them. Other cultural practices, such as removing damaged fruit, keeping the strawberry patch and the rest of your yard free of excess ground litter, and regular renovation are also important for sap beetle control. There are currently no insecticides known to control them.

Spittlebugs are insects, commonly found on strawberries, that pose more of a nuisance than a harm. The nymphs hatch from late March through May and surround themselves with a frothy, white spittle that is a familiar sight to most gardeners. They feed on new plant growth by sucking the sap, weakening the plant. Stunting of fruit occurs only when pest populations are high. They rarely cause major damage.

124 the Backyard Berry Book

Diseases

Fungus diseases can effect your strawberries in two ways, one by infecting the leaves of the plant and second, by actually infecting the developing fruit. One of the primary steps in controlling fungus diseases is the use of cultural practices that keep the plant and fruit dry. Don't allow tall weeds that hold moisture to grow in the berry patch. Mulch to keep rain and dirt from splashing back up on the berries and irrigate during the day when foliage dries more quickly.

Leaf spot and **leaf scorch** both infect, as the names imply, the plant leaves. Leaf Spot appears on the plant as small tan spots surrounded by purple halos. It is particularly prevalent in cool, wet seasons. Leaf Scorch lesions show up as irregular 1/4 inch purple spots on the leaves' upper surface. Many varieties are resistant to one or both of these diseases, and planting these varieties is the first step toward control. Under most circumstances, these two diseases do not seriously affect the plants and can be sufficiently controlled by regular renovation of the bed.

Figure 50. Leaf Spot & Leaf Scorch

Fungus diseases of the fruit are more serious because the fruit is normally rendered inedible. Where preventive fungicide programs are used for control, it is important to start early. This will protect the first blossoms, which are the ones that produce the largest size fruit and represent the bulk of the harvest.

Gray mold and **leather rot** are the most likely to cause problems in the home garden. Gray mold (or *Botrytis*) is the familiar fuzzy gray mold that most gardeners find on overripe strawberries. It develops quickly from its initial watersoaked spots to the gray spore masses that are typically seen. Fungicides at bloom and continuing weekly until harvest are the most effective control. Leather rot appears first as mushy gray-brown areas on fruit clusters that are touching wet ground. As the fruit dries, the area becomes leathery. Leather rot has a distinctive rancid odor and insipid taste that is not easily forgotten.

Keeping berries well mulched with straw will help to control this disease by keeping berries up out of puddles. Do not mulch with plastic however, since it encourages rain water to pool.

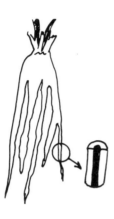

Red stele root rot is a particularly serious problem when strawberries are grown on heavy soil or poorly drained sites. The root core (the stele) of affected plants turns a rusty red or brown. (This can be viewed by cutting the roots longitudinally.) The roots take on a "rattail" appearance due to death of the small root hairs. Discoloration affects only the roots not the plant crown. (A discolored crown may be a sign of cold injury.) Symptoms are not usually evident until the second growing season when old leaves turn red or yellow and new leaves may turn bluish green. Often the plant dies. This disease is actually caused by five different races of the pathogen. The most effective control is to plant varieties resistant to as many races as possible. Few are resistant to all races, so control may still be incomplete. The pathogen can remain in the soil for over ten years, so do not replant known infected sites.

Figure 51. Red Stele root rot

Harvest

Predicting harvest times for strawberries is relatively easy. In a normal growing season, harvestable berries will be ripe about one month after blossoms have started to appear. Harvest berries as they ripen. At first, harvesting twice a week or every other day will probably be sufficient. If temperatures become very warm, berries will ripen literally overnight and you should pick them daily. Each variety will likely require three to four pickings and will continue to provide ripe fruit for about a week, depending on weather conditions. Most nursery catalogs classify June bearing strawberry varieties as early, mid-season, or late varieties, referring to when they ripen relative to the earliest ripening variety (usually Earliglow). In practical terms, there may only be a few days difference from one part of the season to the next. However, by choosing varieties from each group, the June harvest season can last several weeks. The season can extend even longer if day neutral varieties have also been planted.

The berries are firmest and best able to withstand handling after cooler overnight temperatures, so morning is the best time to pick them. Normally after 2:00 P.M. or so, even in northern climates, the berries have picked up enough field heat that they will practically turn to juice between your fingers.

For longest shelf life and to avoid pinching berries, pick them with the stems and caps on. Picking into quart baskets, that don't have sharp edges, is ideal. Otherwise, most any shallow container will do, as long as berries are no more than three or four layers deep. Refrigerate the freshly picked berries as soon as possible and do not wash them or remove the caps until you are ready to use them. This will help keep them fresh and give them a shelf life of at least four or five days, if they have not all been eaten by then.

To keep fungus diseases from spreading throughout the berry planting, and they can spread quickly on ripe, sugar filled berries; carry a separate container along as you harvest. When you encounter berries that have rot or mold spots on them, pick them into the container and dispose of them away from the strawberry patch. This will make disease control a relatively easy job and also minimize the amount of spraying you will have to do.

11. Rhubarb

Although obviously not a berry, rhubarb is included in this book because so many gardeners include it as a part of their "small fruit" garden. An early spring treat by itself or combined with strawberries, it is also a novice gardener's dream. Rhubarb, which is actually a vegetable, seems almost to grow by itself. There are however, ways every gardener can encourage this first garden goodie of spring.

Rhubarb or "pie plant", as it's fondly known, is very winter hardy, surviving temperatures to -20°F. This large leafed perennial is grown for its astringent leaf petioles or stalks. Grown primarily in northern areas because it requires a cold dormant period,. it is also most productive in climates with a long, cool spring. Once established, the plant will produce for twenty years or more.

Site Selection, Preparation, and Planting

Although quite tolerant and willing to grow in most places, rhubarb prefers a fertile, well drained loam or sandy loam soil with a pH of 5.5 to 6.5. It also prefers a location in full sun. This is especially important for the red stalked varieties, which will be better colored with greater sun exposure.

To prepare a site for your rhubarb, select a spot where it can be left undisturbed for many years, since rhubarb remains productive for twenty years or more. A corner of the vegetable garden or alongside other perennial food crops, such as asparagus, is often suitable and convenient. Allow enough space for the mature plant which can grow to as much as two feet high and six feet wide. Dig a hole about two feet around and at least a foot deep. Spread a layer of well rotted manure or compost in the bottom and mix more manure or compost with the dirt you have taken out of the hole. Plant crowns three feet apart. The dormant "plant" you buy from the nursery will probably look like a big fleshy, brown chunk of root, possibly with a few small, crinkly leaves starting to grow out of it. Place this crown in the hole deeply enough so that, as you shovel dirt in around it, it will end up two to three inches below the soil surface. Refill the hole, covering the new crown, water it in well and cover it with a layer of mulch. Water and mulch throughout the season as needed.

Rhubarb plants can also be grown from seed, but in most cases, since only a small number of crowns will provide you with more than enough rhubarb to give away, codling seeds is hardly worth the effort. A typical mature rhubarb plant can produce up to six pounds of stalks in a season. If you plan on two plants per person in your household, you will surely have plenty.

General Care

In addition to its early appearance in spring, another attribute of rhubarb is its minimal need for attention. It requires no pruning, little pest control, and only a yearly spring feeding. If you spend the small amount of effort needed to fertilize your rhubarb plant, it will reward your tender loving care with more and larger stalks in proportion to your efforts. As plants go, rhubarb does require a high dose of nitrogen. This can be supplied in one of two ways. Each spring, before the leaves emerge from the ground, pile two to three inches of well rotted manure over the plant. Lacking a manure source, nitrogen can be provided in a synthetic form. For the young plant that is not being harvested, 1 1/2 to 2 ounces of 21% nitrogen fertilizer per square yard of garden area will meet its needs. Once stalks are being harvested regularly, nitrogen applications should be doubled to 4 ounces per square yard. Water as needed, but don't overdo it. Rhubarb crowns don't particularly like standing water.

Varieties

Several rhubarb varieties are available through nurseries today. Some still have the greenish stalk common to the old-fashioned rhubarb, but several of the more recent introductions have quite red stalks.

Victoria is an old garden standby that grows to a big vigorous plant. Its stalks tend to be the old-fashioned green.

MacDonald, a quite productive variety, has tender, red-stalks. It is resistant to root rot.

Canada Red is of course also red stalked. The stalks are known for retaining their red color when cooked.

Valentine is an especially disease resistant red stalked variety. It produces few seed stalks and in a Canadian trial of twenty-five rhubarb varieties was rated as the having the best overall quality. **Cherry Red** is also a red-stalked variety, but the one most suited to growing in warmer climates. It does well as far south as northern California.

Pests and Diseases

Amazingly pest and disease free, rhubarb's only insect pest is the rhubarb curculio. This small snout nosed beetle will occasionally bore into the stalks, crown, and root, leaving a telltale black spot. The easiest control is to pick the insect off by hand if you can see it (they can be elusive and like to fall to the ground and play dead). Otherwise, trim damaged spots on the stalk and don't worry too much about it.

Crown rot is the only disease to plague rhubarb, and that happens most commonly on poorly drained sites. The only cure for this disease is complete removal of the plant. When you set new plants, do not start them where old, infected plants have grown.

Harvest

For the first two years rhubarb should be harvested only sparingly, taking just a few stalks at a time and only for a few weeks in the early part of the season. Once the plant reaches its third growing season, pick the now mature plant at your pleasure. You can continue picking until the beginning of July or until the stalks start to decrease in diameter. The stalks can be used for cooking throughout the season, however, only the early season stalks freeze well. The late season stalks tend to have fibers that become tough when frozen.

Figure 52. *Rhubarb seed stalk*

Harvest from several plants at a time, never picking more than half the stalks from a given plant at any one time. If flower stalks begin to appear (you'll notice their scepter like appearance rising on a stalk above the foliage), remove them as long as you would like to continue harvesting. If the plant has to put its energy into flower production, it will do so at the expense of leaf and stalk production.

Rhubarb stalks are usually harvested when they are twelve inches or longer and an inch or more in diameter. Don't cut them from the plant. Rather twist the base of the stalk away from the crown while giving a little upward pull. The stalk should come free from the plant fairly easily. Cut the leaves from the stems and leave them as mulch in the garden or throw them in the compost pile. Under no circumstances should they be eaten as they contain oxalic acid, a poison.

Figure 53. *Picking rhubarb*

Section III.

Brambles

12. Bramble Basics

Blackberries, dewberries, and raspberries, all members of the genus *Rubus*, are collectively known as brambles. Originally the brambles derived their name from the fact that they had thorny or spiny canes and branches. Fortunately, today a number of varieties also exist that offer the same delectable fruit as the old brambles, but without the thorns. The genus *Rubus* is divided into two subgenera, one containing the raspberries, the other blackberries. These subgenera and their related species have different growth habits and are managed in slightly different ways. Awareness of these variations will help the different cultural practices make sense as we discuss them.

Found growing in most parts of the world, brambles thrive in conditions as diverse as the tropics and the tundra. Different varieties are quite specific in which climatic conditions they will perform best. As you read through the next three chapters, pay particular attention to those types and varieties that best match your conditions.

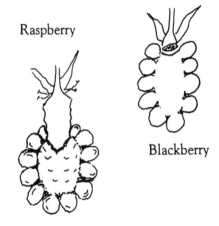

All brambles have a perennial root system which produces canes that are biennial. During their first growing year the canes are vegetative and are known as primocanes. In the second growing season, the floricanes, as the canes are then known, become reproductive and bear fruit. Following fruiting, the floricanes die. At the same time, the bramble plant is also producing

Figure 54. Raspberry and Blackberry fruit

new primocanes. Under good care the plant will normally grow and produce for about ten years.

While the brambles share some common characteristics in how they produce fruit, they differ slightly in the structure of that fruit.

As mentioned in an earlier chapter, all brambles are aggregate fruit made up of drupelets that adhere to a single central receptacle. Blackberries and dewberries continue to adhere to the receptacle when ripe. Raspberries pick free of the receptacle yielding a hollow thimble-shaped berry. The different brambles also vary in the location at which they produce new canes, as will be explained later.

Site Selection and Preparation

Brambles are relatively shallow rooted plants. Therefore, it is very important to pay attention to soil type when selecting a planting site. Brambles definitely grow best in a well drained loam or sandy loam soil with a minimum of three percent organic matter. Though they need a soil with adequate moisture holding capacity, they cannot tolerate saturated soils or standing water. Extended exposure to standing water can suffocate and kill raspberry roots. Certain root rot fungi that affect brambles flourish in heavy, poorly drained soils. Brambles grow best when soil pH is between 6.0 to 7.0.

Like most berries, brambles compete poorly with weeds. Therefore, site preparation a year ahead of planting is very beneficial.

In northern climates where cold, drying winter winds are common, select a planting site that is well protected or plant a hedgerow to slow the wind. Remember that some air circulation around the plants during the growing season helps prevent fungus diseases. This is especially important in areas with humid summers.

Be on the lookout for sites that might harbor soil borne diseases. Verticillium wilt can be found on sites that have grown tomatoes, potatoes, melon, eggplant, or strawberries in the last five years and crown gall can be a problem on sites that have previously grown tree fruit, grapes, or brambles. These sites should be avoided when establishing a new bramble planting, unless they are known to be disease-free. Neighboring wild brambles can harbor viruses that cause poor fruit quality and plant decline. If at all possible, establish new plantings at least 400 to 600 yards away from any wild brambles.

Many home gardeners are inclined to turn a piece of the garden that was formerly lawn into a berry patch. If you are planning on doing so, check to see that white grubs or wireworms will not be a problem. If you find many, consider planting a pumpkin patch or sweet corn on the site of your future berry patch for a year or two in order to reduce the population of these damaging soil borne insects.

Selecting and Caring for Bramble Varieties

Raspberries are normally considered suitable for growing in USDA plant hardiness zones three through eight. Raspberry canes are fairly tolerant of the cold. The fruit, however, does not withstand high heat and humidity well - becoming soft and hard to handle when ripe. Almost the opposite is true of blackberries. While most blackberry roots can survive air temperatures to -40°F, the canes are often killed when the thermometer drops below zero (or in the case of some new varieties still being tested -10 to -20°F). In contrast to raspberries, blackberry fruit remain firmer and are less susceptible to fungus diseases when exposed to warm, humid conditions.

Once you have determined which brambles will grow in your climate and soil conditions, you will want to start picking specific varieties. To narrow the choices, ask yourself these questions:

1. When do I want my berries to be ripe, during the traditional summer harvest period, fall, or at both times?

2. Do I have a strong taste preference for raspberries, blackberries, or am I open to experimenting with some of the crosses?

3. Can I tolerate thorny canes or is a thornless variety an absolute necessity?

4. Do I understand the various cultural requirements of each type of bramble and do I have the irrigation or trellis needed by some varieties (or am I prepared to install it)? Don't worry if you are not completely able to answer this question quite yet - by the end of this book you should be able to.

5. Finally, what do I plan to do with my berries - eat them fresh, freeze them, or make jam? (After all, this is the real reason you are growing them!)

To help you answer these questions, let's take a look now at the requirements and specific varieties of each type of bramble.

Planting and Spacing

If proper site preparation was done in advance, planting a small bramble patch should be relatively quick and easy. How your plants are packaged will determine when it is best to plant them. If you have bareroot mail order plants that arrive before you are ready to plant them, they may be held by "heeling-in". In a well drained location, dig a trench deep enough to accommodate the plant roots.

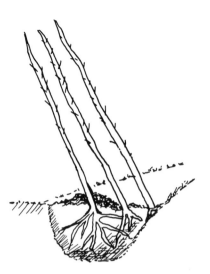

Lay the plants on their side as shown in Figure 55 and cover the roots with moist soil until planting.

It is generally best to plant bareroot and pot grown brambles as early in the spring as the ground can be worked satisfactorily. The air temperature is still cool but the soil is dry enough not to be muddy. Pot grown plants can be planted throughout the growing season, but will have to be watched more closely and watered more regularly in hot weather to accommodate their restricted root system.

To plant green, actively growing tissue cultured plants, wait until all danger of frost is past. Although the plants have been acclimated,

Figure 55. Heeling in canes while awaiting planting

they have been raised in a controlled environment and thus their tissue is much more sensitive to cold and also more sensitive to drying sun and wind.

A few nurseries are now selling "nursery mature" plants. These are tissue cultured plants that have been planted in an outdoor setting for two and a half to three months and then harvested and shipped as dormant plants. Nursery mature plants have all the benefits of tissue culture plants and usually come into production a year sooner as well. They can be planted early in the season, much as one would plant bareroot stock.

When planting brambles, it is best to choose a cloudy, wind-still day. Bramble roots dry out quickly when exposed to the elements. Dip the roots in water or a thin mud slurry and keep them covered with plastic to protect them. Special care needs to be taken when planting blackberries. Roots of trailing and semi-erect blackberries should be kept in the dark until planting. This is especially important. For some reason, their roots are very sensitive to sunlight, and they will often suffer high transplant losses if planted on a bright sunny day when their roots have been exposed to light. Even when planting on partly cloudy days, it is wise to take extra precautions to see that their roots are kept in the dark.

Brambles are usually grown in rows, in a part of the garden where they can stay for ten or more years. To allow for rototilling and easy movement when caring for and harvesting the plants, raspberries should be planted in rows spaced six to twelve feet apart. Plants of summer fruiting varieties are planted two to three feet apart within the row. Primocane fruiting varieties are planted nine to fifteen inches apart, to fill in the row quickly.

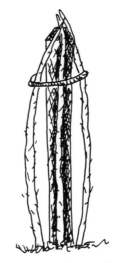

Blackberries, being larger plants, should be planted in rows

Figure 56. Canes planted in hills

that are ten to twelve feet apart. Erect growing varieties can be spaced two to four feet apart within the row, while trailing types are better spaced five to six feet apart.

Sometimes brambles are grown in "hills". To create a hill, two or three plants are planted six to twelve inches apart, often with a support stake between them. Five to six feet of open ground is then left around the hill on all sides. The area is then cultivated regularly in both directions, unlike plantings in rows that are only cultivated parallel to the row. This planting system works best for varieties that don't sucker much, but rather produce all their canes from the plant crown. It is usually less productive than planting in rows.

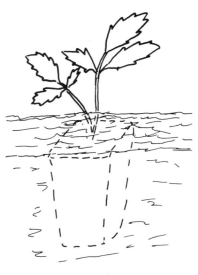

When setting plants in the ground, dig a hole large enough to spread the roots out well. Bareroot raspberries should be planted one inch deeper than they grew in the nursery. Place blackberry plants in the hole at the same depth that they grew in the nursery.

Tissue cultured plants should be set so that the soil plug is just level with the ground, but covered with soil. Refill the planting hole with soil and firm dirt with your hands or heel.

Figure 57. Planting depth for tissue cultured plug

Bramble Basics 139

Cut the tops of bareroot and dormant, nursery mature tissue culture plants back to ground level. This will help prevent the spread of diseases that may be present on the cane and also give the root system time to start growing before it has to support a large number of leaves. This also reduces stress to the plant since it will not produce flowers or fruit during the first growing season. Tissue culture plants are typically three to four inches tall at planting time. If they are green and actively growing at planting time, they should not be cut back.

Water

Although brambles need well drained soils to grow in, they also require a regular supply of water. This is especially important when the young plants are becoming established and also in the three to four weeks preceding harvest. If possible, trickle irrigation should be used where natural rainfall is less that one inch per week. Mulching heavily with straw helps preserve soil moisture and improve fruit yields. If you are not able to irrigate, you may find that over the years, purple raspberries will produce most consistently, black raspberries will do reasonably well, and red raspberries will be the poorest bearers in areas with low natural rainfall.

Fertilizer

Since brambles are relatively shallow rooted, (normally distributing 90% of their root mass in the top foot and a half of soil surface - at least raspberry), both nutrient and water management are quite important. Nitrogen is of course very important for proper shoot growth and should be applied annually. Raspberries require regular applications of potassium as well to properly use the nitrogen and other nutrients taken up from the soil. It is not uncommon to find potassium deficiency as a problem with raspberries in certain parts of the country.

Unlike most other small fruit plants that are not given much fertilizer in the year of planting, brambles benefit from receiving fertilizer during the first growing season. About a month after planting blackberries, a two foot wide circle of nitrogen can be applied at the rate of 1/2 pound per 100 foot of row. These same rates can be applied to raspberries about six weeks after planting.

The fertilizer should be spread at least three to four inches from the base of the plant to avoid burning the tender, young roots.

The following spring, nitrogen application rates for raspberries and erect growing blackberries can be increased to 3/4 pounds of actual nitrogen per 100 foot of row applied in a four foot wide band along the row. Trailing blackberry varieties can receive up to one pound of nitrogen.

Once the planting is three years old, fertilizer rates should be increased again. One and a half pounds of nitrogen per 100 feet of row is applied to raspberries and trailing blackberries. Erect blackberry varieties can receive up to two pounds of actual nitrogen. Some variations of these rates will apply in that vigorous growing varieties and primocane fruiting varieties may require up to double these amounts, particularly on sandy soils. In shorter growing season areas such as the northeast and upper midwest, as a rule of thumb, new black raspberry canes should grow to a height of two and a half to three feet in a season, red raspberries should reach five feet, and purple raspberries should grow to six feet or more. Cane growth will exceed these guidelines in long growing seasons, such as those found on the west coast.

Pruning and Trellising

The various brambles have diverse growth habits and consequently require assorted pruning and trellising techniques. Purple and primocane fruiting raspberries, as well as blackberries, tend to bend over when weighted with a fruit crop. These brambles benefit from the support of a trellis. Not only does trellising keep the fruit off the ground, it can also make picking and pruning easier. One permanent trellis design being studied is a T-bar construction. Primocanes are trained up to a high central wire while floricanes are trained horizontally across both sides of the "T", as shown in Figure 58. This method has shown increased production, higher quality fruit due to better sun exposure and easier pruning. Once floricanes have fruited, they are quickly removed and the floricanes are dropped down to the horizontal plane in anticipation of next season's crop.

The V-trellis also works on the concept of segregating the primocanes and floricanes. Primocanes are sandwiched between plastic monofilament or wire on one side of the trellis while floricanes are trained to the other side. When the floricanes have been pruned out

Bramble Basics 141

Figure 58. T-bar and V-trellis design

the newest primocanes are trained to that location. This system has also shown increase yields over conventional plantings.

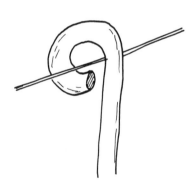

Figure 59. Movable trellis posts

Primocane fruiting varieties will need a removable trellis if they are mowed annually. Simple rebar bent to hold baling twine or fence wire is quick to put up and take down. For all types of trellis, light weight line posts may be needed to keep wires from sagging.   During the year of planting and the first year of growth thereafter most brambles are just sending out their initial canes and very little pruning needs to be done. Pruning really begins in earnest after the first crop has been produced. Specific pruning techniques are detailed for each type of bramble in the respective chapters that follow.

Insects and Diseases

Brambles are among the small fruit that are host to numerous insect pests, fungus diseases, and viruses, yet they are one of the easier fruit to raise without pesticides. Most bramble pests do not do direct damage to the fruit crop. Many are more likely to indirectly affect the crop by weakening the plant, thereby reducing the size and quantity of fruit produced. For most home gardeners this is not as serious a problem as it is for commercial growers. None the less, it is worthwhile to be familiar with the various insects and diseases and the steps that can be taken to minimize the problems they may cause. Insects such as cutworms, tarnished plant bug, Japanese beetles, sap beetles, borers, mites, and aphids have already been discussed in chapter 7 since they commonly affect many fruit including brambles. The diseases anthracnose, gray mold, powdery mildew, and verticillium wilt are discussed in chapter 8. The pests and diseases in the sections that follow are among those most commonly encountered by the home gardener and are specific primarily to brambles.

Insects

Raspberry cane borer causes damage to developing canes. The life cycle of this insect spans two years. During the first year, the adult beetles are present in the raspberry patch from June through August. The adult is black with a yellow or orange thorax and about 1/2 inch long. Damage is done when the female makes two rings of punctures in the shoot tip in preparation for egg laying. The rings are usually located about six inches from the tip and about 1/2 inch apart. Cane tips usually wither and developing larvae bore down the cane. Although damage to the plant is minimal, its appearance often alarms the novice bramble grower. Cane borer is easy to control by pruning out affected canes below where the larvae are situated.

Figure 60. Raspberry cane borer damage symptoms

Raspberry crown borer adults are clear winged moths that look much like yellow jackets. They also have a two year life cycle. During the first year, larvae of the crown borer feed on buds and new canes at the base of the plant, where they also overwinter. During the second season they move into the plant crown to feed, causing extensive damage before emerging as adults in August. Damage symp-

Figure 61. *Raspberry crown borer*

toms are often confused with disease symptoms as the canes wither and die. However, damaged canes often break easily and can be pulled off the plant. Removing damaged canes and destroying the insect should help control this pest the following season.

Nematodes, especially dagger nematode, can act as vectors for tomato ring spot virus and eventually "crumble berry" of red raspberry. The virus is commonly transferred from numerous weeds, especially dandelion, curly dock, chickweed, and plantain.

Yellow jackets are a serious problem in some areas of the United States, particularly in yellow raspberry plantings. In some years they have been reported to feed on and destroy as much as half of the tender skinned crop.

Diseases

Prevention is the best medicine for fungus diseases in brambles. Keeping canes pruned to no more than three or four per square foot aids air circulation, which in turn encourages quick drying of plant tissue, and reduces disease development. Removing fruiting shoots in the lower foot and a half of the canes also helps to improve air circulation and disease control. What fruit is removed is unlikely to be missed, as fruit in that area of the cane is most apt to be sandy or lower in quality anyhow. Pruning only when foliage is dry will also help prevent the spread of fungus diseases. Most fungus diseases in brambles are also controlled by diligent field sanitation, pruning out floricanes immediately after harvest and burning them. Unfortunately, few disease resistant bramble varieties exist yet. At best, avoid planting varieties that are highly susceptible to the major disease problems in your area.

Gray mold is the most serious fungus disease affecting bramble fruit. Its symptoms have been discussed in chapter 8. Maintaining adequate air circulation and removing old floricanes are the most effective control methods.

Anthracnose, as well as affecting the canes and leaves, will on occasion also affect the fruit. It is most serious on black and purple raspberries, but also occurs on red varieties and blackberries. Sanitation, that is removing old floricanes, is an effective control. Lime sulfur sprays early in the spring, when the foliage is between 1/4 to 1/2 inch leafed out, are also effective and meet organic growing guidelines. Spraying earlier in the season than the 1/4 inch green stage is not very effective. Likewise, spraying when foliage is more developed can cause severe burning of the leaf tissue.

Spur blight appears as small brown or purple spots around the nodes on the lower part of red raspberry canes. Canes turn brown and leaf and flower buds shrivel and die. Disease spread starts with May rains and continues during rainy periods throughout the season.

Cane blight usually starts at a wound near the base of the cane and eventually girdles the cane. It looks much like spur blight with brown-black diseased areas extending several inches down the cane. The best control method is to prune only during dry weather. Then try to keep canes dry for several days following pruning to allow cuts to callus. Diseased canes should be removed and burned.

Double Blossom Rosette is found mainly in the southeast. Symptoms appear as a misshapen compressed bloom that does not set fruit. Mowing off the planting in spring before bloom and disease spore release is the only cure. The following year's canes probably won't be infected. The old variety Humble is resistant to double blossom rosette. Shawnee is very susceptible.

Leaf rust can be a problem on long growing fall bearing varieties. Heritage is particularly susceptible. There are no known controls.

Orange Rust is a serious, but isolated problem in the eastern United States. Symptoms include orange powdery spores on the leaf undersides; chlorotic, spindly, bunched shoots; and scaly canes. The cure lies in identifying the disease in early spring, completely removing, and immediately burning the plant. Fungicides are not an effective control. Black and purple raspberries are susceptible, but red raspberry is not.

Crown gall is a soil borne bacterial disease of the roots and crown that can affect all brambles. It enters through tissue wounds and appears as cancer or wart-like growths on the roots. Controls for this disease are purely preventative; planting disease free plants and avoiding replanting in old orchard, grape or bramble sites. *Agrobacterium radiobacter* acts as a competitive biological control and offers yet another means of prevention, although a rather expensive one for the home garden. Once established, there is no cure for the disease.

Numerous virus diseases affect brambles. They are easiest to identify in cool spring conditions. As the weather gets warm and the plant grows more actively, the symptoms are often masked.

Raspberry Bushy Dwarf is quite widespread, but is often symptomless. Plants that do display symptoms may show yellow leaf veining, crumbly berries, reduced yields, or stunted growth.

Raspberry Mosaic, a very damaging and at one time widespread virus found in raspberries, is spread from wild and diseased plants by the common raspberry aphid. Its symptoms first appear as mottling and blistering on the leaves. Eventually, the virus stunts the plant and causes small, crumbly berries. Fortunately, many of the varieties cultivated today are residant to the aphid vector. Autumn Bliss, Canby, Chilcotin, Chilliwack, Haida, Killarney, Nootka, Nordic, Royalty, Skeena, and Tulameen are all resistant varieties.

Raspberry Leaf Curl causes rounded, downward curling leaves that look dark green and greasy. Fruit production is decreased and plants are stunted. This virus is also spread by an aphid.

Tomato Ring Spot, although quite common in tree fruits and grapes, does not cause severe symptoms on raspberries. It causes a general stunting of the plant and yellowing of the leaves. Fruit of infected plants is crumbly. All varieties are susceptible. As mentioned earlier, it is spread by the dagger nematode.

Other virus diseases affect brambles as well, mostly causing general weakness of the plant and diminished production. Unfortunately, there are no effective cures for virus diseases, so it is best to keep them from becoming established when possible. Purchasing virus free plant stock is the best insurance against contaminating your new berry patch. Keeping weeds that serve as virus host plants pulled out and aphids and leafhoppers that transmit viruses under control will also help minimize virus problems.

The preceding sections have outlined the basic principles that apply to growing brambles. They can generally be applied to either raspberries or blackberries. In the two chapters that follow, more specific details and the differences between these brambles will be examined. Variety selection, pruning, and harvesting are the major topics that are covered.

13. Raspberries

As a group, raspberries are the most commonly grown bramble in home gardens. Having a somewhat wider geographic adaptability than blackberries, they are probably the easiest for the novice bramble grower to start with. Depending on the variety chosen, raspberries provide a harvest season in the summer or the fall. They also provide fruit of several colors and flavors. One species of raspberry (*R. idaes*), represents the red and yellow raspberry varieties, another (*R. occidentalis*) denotes the black raspberry. If this family tree isn't confusing enough, purple raspberries are a third species (*R. neglectus*) that has resulted from crossing red and black raspberries.

Raspberries grow best in climates with cool summers and mild winters. Although they can also be grown in warmer regions, the ripe berry becomes very soft and difficult to harvest, making the more heat tolerant blackberry a better choice in warm climates.

Red Raspberries

Red raspberries are a fairly shallow rooted plant. About ninety percent of their roots can be found in the top two feet of the soil profile. Typically the roots spread out laterally for three to four feet in all directions. Buds of new canes are produced randomly along the roots from fall until early spring. New shoots do not usually appear until spring, though, continuing to grow throughout the summer. In their first season of growth, these canes are called primocanes. During the primocanes' growth season, they grow fairly straight up with few buds breaking at the nodes. Under good growing conditions, these canes can easily reach six feet high, achieving twice that size in the favored bramble growing regions of the Pacific northwest.

With the shortening day length and cooler temperatures of fall, the axillary buds on the cane begin to differentiate. Starting from the shoot tip, most of these buds develop into flower buds. The last two or three buds just below ground level remain vegetative. They will produce primocanes the following season. Cane growth also ceases and the cane becomes dormant.

In the cane's second growing season, the differentiated axillary buds grow to form flower bearing shoots. Weather conditions the previous fall and cane strength seem to have a direct effect on how many flower buds are actually produced and how many flowers there are in each bud. Typically, the middle sixty percent of the cane will produce most of the flower buds. After harvest, the floricanes have outlived their usefulness and die.

Red raspberries are generally the hardiest of the brambles, with some varieties withstanding temperatures to -30°F. Easy to care for and quick to fill in the garden rows, they are useful for everything from fresh eating to jam. A number of varieties are available, most of which bear full crops within three years of planting.

Summer Fruiting Red Varieties

Variety	Hardiness	Season	Comment
Algonquin	Fair	Midseason	Spineless. Disease resistant.
Boyne	Excellent	Early	Heat & drought tolerant. Vigorous. Fair flavor.
Canby	Fair	Early	Excellent flavor.
Chilliwack	Fair	Midseason	Tolerates heavy soil, root rot resistant. Short bearing season
Dorman Red	Poor	Early	Developed for south, thrives in heat.
Festival	Good	Midseason	Resistant to most diseases. Fair flavor.
Haida	Good	Late-mid	Fairly disease resistant.
Killarney	Excellent	Midseason	Good flavor.
Latham	Excellent	Midseason	Older variety, fair fruit quality. One of the most hardy, but also grows well in south.
Meeker	Poor	Midseason	Older variety. Pacific northwest
Newburgh	Good	Midseason	Excellent flavor.
Nootka	Good	Midseason	Similar to Haida.
Reveille	Excellent	Early	Good flavor, soft fruit.
Taylor	Fair	Midseason	Excellent flavor.
Tulameen	Fair	Late	Large fruit, high yield. Very long harvest season. For Pacific northwest.
Willamette	Fair	Early	For Pacific northwest.

Fall Fruiting Red Varieties

As with strawberries, there are "everbearing" or fall fruiting raspberries. These are also referred to as "primocane fruiting". Unlike the typical summer bearing bramble, the fall bearing raspberry produces fruit on the top ten to twelve buds of the primocane during the fall of the first growing season. During the following season, an additional summer crop is produced on the floricanes. Other growth and development is similar to the summer fruiting types.

Many of the fall fruiting red raspberry varieties become quite top heavy as the fruit matures. To keep the fruit from getting dirty and the canes from breaking, support them in some way. Remember that any trellis system you use will need to be easy to put up and take down if you are planning to mow the canes off and only harvest fruit from the primocanes.

Variety	Flavor	Season	Comment
Amity	Good	Midseason	Firm berry.
Autumn Bliss	Good	Very early	Widely adapted. Heat tolerant.
Bababerry	Good	Very late	Discovered growing wild in California. Grows well in hot climates where other raspberries do not. For hot, long season, low chilling areas.
Fallred		Very early	Tolerates heat to zone 9.
Heritage	Good	Late	Most planted red primocane fruiting variety. Suited to most climates. Bears heavily on cane tips for easy picking.
Nordic		Very Late	Only grown for fall crop in long season areas. Excellent hardiness.
Redwing	Good	Very Early	Hardy, but heat resistant.
Southland	Fair	Very Late	Heat and drought tolerant.

Yellow Raspberries

Yellow raspberries are basically identical in their growth habits and care to red raspberries. When it comes to their berry, though, they are slightly more fragile and even more delicious. Yellow raspberries are grown almost exclusively for fresh eating. Their flavor, when eaten fresh is honey sweet and they certainly add an interesting touch of color to a mixed bowl of fresh berries.

Yellow raspberries tend to yield less than the red varieties and until recently the reasons were unclear. Numerous virus diseases have been implicated as a cause. New research is also finding that yellow raspberries may prefer to grow in a slightly higher soil pH than other brambles. A side dressing of wood ash seems to help plant vigor too, pointing to the idea that they may have a higher requirement for potash than was formerly believed.

There are only a few yellow raspberry varieties to choose from. For some reason, yellow raspberry cultivars have tended to harbor more virus diseases than the other brambles and it has been difficult to obtain truly virus free plant stock. This has often made them comparatively less productive and contributed to their shorter life span. Although you may find more varieties than those listed below in some nursery catalogs, the varieties listed below are the only ones that at this time appear to have certifiably virus free foundation stock. You may be tempted to shrug and say "so what?" Remember that eventually the virus from contaminated stock can be spread to all your raspberries, resulting in crumbly berries, weakened plants, and reduced productivity.

The following varieties are all suited to the home garden:

Honey Queen is a summer bearing variety with pale yellow color and very mild taste. It is well adapted to the climate in northern prairie areas.

Golden Harvest is a primocane fruiting variety. Discovered in New York, it is adapted to zones 4 through 7B.

Goldie is the newest yellow raspberry variety available. This primocane fruiting variety is a gold mutation of Heritage red raspberry. It is high yielding, bearing an almost orange berry on semi-erect five to seven foot canes.

Black Raspberries

Black raspberry canes have the same type of two year fruiting cycle as red raspberries have, but their manner of producing canes is somewhat different. First, the black raspberry's root system does not spread as extensively, tending to remain where it was originally planted. While red raspberry primocanes are produced from buds along the length of the roots, black raspberry primocanes are primarily produced within the plant crown. After the primocane has achieved four to five feet of upright growth, it starts to arch over, eventually touching the ground. By late summer the cane tip is stimulated to produce roots and if the tip is covered with soil or mulch, rooting will occur. In spring, a new shoot will grow at this spot. This method of rooting, called tip layering, is how black raspberries are often propagated.

To encourage the formation of lateral branches that will produce fruit, black raspberries are often cut back or "tipped", when they reach a thirty to forty inch height rather than being allowed to tip layer. During the cane's second growing season, the floricane will bear fruit and then die, as with the red raspberry.

Black raspberries, also known in some areas as "black caps", are not quite as winter hardy as the red varieties. Most black raspberry varieties will tolerate temperatures to about -20°F, but the canes can be damaged at zero degrees F if hard, drying winds occur. All of the current black raspberry varieties are summer fruiting. Black raspberry plants are a little quicker to reach maturity than red raspberries. They can be expected to produce bountifully from their second growing season on.

Variety	Hardiness	Season	Comment
Allen	Moderate	Early	Mild flavor, uniform ripening.
Black Hawk	Excellent	Midseason	Hardiest black raspberry.
Bristol	Good	Early	Excellent flavor.
Cumberland	Fair	Midseason	Good flavor & firmness.
Dundee	Good	Midseason	Excellent flavor. Productive, for northeast. Disease susceptible.
Haut		Early	New variety, recommended for trial in northeast.
Jewel	Good	Midseason	Large fruit. Fairly disease resistant.
Lowden	Good	Late	Fairly disease resistant.

Purple Raspberries

As a cross between red and black raspberries, purple raspberries show some of the characteristics of both species. They will produce a few sucker canes along the roots as well as tip layer. Fruit is produced on the floricanes and is typically ripe in mid-summer, ripening somewhat later in the season than either of their parents. Purple raspberries grow vigorously and are quite tolerant of diseases and pests.

Purple raspberry plants, like their black raspberry parent, reach maturity quickly and will often produce full size crops in their second growing season. Of all the raspberries, they are the most consistent in their production under drought conditions. Although they benefit from irrigation, they are the bramble most tolerant of its absence.

Although several older purple raspberries may still be found in nursery catalogs, the following varieties are considered the best current choices. All are hardy to -25°F.

Brandywine bears a very large, tart berry which some people find too tart for fresh eating. It is excellent for jam and pie. The plants are very consistent producers with high yields from year to year.

Estate is a new variety that bears large, uniform sweet fruit. The berry is redder in color than other purple raspberries.

Royalty produces late ripening fruit that can be picked at one of three stages. Picked when fully red, it has the red raspberry flavor. Picked later, when the berry is purple, it has the sweet purple berry flavor or when overripe, the flavor is similar to a black raspberry.

Along with the popular raspberry types already mentioned, the adventurous berry grower may want to try several lesser known and unique raspberries - the thimbleberry and the wineberry.

Thimbleberries

Figure 62. Thimbleberry leaf & flower

The thimbleberry (*Rubus parviflorus*) has both a distinctive appearance and fine flavored berry. It grows native as an understory plant in Michigan's Upper Peninsula, northern lower peninsula and the Pacific northwest. It prefers moist soils and is found mostly at the edges and in clearings of mixed hardwood forests. An upright growing plant with smooth stems, its large palm shaped leaves give it an appearance unlike the other brambles. Its large blossoms have contributed to it also being called the "flowering raspberry". Its unique appearance make it an execellent plant for incorporation into an edible landscape design. Although it yields only a moderate amount of fruit, residents of its native areas commonly use it to make prized jams and tarts. The fruit is sweet and subtle flavored. Red in color, the ripe fruit easily separates from the receptacle to yield a shallow bowl-shaped berry.

Wineberries

The wineberry (*Rubus phoenicolasius*) has a flavor quite distinct from the other raspberries. It can best be described as "musky" with a complex bouquet, like one might describe a wine, although the flavor is not wine-like. Nor are the berries used specifically to make wine. A bit tarter than the common raspberry, the wineberry can be sweetened with a bit of sugar to closely resemble other raspberries. Most connoisseurs of wineberries, however, enjoy them for their own distinct taste. They can be used in any of the ways that other raspberries are commonly used.

Wineberry plants spread quickly, and since they tip layer, will easily become overgrown. A regular annual pruning will keep them in check. Originally native to China and Japan, wineberries now grow wild in the Mid-Atlantic states and Appalachia. Their normal growing range spans USDA zone 5 to zone 8. Although, considered hardy to zone 5, wineberries will occasionally suffer some winter injury when grown in this zone.

Figure 63. Wineberry fruit

The wineberry plant's appearance can be distinguished from other raspberries in several ways. First, the husk, a remnant of the flower calyx that looks like little leaves at the base of the fruit, has red, fuzzy bristles and is quite large. It surrounds the fruit rather attractively. The fruit itself is an almost luminescent orange-red. Most of the fruit is borne in clusters at the cane's tip. Second, the canes are somewhat sticky with hairy red-orange bristles. The leaves are downy white underneath with prominent purple veining, making them attractive landscape plants as well.

Pruning

Raspberries are one of the easiest fruit to prune once the gardener has learned the fundamentals. Following fruiting in red raspberries, immediately remove all the floricanes. The floricanes will be easily recognizable as the woodier canes with silvery brown coloring and light green leaves. The primocanes that will remain are green in color and more succulent with darker green leaves. If the plants have filled the rows, also remove all but the strongest three to five canes per linear foot of row. In the spring, you may want to shorten the height of the tallest canes to between four and five and a half feet. This will help keep the cane growing erect when it becomes weighted with fruit later in the summer. Tipping the canes in this manner will remove some fruit buds, so cut the canes back only as much as needed to keep them growing upright. After fruit harvest, start the pruning cycle over again by removing old floricanes. Red raspberries pruned in this manner normally do not need trellising.

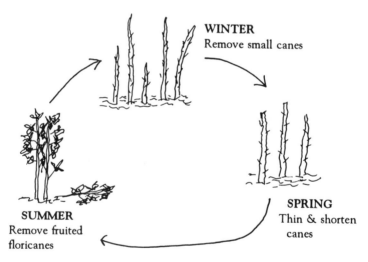

WINTER
Remove small canes

SPRING
Thin & shorten canes

SUMMER
Remove fruited floricanes

Figure 64. Pruning red raspberries

Black raspberries are pruned somewhat differently than red varieties. In the first growing season, when the primocanes reach twenty four to thirty inches, pinch off at least the top two inches of the cane. This will encourage side branches to grow. It is these side branches that will produce most of the fruit next summer. Since the canes grow at different rates, you may need to repeat this pinching several times throughout the growing season as more canes reach the two foot height. The following spring, while the canes are still dormant, trim lateral branches back to eight to ten inches. Although you will remove some fruit buds, the remaining buds will produce larger fruit. After fruiting, immediately remove the floricanes and continue the pruning cycle already in practice on the primocanes. Black raspberries that are kept properly pinched can be grown without trellis support, but suffer less wind-whip stress when trellised.

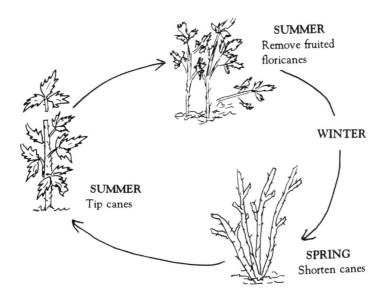

SUMMER
Remove fruited floricanes

WINTER

SUMMER
Tip canes

SPRING
Shorten canes

Figure 65. Pruning black raspberries

Purple raspberries are best pruned like their black raspberry parent, with the exception of Royalty, which is treated like a red raspberry. Royalty should be thinned more aggressively than red raspberries, leaving only two to three purple raspberry canes per running foot of row. The other purple varieties, which tend not to sucker heavily can be grown in hills, three feet apart. Since purple raspberries grow vigorously, they need to be supported by a trellis.

If you are managing your purple raspberries like black raspberries, tip the primocanes when they reach three feet in height and shorten lateral branches as you would with black raspberries.

Primocane bearing raspberry varieties are usually pruned in such a way that only their fall crop is harvested. They produce their best quality crop when managed this way and pruning is a very easy affair. In very late fall or in late winter before budbreak, all the dormant canes are simply mowed off at ground level. This can be done with your home lawn mower in a small planting. New primocanes are then allowed to grow and fruit each season.

If the planting of primocane fruiting raspberries grows vigorously, a trellis support is very helpful in keeping the berries off the ground. This can be something as simple as a single wire supported to a height of about three feet. Be sure to choose a system that is easy to install and remove to accommodate annual mowing of the canes.

Harvest

Raspberry harvest typically occurs during July and August in most areas of the United States, with some overlap between colors. Black raspberries will be first to ripen, with the harvest season spread over about two weeks. Red and yellow raspberries will be next to ripen over a four to six week period, followed by purple varieties for an additional two week period.

Raspberry yields range from one to two pounds per lineal foot of row. Black raspberries yield on the low end of this scale, red varieties fall in the middle, and purple raspberries normally produce on the high end of this range.

A good ripeness test for raspberries is just how hard you have to pull to remove the berry from the cane. If you have to pull hard, the berry is not ripe yet. A truly ripe raspberry will pop right off its receptacle with gentle pressure. Gently lift the berry from the plant between two fingers.

To keep fragile berries from being crushed by the weight of those above them, pick into containers no larger than 1/2 pint or no deeper than three layers deep.

14. Blackberries

Just as the raspberries can be broken into several groups with distinct growth habits, there are several groups of blackberries. There are the erect growing type, the trailing type, and the evergreen blackberries. Trailing types are sometimes divided further according the geographic regions in which they grow best. Dewberries, sometimes referred to separately, are actually a trailing blackberry type.

Blackberries follow the same primocane/floricane fruiting cycle that raspberries do, but produce canes at several locations depending on the type of blackberry they are. Like black raspberries, trailing blackberries produce canes only at the plant crown. Erect growing blackberries will produce canes from both the roots and the crown.

Blackberries prefer a warmer climate than raspberries and grow well in the southern United States. The ripe blackberry is better able to tolerate the heat than the raspberry and is therefore a better choice of bramble to grow where the summer is hot. Blackberry canes are less cold hardy than raspberries and, therefore, can be more challenging to grow in northern climates. However, the effort is certainly worth the reward. Blackberries are excellent for fresh eating, pie, freezing, jam, and wine. They are ripe, just after summer raspberries, when few other fruit are available in the garden.

It normally takes three years for a blackberry plant to reach its production potential. Each plant will typically yield from three to six pounds per plant for the erect types and up to four times that for the trailing types. Yes, trailing types can indeed yield twelve to twenty five pounds per plant under optimum climate and proper management. Fruit normally ripens between July and September, depending on variety and geographic location.

Planting

Planting blackberries has already been covered in detail in chapter 12 on bramble basics, but one important point bears repeating. It is very important to protect blackberry roots from sunlight during the planting process. While the plants are out of the ground, be sure to keep the roots covered and if possible, plant on an overcast day. Although the reasons remain uncertain, blackberry plants suffer a high mortality if their roots are exposed to sun light during planting.

Erect Growing Blackberries

Erect growing varieties are generally considered to be the best flavored of the blackberries. They produce sturdy, thorny canes, which don't require the support of a trellis. Typically more winter hardy than the trailing types, the canes of some erect growing blackberries can tolerate cold temperature to -10°F. The stiff erect canes are too inflexible to bend over and be covered with mulch for the winter, but several feet of snow can often provide some winter insulation. These varieties are more commonly grown in the eastern and northern regions of the United States and are the ones that will survive best, provided winter snow cover is reliable.

Variety	Use*	Zone	Season	Comments
Arapaho		6-10	Very Early	Thornless. Hardy to -10°F
Brazos	J	4-9	Midseason	Disease resistant. Productive. For Gulf Coast/S. west
Cherokee	E,F,J	5-8	Early	
Cheyenne	F,J	6-8	Early	Large berry
Choctaw	E	6-8	Very early	Small seeds. Very thorny.
Comanche	E,F,J	6-9		For Central U.S.
Darrow	E,F,J	5-9	Early	Productive. For Northeast and Midwest
Illini Hardy	E,F	5-9	Midseason	Wild berry flavor. Hardy to -23°F. For northern areas.
Lochness				New variety for trial.
Navaho	E	6-10	Very Late	Thornless. Small berry. Best flavored blackberry.
Rosborough	E	5-9	Early	Heavy cropper. Long season. Hardy to 0°F.
Shawnee	E	6-9	Very Late	Consistent high yield.

*E=Eating, F=Freezing, J=Jam and cooking.

Trailing Blackberries

Trailing blackberries are commonly grown on the west coast and in the southern United States. They are only winter hardy to zero degrees F, but can be protected with mulch. The fruit is often sweeter and larger than that of the erect growing varieties. Several varieties are available today that are genetically thornless.

Variety	Use	Zone	Season	Comments
Black Satin	E,J	6-9	Late	Thornless. For Pacific NW, midwest and south
Chester	E,J	5-7	Very Late	Thornless. Doesn't lose color in heat & sun
Dirksen	E,J	6-10	Midseason	Thornless. Older variety. Disease resistant
Gem	E	6-9	Very Early	Excellent quality, large fruit. Disease resistant.
Hull	E,J	5-8	Late	Thornless. High yield. For East & Pacific NW.
Marion	E		Midseason	For Pacific NW.
Olallie	E		Midseason	Pacific NW. California.
Smoothstem	E		Late	Thornless. For south & lower midwest, not hardy in north.
Thornfree		5-9	Late	Thornless. Grows best in fertile soil.

Blackberry - Raspberry Crosses

Several crosses between blackberries and raspberries are also available. These include Loganberry, Marionberry, Tayberry, and Youngberry. Most of these plants have growth characteristics and hardiness similar to blackberries. Yet, their fruit is often redder in color and somewhat sweeter. In most cases they grow best primarily in the Pacific northwest. Since they are so regionally specific, the individual varieties will not be described in detail.

Pruning Erect Growing Blackberries

During the first growing season, erect type blackberries are usually allowed to grow unpruned. In the second growing year, once the primocanes reach three to four feet high, they are tipped just like

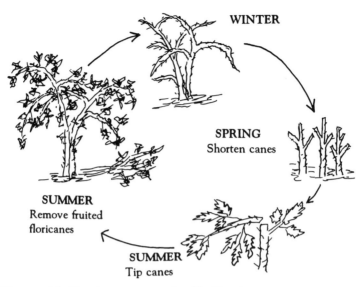

WINTER

SPRING
Shorten canes

SUMMER
Remove fruited
floricanes

SUMMER
Tip canes

Figure 66. Pruning erect growing blackberries

black raspberries. Weak, spindly canes should also be removed in the early spring and the remaining canes thinned to a distance of six inches apart. If you maintain plant rows about twelve inches wide, this means you can usually save four to six canes per lineal foot of row. Lateral branches on the floricanes are cut back to a length of twelve to eighteen inches before bud break in the spring. Old floricanes are removed after fruiting. Erect growing blackberry varieties can normally be grown without needing a trellis for support.

Pruning Trailing Blackberries

Trailing blackberries usually need only to have their canes positioned in the direction of the row during the first growing season. Little or no pruning is required. Since trailing blackberries require trellising, it is best to install the trellis at planting time, but if this was not done, a trellis definitely needs to be installed before growth starts in the second season.

As canes grow in the second season, unlike erect growing blackberries, do not tip the primocanes of the trailing types. Just pull the canes up and tie them to the trellis. Special plastic ties that resist the sun's UV rays are available. Strips of old cloth or panty hose work very well too, (and the price is right) although they may need

160 the Backyard Berry Book

to be replaced every few years as they weaken with exposure to the weather. In warm climates, floricanes are removed after fruiting and primocanes are tied to the trellis in early fall. Where winter temperatures may injure cold sensitive canes, it is best to leave primocanes on the ground where they can be protected with mulch and snow cover. In these areas, remove the previous season floricanes in the spring of the third growing season and select the six healthiest primocanes to tie to the trellis. Leaving the floricanes in place until spring will help trap snow that can protect the plant crown and the primocanes.

After the six primocanes have been selected, gather and tie them together in groups of three. Then train the canes, one bunch in each direction along the wire, by lightly wrapping them around the wire several times as you proceed to tie them in place. Only allow adjacent plants' canes to overlap two to three feet. Remove the rest of the cane tip.

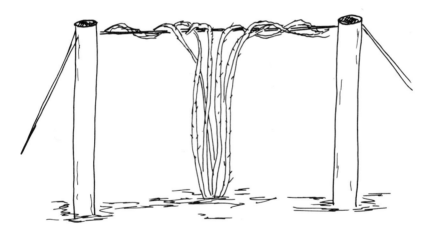

Figure 67. Training primocanes along the trellis wire

Next, remove all lateral cane branches up to three feet from the ground. Any laterals growing higher than three feet on the canes should be shortened to a stub of two to four inches. Most stubs will produce several clusters of fruit.

Blackberries 161

Harvest

Blackberries often begin to bear a partial crop in their second year of growth and a full crop by their third growing season. Fruit is usually ready to harvest starting in May in the southeastern United States, July in the Pacific northwest, and as late as September or October in the upper midwest. One way to judge the timing of harvest in your area is to keep in mind that blackberries usually ripen between forty and sixty days after bloom. The harvest season often extends over a four to seven week period. Picking ripe berries every two to three days usually works well as long as temperatures are cool and dry. In very warm areas, blackberries will sometimes turn red and become bitter if exposed to excessive sunlight. Covering lightly to shade them can help alleviate this problem.

First time blackberry growers are tempted to pick their berries as they first turn shiny black. At this point, they are still quite tart. If you wait a few days, the berries will soften and loose their shine, appearing almost overripe. At this point, the now sweet, juicy berries are at their flavor peak and will almost fall into your hand.

Section IV.

Bush Fruit

15. Blueberries

Blueberries are one of only a few native North American fruit now grown as cultivated varieties. They have provided food for many centuries and are one of the easiest fruit to prepare. Their flavor is sweet, making them excellent for fresh eating. Yet, they have just enough tartness, adequate shelf life, and small seeds to make them versatile for use in cooking and preserving. The advantage of being a native fruit stands out in that blueberries are not overly plagued by pests and diseases. As a final attribute, they also provide an attractive landscape focus with their red fall color.

Blueberries grow best in sunny areas where the growing season is at least 160 days and temperature and humidity are not extremely high. As a result they are most commonly grown in USDA zones 5 through 7, but can be grown as far north as zone 3 when the proper microclimate exists and early maturing varieties are selected. Depending on what part of the country you live in, you will find one or more of the main cultivated types of blueberries growing successfully. In far northern areas, lowbush blueberries are most common. Highbush blueberries are popular in the Eastern states and into the midwest. Characteristics of highbush and lowbush are found in the new hybrid "half-high" varieties that have been developed to withstand harsher climates and still provide a productive harvest. In the deep south rabbiteye blueberries are the varieties of choice.

Types and Varieties

Highbush
The highbush blueberry is the most widespread of the three main types of blueberry and probably the one most often grown in the home garden. It is commonly grown along the Eastern seaboard, throughout the lower and central midwest and in the Pacific northwest, in areas with a growing season of 160 days or more. The root system of the highbush blueberry is composed of a thread-like root mass with no root hairs. Most of the root zone lies within the

drip-line of the plant, typically extending out to about six feet and down as much as thirty-two inches deep. The highbush blueberry plant can grow as large as six to eight feet tall. The original highbush blueberry varieties typically had chill requirements of anywhere from 600 to 1000 hours below 45°F.

Variety	Use*	Zone	Season	Comments
Bluechip	E	6-7	mid-June	Resistant to canker & leaf spot.
Bluecrop	E,F,J	4-7	Midseason	Standard against which other varieties are judged. Long harvest period.
Bluejay	E	4-7	Early	Resistant to mummy berry.
Blueray	E	4-7	Early-mid	Good for home garden, hot areas. Similar to Bluecrop with more acid sweet flavor. Only needs 800 hrs. chilling.
Cape Fear		6-10	Early-mid	Low chill 500-600 hours. Heat tolerant. Disease resistant.
Coville	F	5-8	Late	Tart until ripe. Tops for flavor. Susceptible to anthracnose.
Darrow	E	5-7	Late	Productive in mild climates. Big berry. Good in Pacific northwest.
Duke	E,F	5-7	Early	Mild flavor, productive. Gets stem canker when grown on East coast.
Elliot	J	4-7	Very Late	Consistent yield. Tart/acid flavor excellent for jam. Long harvest season. 800 hours chilling. Not good for Pacific northwest.
Herbert	E	4-7	Late	Excellent flavor. Tip bearer. Small bush, good for home garden.
Jersey		5-8	Late	Hardy to -30.
Meader	E,F		Midseason	Similar to Bluecrop but hardier.
Olympia	E,F		Midseason	Needs pollination & heavy pruning. Adapts to most soils. For Pacific northwest.

Patriot	E	3-7	Early	Large berry. Resistant to root rot, tolerates wet/clay soil.
Sierra	E	5-8	Early	Very large berry. Ripens with Bluejay. New variety worth trial.
Toro	E,F	4-7	Midseason	Tolerates temperature fluctuations. Huge, crisp berry.

*E=Eating, F=Freezing, J=Jam and cooking.

In the 1970s some low chill highbush varieties were developed that require only about 200 to 250 hours below 45°F. This has allowed the introduction of highbush blueberries as far south as central Florida. These berries are ripe in late April/early May, much ahead of the typical season of commercial availability. Due to some of the genes inherited in the process, the low chill highbush blueberry is hardier than the rabbiteye varieties that are native to the southern growing areas. The best currently available varieties include:

Avonblue produces medium size berries and is well suited for USDA zones 6-9.

Blue Ridge grows well in North Carolina, producing excellent quality berries. It ripens early midseason. The bush is quite ornamental and can grow to seven feet.

Flordablue is one of the original low chill highbush varieties.

Georgiagem is an early ripening, new variety release for USDA zones 7-9.

O'Neal is another new release for zones 7-9. It is tolerant of high heat, ripens early and needs only 200 hours of chilling.

Sharpblue, considered the best flavored in this group, is a productive variety that bears large fruit. It is suited to zones 7-10.

Sunshine Blue is adapted to zones 6-9. It is more tolerant of higher soil pH than other southern varieties.

Lowbush

On the other end of the spectrum is the lowbush blueberry. Originally native to the cold northern climates, it is now grown as a cultivated crop, but still planted primarily only in extreme northern areas. Often these areas experience winter temperatures that are too harsh for tall highbush blueberry plants that are not completely covered with an insulating blanket of snow. Lowbush varieties survive the winter in these areas, not because they are so much hardier than the highbush plants, but because their short stature allows them to be fully covered by the snow.

The lowbush blueberry can be grown successfully from zone 7 north through zone 3. However, plants are sometimes hard to find, since only a small number of nurseries sell them. Two varieties are currently available:

Early Sweet is considered the best lowbush variety. It is early ripening and hardy in zones 2 through 7.

Bloodstone ripens in late July. Suitable for zones 5 through 7, it does not grow well in high moisture or humidity situations due to susceptibility to both *phytophthora* root rot and anthracnose.

Lowbush varieties grow as a ground-cover-like small bush, usually growing no taller than one and a half feet. The fruit is generally small, about 1/4" in diameter and slightly tart. Often considered the best for baking and preserves, the lowbush blueberry's piquant flavor is strong enough not to be overshadowed in the cooking process.

Half-high

Half-high blueberries are the result of breeding programs that sought to achieve a plant with the hardiness of the lowbush varieties and the larger, sweeter fruited berry of the highbush types. Most of these varieties came from breeding programs in Michigan and Minnesota and are most adapted to northern climates. South of zone 7 they do not receive sufficient chilling to grow well. The half-high blueberry bush usually grows from three to five feet tall and bears small to medium sized fruit.

Variety	Height	Zone	Season	Comments
Friendship	3 feet		Late	A Wisconsin selection with sweet Flavor
Northblue	30 inches	3-7 to -35°F	Midseason	Excellent quality, easy to pick.
Northcountry	2 feet	3-7 to -35°F	Midseason	2-3 week harvest.
Northland	3-4 feet	3-7 to -25°F	Early	Needs cross pollination. Concentrated harvest.
Northsky	18 inches	3-7 to -40°F	Midseason	Smaller berry & yield. Good home garden variety.
St. Cloud	4 feet	3-7	Midseason	Needs cross pollination. Newest release.

Rabbiteye

Rabbiteye blueberries are more tolerant of high pH soils than the other types of blueberries and will also tolerate high temperatures better. They are more sensitive to cold winter temperatures than the other blueberry types, however, and are grown no further north than the Carolinas. Most have low chill requirements, many ranging from 360 to 500 hours below 45°F. Consequently, they begin growing early and do not produce well where late spring frosts are common.

In the wild, they can grow more than thirty feet tall, but cultivated varieties typically range from five to twenty feet tall. The pink blush found on the blossom end of the berry has an appearance much like a rabbit's eye, thus their name. The berry quality is not as good as that of the other types of blueberries, being smaller and seedier. Now that low chill highbush varieties are available, more gardeners are turning to growing them instead. Most rabbiteye varieties are self-sterile and require suitable cross pollination.

Variety	Zone	Season	Comment
Aliceblue	6-9	Early	
Beckyblue	6-9	Early	Produces in high & low chill
Bluebell	6-10	Midseason	Extended 3-4 week harvest. Recommended for home garden.
Bluegem		Midseason	Large berry.
Brightwell	7-9	Early	Excellent flavor. Concentrated harvest. Late blooming,
Briteblue	6-10	Late	Excellent flavor/quality. Tolerates wide range of conditions.
Centurion	6-9	Late	Excellent jam berry. Easy to manage, upright bush
Choice	6-9	Mid-late	
Climax	7-9	Early	Ripens uniformly.
Delite	6-10	Late	Excellent flavor. Recommended for home garden.
Powderblue	6-9	Midseason	Very productive. Good for home use.
Premier	7-9	Early	Very productive, large berry. Good for home use.
Southland	6-10	Midseason	Tough skin on later pickings.
Tifblue	7-9	Midseason	Standard for judging rabbiteyes. Most cold hardy. Pollinate with Woodward.
Woodward	7-9	Early	Very large berry. Good for home use. Pollinate with Tifblue.

Site Requirements

The most general site requirements of blueberries are determined by the severity of winter temperatures and the length of the growing season. Most highbush cultivars require a growing season of at least 160 days and withstand minimum winter temperatures no lower than -15°F when fully dormant. Half-high varieties will tolerate temperatures from -25°F to -40°F. The rabbiteye varieties can typically only withstand zero degrees F. The soil requirements of blueberries are more specific than for most other berries and often become the limiting factor in whether your site is suitable for blueberry growing, once climatic conditions are acceptable.

Soil Requirements

Blueberries have more exacting soil requirements than most other small fruit. As members of the Ericaceae family, blueberries are related to a number of popular landscape plants such as rhododendron, azalea, and heath. Other fruit in the Ericaceae family include cranberries, lingonberries, whortleberries, and bilberries. Like most of these plants, blueberries favor an acid soil. Although acid soil conditions are not as widespread as the more alkaline soils favored by other fruit crops, they can often be created on a small scale by diligent soil modification.

What has not been stressed nearly as often as the blueberry's need for acid soils, is the blueberry plant's need for high organic matter. Soil organic matter content between 3% and 20% will contribute greatly to your success in growing blueberries and also enable the plant to tolerate pH ranges from 3.8 up to 5.5.

Muck soils, which are typically characterized as having high organic matter content, very fine particle size, and high nutrient exchange capacity would appear to be ideal for growing blueberries. However, while some muck soils with organic matter content from 20% to 50% are suitable for raising blueberries, they often have a high water table not easily tolerated by blueberries. Muck soils with organic matter greater than 50% tend to have very low pH, often less than 4.0 and have the disadvantage of releasing excess nitrogen from organic matter breakdown. This encourages late season plant growth that is susceptible to winter injury. Muck soil is also slow to warm up in the spring.

Good soil drainage is essential to a favorable growing site as blueberries' shallow, fibrous roots are easily starved for oxygen. Be sure that the water table is at least eight to twelve inches below the surface, within twenty four hours of a rain. At other times, the water table should be at least twice that deep. Sandy soils tend to be the best drained soils, but they are often low in organic matter. This can be corrected, however, by growing green manure cover crops prior to planting. Buckwheat and oat cover crops will both grow well in the pH range required by blueberries. Oats will add more organic matter though. Additionally, organic matter can be added by using compost, leaf litter or peat.

Traditionally, it has been recommended that blueberries be grown in soils with a pH of 4.5. A soil pH range from 4.5 to 4.8 is considered optimum for blueberry production, but blueberries will grow reasonably well in a soil pH as high as 5.2. Sandy loam soils, which typically have low cation exchange capacity, tend to be naturally more acid and are consequently preferred soils for blueberries. For this same reason, blueberries in the wild may seem to grow reasonably well on fairly poor soils. It is also these sandy soils where it is easiest to change the pH.

In most cases where pH is being modified to accommodate blueberries, the pH is being lowered. Several available materials will accomplish this task. Powdered elemental sulfur is the most economical. Elemental sulfur in prill form is also available and less dusty to spread than the powdered form. It is more expensive, however. Aluminum sulfate and iron (ferrous) sulfate will lower soil pH, but should be avoided since they can cause plant toxicity in certain types of soil. Also, much greater quantities of the sulfate materials will be needed to accomplish the same job that the elemental sulfur will do.

The chart that follows provides a general guide to the amount of sulfur needed for various modifications in pH. Changes in pH occur slowly as chemical reactions take place within the soil, so it is best to add any of these soil amendments at least six to twelve months before you plan to do your planting. Extreme caution is advised when trying to change pH in increments of more than .5 on heavy soils. High amounts of sulfur will damage bushes that are already planted. If changes need to be made after bushes are in the ground, do so very gradually over the course of several years.

Amount of sulfur (#/100 sq. ft.) to lower pH to 4.5

Current pH	Sand	Loam	Clay
5.0	0.4	1.2	1.85
5.5	0.8	2.4	3.66
6.0	1.2	3.5	5.33
6.5	1.5	5.6	6.95
7.0	1.9	5.8	8.80

On rare occasions, where the pH is below 4.0, it may be necessary to raise the soil pH before planting blueberries. In that case it is best to take a soil test first and determine whether magnesium also needs to be added to the soil. Where magnesium is needed, it is best to lime with dolomitic lime. Otherwise high calcium lime can be used. Generally, to raise the pH one point, lime can be applied at a rate of 50 pounds of lime per 1000 square feet on sandy soils; 60-70 pounds per 1000 square feet on loam soils; and 80 pounds per 1000 square feet on clay soils.

Blueberries are more sensitive to micronutrient deficiencies and toxicities than most other small fruit. Iron deficiency is quite common in soils with pH above 5.5 while aluminum and manganese toxicity can be a problem in some soils, especially in the southern central United States, when the soil pH is modified below 5.2.

Plant Selection and Planting

Most blueberry plants available to the home gardener are either container planted stock or bare root stock. In both cases, to find plants that will grow best and be most productive, look for healthy two or three year old plants. One year old rooted cuttings are sometimes available. They may be less expensive, but will take longer to mature and produce fruit.

With bareroot stock, it is important that the plant be dormant when set into the ground. This usually means planting in early spring (April to early May). To keep bare root plants dormant, they should be refrigerated or kept as cool as possible until planting time.

In most areas of the United States, spring planting is also recommended for container grown plants. In warmer areas, where frost heaving and winter injury is not a problem, fall planting is possible.

If container grown plants are not planted shortly after purchase, they can be kept outdoors in their pots and watered until planting time. At planting time, check the root ball to be sure it has not become pot-bound. If it has, it is advisable to root prune it moderately, as you would when repotting a root-bound house plant.

Blueberries can be planted individually or in small groups as specimen plants in the home landscape. Most commonly they are planted in rows as part of the food garden. Select a site where they will receive full sun. It is wise to plant at least two varieties near each other to insure cross pollination. Although most blueberries are self-fertile, cross pollination produces larger fruit that ripens earlier.

How far apart to space plants will depend on the type of blueberry you are growing. Highbush berries are generally planted four to five feet apart, while half-high plants are commonly set two and a half to three feet apart. Lowbush blueberries are normally planted one foot apart. Eight feet between plants is recommended for rabbiteye varieties. Space between rows is typically eight to twelve feet, depending on what garden equipment needs to be accommodated.

Prior to planting, you will need to prepare some peat that will be used in the planting hole. It will be easiest to start getting the peat ready several days before you intend to plant. Start by breaking the peat bale apart and wetting it with a hose. You will find the peat quite difficult to wet. To make the process easier, you may want to soak it for several days in a tub of water. Once your peat is soaking wet, it will do a good job of holding soil moisture for your plants. You can now use it in planting. Don't, however, be tempted to think that you can throw dry peat in the planting hole and then water it in. The dry peat will actually draw moisture away from your newly planted blueberry plant, weakening or possibly killing it.

When digging the planting hole, remember that blueberry plants have dense, shallow root systems. A wide hole will be more important than a deep one. To prepare the planting hole, dig it deep enough to allow the plant to be placed in it at the same depth as it grew in the nursery (you can often see a soil line on the branches) and wide enough to allow the roots to be spread out completely. Add five to six gallons of soaking wet peat to each planting hole and mix it 50-50 with the soil. Make somewhat of a dirt mound in the middle of the hole to set the plant on. Adjust the plant to set at the proper height, spread the roots out fully, and fill the hole back in with the soil. Firm the dirt with the heel of your foot and water it well.

Much of the water and minerals supplied to the blueberry roots is done so with the aid of natural soil occurring fungi. Some growers advocate "inoculating" the new planting with these fungi. If you are fortunate to have wild blueberries in the area, simply mix some of the soil and leaf litter you find at their base into the soil around your new plants. The fungi will soon establish themselves.

Care After Planting

After planting, prune off about one third of the branch growth to reduce the transpiration area while the roots adjust. Also remove any fruit buds or blossoms that appear during the first two years. This will allow the plant to put its energy into strong healthy branch growth that will be more productive in the long run. It is also important to keep an area at least three feet around each bush weed free. If you hoe or cultivate near the blueberry bush, remember that its roots are within inches of the surface and keep cultivation very shallow.

Mulch, four to six inches thick, will help control weeds and keep the soil cool and moist. Mulching also helps to add organic matter to the soil and moderate changes in pH as fertilizer is added. When possible, choose a mulch that is slow to break down, as this will not deplete the soil nitrogen so quickly. Sawdust is one of the best mulch materials for blueberries. It can often be obtained free or inexpensively from a local sawmill. Attention needs to be paid to the quality and age of the sawdust being used, however. As a pile of sawdust ages, the interior of the pile has decreasing amounts of oxygen available to it and consequently will eventually begin undergoing anaerobic respiration (also known as fermentation). As a by-product of this reaction, alcohols, formaldehyde, and methane gas are produced. All of these are harmful to plants. So, be sure the sawdust to be used is *well aged but from the outside of the pile* where it is able to decompose under aerobic conditions. Also avoid mulch materials, such as leaves, grass clippings, and/or layers of newspaper, that mat down and will deprive the blueberry roots of needed oxygen.

About a month after planting, usually in early June, an ounce of fertilizer per plant can be applied in a ring at least a foot away from the bush. One exception to this is the rabbiteye blueberry. These young bushes are very sensitive to fertilizers and should not be fertilized until the second growing season. A complete fertilizer specially formulated for acid loving plants can be used.

Water the plant regularly, as local rainfall dictates. As with most other fruit plants, about an inch of rain per week is needed. If moisture is not provided by normal rainfall, irrigation should be provided. Do remember that you may have to check your blueberries more frequently than other plants during their first year of growth since their shallow roots are not particularly good at taking water from the soil. Also be sure to water evenly on all sides of the plant. Irrigation studies have shown that where the blueberry plant is only irrigated on one side, it grows more vigorously on that side.

Ongoing annual care of your blueberries will include pruning, pest control, and applications of fertilizer and water as discussed in the following sections. If the blueberry plants were mulched originally, this practice will need to be continued since the plant roots grow primarily in the interface between the soil surface and the mulch. Every two or three years, mulch should be added to maintain a six inch deep layer. To compensate for the additional nitrogen used in the decay process, fertilizer application rates may need to be doubled when new mulch is added.

Planting in Containers

Although typically planted as a fruit garden or landscape bush, blueberries can also be planted in a container as a patio plant. Dwarf varieties, specifically adapted for container planting grow well in a twelve to fifteen inch diameter pot. The most popular variety today is Tophat. General aspects of caring for the potted blueberry are similar to that of most potted perennials. Potting soil specially formulated for acid loving plants should be used. Extra attention will need to be paid to regular watering and possible split applications of fertilizer. Pruning the dwarf bush will be much like the field grown one, but require less effort. The fruit yield per bush will also be less than from the larger bushes.

Fertilizer and Water

Blueberries will respond well to annual applications of fertilizer and in dry periods will also require regular watering to be productive. Unlike many fruit that do just fine with a single fertilizer application each season, blueberries will grow and produce better if they are given a "split application", two smaller doses, of fertilizer per season.

Apply the first dose in early spring, as the buds begin to open and then give a second dose about a month later.

A complete fertilizer, specifically developed for acid loving plants, with a 1:1:1 ratio of nutrients best meets the needs of the blueberry plant. Typically you can use a 10-10-10 prepared fertilizer from your garden center or farm supply store. (If you are having trouble finding fertilizers specially formulated for blueberries, try looking at a nursery that specializes in rhododendrons, azaleas, and other acid loving plants.) The mixed fertilizer will likely contain a nitrogen in the ammonium form, such as ammonium sulfate. If applying a "triple mix", start with about one ounce of fertilizer per young plant, gradually increasing the rate by an ounce per year of age until the plant is around eight years old. Alternately, about 1/2 ounce of ammonium sulfate per young plant is adequate. On very low pH soils - less than 4.0 - use 1/4 ounce of urea as a nitrogen source instead. On soils very low in organic matter (less than 3%) a light additional application can be made in early July if the plant is growing weakly. Avoid chloride containing fertilizers, such as muriate of potash (also known as potassium chloride), since blueberries are quite sensitive to chloride and will show toxicity symptoms.

Magnesium deficiency is common on blueberries, so you may find it worthwhile to use a fertilizer that includes 3% magnesium (MgO). Epsom salt (magnesium sulfate), which is 18% magnesium, can be applied as a foliar spray if your plants are showing signs of magnesium deficiency. Magnesium oxide (5% Mg) or Sul-Po-Mag (11% Mg) can be used as ground applied fertilizers where magnesium is needed. Potassium may also need to be supplied occasionally, based on soil test results. Sul-Po-Mag (22% K_2O) or potassium sulfate (50% K_2O) are the most recommended source for use on blueberries.

Distribute the fertilizer in a wide band about six inches from the base of your young plants or under the drip line of older plants. As a gauge, you should expect a highbush blueberry to grow new shoots with fifteen to eighteen new leaves per year. If yours are not doing so, adjust fertilizer and water applications accordingly.

As mentioned earlier, blueberries require a regular supply of water due to their very shallow root system's inefficiency in water uptake. This is especially true for the highbush and half-high varieties. An inch of water per week is typically needed by most fruit plants. When fruit is developing, blueberries may need as much as two inches of water per week.

Rabbiteye blueberries, although also shallow rooted, are better adapted to hot summer temperatures and will produce in areas too dry for other blueberries types.

Pruning

Once the blueberry bush is mature, usually at around five to eight years, depending on your growing location, it should be pruned annually. Annual pruning has the advantage of opening up the bush to light, which encourages flower bud and fruit development. It also facilitates air circulation which reduces the growth of fungus diseases. A well pruned bush is easier to pick. Blueberry bushes that are not pruned regularly will produce an excess of small fruit and their branches will become weak and spindly.

Two types of pruning cuts are generally used when pruning fruit bearing bushes. First are major cuts into the larger diameter branches. These cuts are often used to remove older branches at their base and are a fast way to thin out less productive wood. The second type of pruning cut involves removing smaller branches with numerous detailed cuts. Detailed cuts are often used on less vigorous varieties to stimulate new growth and fruit bud production.

An ideal time to prune blueberries is in early spring, while the bushes are still dormant. At this time the plant has had maximum time to store food reserves for the coming growing season. Winter cold injury is also easy to identify at this time of year, often appearing as dried out grayish branches.

The best quality fruit is produced on vigorous, young branches. These are typically four to six years old and from one to one and a half inches in diameter at their base. The easiest way to encourage this type of growth is by pruning out canes that are older than six years old. Remove these older canes at ground level. Also prune any other weakly growing wood back to healthy, larger diameter lateral branches. Varieties with dense, upright growth (such as Elliot, Lateblue, Bluecrop, Collins, Darrow, Jersey, and Earliblue) should have excess canes growing from the center of the bush thinned out. Varieties with weak growth (such as Bluetta and Weymouth) need to be pruned heavily with detailed cuts to encourage vigorous growth.

Blueberries typically produce fruit on one year old wood. Detailed pruning removes a greater portion of this type of wood and will not be necessary in a vigorous growing bush. As the bush ages, becomes

Blueberries 177

less productive, and bears smaller size berries, it may be helpful to do more detailed pruning. Although the number of berries per bush will be reduced, berry size and quality will be better and overall yields will not be badly reduced.

How much to prune will vary somewhat, depending on whether you are in a northern or southern growing area. In the south, blueberry plants can reach maturity by five years of age and should have about twenty healthy growing canes. Ideally, twenty percent will be young canes of less than one inch diameter at the base, another fifteen to twenty percent will be old canes over two inches in base diameter, and the balance will fall between them in age and diameter. Each year from that point on you should try to remove three or four of the oldest canes (more if many healthy new canes are being produced). By the time the bushes are eight or nine years old, they will have reached their peak and no more than 20% of the oldest wood should be pruned out at a time.

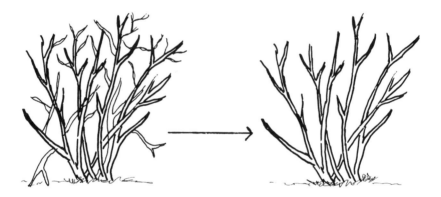

Figure 68. *Pruning blueberries*

In the north, blueberry plants may be anywhere from three to eight years old before they reach maturity. From years three through eight, generally prune out all but two or three of the new canes produced the previous season. Leave older, healthy canes to continue fruit production. By the time the bush is eight years old, it will have between ten and twenty healthy canes of various ages. Continue to maintain a similar number of canes in subsequent years, thinning out the oldest, least productive ones.

178 the Backyard Berry Book

Lowbush blueberries can be pruned by mowing half of the planting every two to three years. This makes the task very easy, but will result in the mowed portion of the planting not producing fruit that season.

Diseases

Mummy Berry is the most common fungus disease affecting blueberries. This disease has a two stage life cycle. In the first stage, the shoots become blighted, wilt, turn dark brown and die rapidly. A creamy colored or light gray mold will cover blighted tissue if conditions are wet. This first stage is rather inconspicuous and often overlooked by the novice berry grower. In the second stage, fruit becomes infected. As the fruit approaches ripeness, it turns a salmon or

Figure 69. Mummy Berry

light pink color, shrivels and falls from the bush. These shriveled, dry fruit are known as mummies (hence the disease name). Six to twelve hours of leaf wetness at temperatures above 60°F is needed for the fungus infection to develop. Control of this disease is achieved by interrupting the first stage of the disease cycle. An early spring application of urea fertilizer coupled with shallow cultivation of the ground surrounding the bushes reduces the development of overwintering disease spores. If infection pressure is not severe, these cultural practices alone may adequately control the disease in home gardens. Where severe disease pressure exists due to high spore levels and optimum climatic conditions, fungicide applications may be needed from the time of bud break until bloom.

Anthracnose, *botrytis,* **powdery mildew,** and *phytophthora* **root rot,** as discussed in chapter 8, also affect blueberries. A combination of cultural practices and fungicides as outlined are used to control these diseases.

Stem canker can be serious in North Carolina and other northern highbush berry areas. While there are few resistant highbush varieties, leading rabbiteye varieties are highly resistant or immune. Little practical control means exist for this disease. Plants wilt and die in a single season.

Numerous viruses affect blueberries, but unfortunately there is little that can be done to control them once they are introduced into the garden. Weak or stunted plant growth with eventual death are the typical symptoms of most blueberry viruses, especially when no other cause is readily apparent. Infected plants should be rogued from the planting and destroyed. To prevent initial introduction of viruses, plant clean nursery stock and control aphids, leafhoppers, and nematodes that typically act as virus vectors.

Insects

Numerous insect pests prey on blueberries. Of all the berries, the pests damaging blueberries are most like those found on tree fruit - maggot, curculio, fruit worms, and leaf rollers. Curculio is mainly a problem on early ripening varieties.

Blueberry maggot, a very close relative of the apple maggot, will cause berries to become soft and mushy as the white larvae eat the interior pulp. Although sometimes touted as a control, yellow sticky boards or red spheres are used commercially mainly to trap the adult fly and target spray timing. They are not particularly effective controls since the adult blueberry maggot fly is highly mobile. Traps need to be kept free of other insects and debris and several traps need to be hung in each bush when used as a control. Imidan, a chemical accepted by many organic spray programs is effective against blueberry maggot.

Figure 70. Blueberry Maggot

Cranberry Fruitworm is one of most serious pests of blueberry in the eastern United States. Yellow-green larvae web the berries together and cause them to shrivel. Frass is visible as the larvae burrow into the stem end of the fruit. Picking and destroying infested berries is the only practical control in the home garden. Once the larvae are inside the fruit, there is little that can be done to kill them. Sprays of rotenone just after bloom can kill some of the newly hatched larvae before they move into the fruit.

Cutworm larvae, usually feeding at night, eat out the interior of the flower buds and later feed on foliage. They are discussed fully in chapter 7.

Harvest & Yields

Blueberries will ripen anywhere from one and a half to two and a half months after they have bloomed. Harvest season usually starts in May in Florida and runs through mid-July in North Carolina. In northern areas, such as New England and the midwest, the harvest season typically runs through July and August. The picking season lasts from six to eight weeks, depending on the varieties planted.

Blueberries are usually ready for harvest about one to two weeks after the first berries turn blue. They will continue to ripen, growing sweeter and larger for a week after they have turned blue. To judge their true ripeness, look for a completely blue fruit. Berries that are not fully ripe will have a pink or reddish ring where the stem meets the berry. Fully ripe berries will also fall easily from the bush when picked.

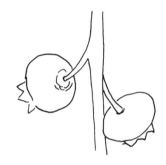

Figure 71. Unripe and ripe fruit

Yields will vary with the type of bush planted. Typically, a three year old highbush blueberry can produce half to three quarters of a pound of fruit per plant. Under good conditions anywhere from five to twenty pounds of fruit can be expected from mature six to eight year old highbush varieties. Half-high varieties yield from two to eight pounds per mature plant, depending on variety and climate. Well cared for bushes can continue to produce for fifteen to twenty years. Rabbiteye blueberry yields on the average range from eight to fifteen pounds per bush. A few highly productive varieties, such as Tifblue, will yield up to twenty five pounds per bush.

16. Lingonberries

The lingonberry, a longtime favorite in Scandinavia, is just now being recognized for inclusion in American gardens. Given the popularity of the cranberry and blueberry, it is somewhat surprising that this close relative of theirs hasn't previously been grown much in the United States. As a native species, growing wild in numerous cool areas of the country it is known as the lowbush or mountain cranberry. This native species (*Vaccinium vitis-idaea* var. *minumus*) bears a single crop each season. The currently cultivated lingonberry, which is of European origin (*Vaccinium vitis-idaea* var. *majus*), is slightly larger in size than the American species and has the unusual habit of bearing fruit twice in each growing season. It is sometimes known by names such as cowberry, partridge berry, and foxberry.

Lingonberry's tart, red fruit make a particularly good syrup or sauce that has traditionally been served over pancakes or pudding. It is similar to the cranberry in tartness and texture, making it well suited as a substitute in baking and other culinary uses. The lingonberry's shiny evergreen foliage, contrasted with the red berries, also make an unusual landscape plant.

Growth Habit

The lingonberry grows as a short, spreading, shrub with branches sprouting from both its base and underground runners, much like a lowbush blueberry. The branch growth is much more succulent and fragile though, not woody like a blueberry branch.

The lingonberry plant has a mature height of twelve to eighteen inches and a spread of up to eighteen inches. It can be grown as a

Figure 72. The lingonberry

ground cover around other acid loving plants, an understory to blueberry plantings, a container plant, or as a short hedge. Its major drawback is that it can be very slow to become established, taking six to seven years to reach mature size and production in some areas.

Site Requirements

Although little research has been done to test how well the lingonberry is adapted to the North American climate, much of what is known about its growth requirements come from its long history in Europe. The plant grows best in a cool climate and is hardy to USDA zone 4. It does need winter protection in areas with little snow cover, primarily to protect it from drying winds. A covering of peat, sawdust, or conifer boughs can be used for protection in the most severe climates. Planting on a protected southern slope is also helpful. Although unproven, it is currently believed that it will thrive as far south as Connecticut. The lingonberry does not grow well in warm southern climates and often dies there due to excessive heat and drought.

Lingonberries will grow in both full sun and partial shade. Sunnier sites will encourage production of a larger crop in growing areas with cool summers. In warmer climate areas, with intense sun, it is best to grow lingonberries where they will be shaded in the hottest hours of the day.

Unlike the sites commonly used to grow cranberries, the lingonberry does not need a bog. It does however need a consistent supply of moisture. Regular watering is helpful, especially during the driest part of the summer. The lingonberry is an acid loving plant that grows best where soil pH is below 5.8, the ideal being a pH of 5.0. The plant requires well drained soil with a minimum of 2% organic matter. It does not compete well with weeds, so it is extremely important to prepare a weed free site prior to planting. Lingonberry roots are so shallow and compete so poorly with weeds that I repeat - plant lingonberries only on a well prepared, weed-free site. Lingonberry's soil requirements are generally similar to blueberry's. Rather than repeating all the details of site preparation here, readers are advised to consult chapter 15. In small scale plantings, lingonberries benefit from having up to seven pounds of moist peat moss incorporated for every 100 square feet of planting area.

Varieties

The lingonberry is self-fertile, but, like the blueberry, it will be more productive if two or more varieties are grown together. There are basically six varieties of lingonberry currently available through U.S. nurseries. All are of European background with similar tasting, medium to large berries. Yields vary somewhat with variety.

Entesegen is of West German origin and yields between one half and one pound of large, mild flavored fruit per mature plant. The plant grows vigorously.

Koralle is a Dutch variety that produces up to 1 1/2 pounds of tart, small to medium-sized fruit per plant. It is the most popular commercial variety. Koralle is very susceptible to *Phytophthora* root rot and requires light soils and excellent drainage.

Moscovia, a new release from Wisconsin, appears to establish itself faster than the other varieties listed here and spreads to over three feet. It holds its berries well into November.

Red Pearl is another recent German variety introduction. The mild flavored fruit ripen a week or two ahead of Koralle. This variety appears to be resistant to *Phytophthora* root rot.

Regal (WI 108) is an American selection from Wisconsin. It produces large fruit that are early ripening.

Sanna is a low growing, six to eight inch tall, variety. It is slow to become established, but is productive once mature.

Scarlet is primarily used as a pollinator for the above mentioned varieties. Although its pollen production is exceptional, its fruit production tends to be scanty.

Splendor is vigorous and grows to a height of up to fifteen inches. Berries are medium size and firm. This variety appears to be resistant to *Phytophthora* root rot.

Susi is a very prolific Swedish variety that produces large size fruit. It appears to be similar to Sanna.

Planting

Once the site is prepared and varieties have been selected, it is planting time. Spring, after danger of frost is past, is the best time to plant lingonberries. Select plants in the one-gallon pot size or two-inches in height. These will adjust most successfully to transplanting.

Make planting holes large to allow all roots to spread out completely.

Plants should be placed at the same depth at which they grew in the pots. Set plants from twelve to eighteen inches apart in rows that are spaced three to four feet apart. In a few years, these will fill in and become attractive evergreen hedges. Firm the soil around the roots and water well to insure that all the soil is settled. A small grouping of plants can also be used as ground cover around azaleas and rhododendrons. Space plants about twelve to fifteen inches apart in all directions.

Lingonberries can also be grown in large decorative containers such as wooden half whiskey barrels. Care must be taken in the winter, however, to adequately protect them from frost heaving and freezing of the roots. The best solution is to dig the barrels into a hole or trench that is mulched well with straw. The plants should not be brought indoors, or their chilling requirement may not be properly met.

Ongoing Care

Mulch the plants well, right after planting, to prevent weed growth. Moist peat moss, two to three inches deep, is the ideal mulch for lingonberries, but other natural mulches suitable for blueberries also work well. As the plants grow in height, continue to add additional mulch. Mulched plants have been reported to produce up to four times as much fruit as those that are not mulched. Any weeds that crop up later should be pulled by hand.

Little pruning is needed in the first few years of plant establishment other than to remove broken or dead branches. At five or six years of age, once the plants are fully established, pruning every two to three years will encourage dense shoot growth and increased fruit production. The easiest way to prune lingonberries is similar to the method used for lowbush blueberries. Alternate rows of plants are mowed every second or third year while they are dormant. Mowed plants will not fruit the season following mowing, but fruit can be harvested from the remaining unpruned plants.

Fertilizer and Water

Lingonberry's requirement for N:P:K fertilizers is minimal. Too much nitrogen will actually reduce fruit production. It will also overstimulate shoot growth that may not harden-down sufficiently, leading to winter kill. Let the plant be your guide in applying fertilizer. Several inches of vigorous, rigid, upright shoot growth indicates that the plant is getting enough nitrogen. Dark green leaves and soft, uncontrolled shoot growth is an indication of excess nitrogen. Plants lacking adequate nitrogen will show typical deficiency symptoms of minimal shoot growth and yellow or red colored leaves. (Do not, however, mistake these red leaves for the red coloration sometimes found on young lingonberry plant leaves. Be sure that other signs of weak growth are also present.) Usually an annual maintenance dose of 1/4 to 1/2 cup of a low nitrogen (5:10:10) triple mix fertilizer will be adequate to meet the plants growing needs. Ammonium sulphate, compost, or organic fertilizers can also be used. Lingonberries, like blueberries, benefit from split applications of fertilizer. Apply half of the yearly fertilizer dose in early spring. Four weeks later the second dose can be applied. Applications should be completed before the end of June to avoid encouraging late season shoot growth.

Like blueberries, lingonberries benefit from magnesium applications when indicated by soil tests. They are also sensitive to chloride damage, so avoid fertilizers such as potassium chloride. For lingonberries planted in the landscape, also be aware of subtle, forgotten sources of chloride injury such as water from chlorinated swimming pools or de-icing salt.

One inch of water per week during the growing season is usually sufficient to meet the plants' requirements. If this is not supplied by rain, provide irrigation or sprinkling.

Pests and Diseases

Lingonberries appear to be pest and disease free when grown in the United States with the exception of possible problems with *Phytophthora* root rot when grown in poorly drained soils. Being botanically close to blueberries, it is possible that lingonberry pests and diseases will be similar as well.

Harvest

The cultivated lingonberry's cropping habit is quite unusual when compared to most of the other berries in this book. The plant blooms twice each season, the first time in spring and again in early summer. The first small crop is ripe in July if the blossoms were not damaged by spring frosts. A second, larger crop ripens in October or November. Lingonberries will start producing a crop when the plant is two to three years old. They typically yield a pound and a half per bush or ten pounds per square yard when the plant is fully mature.

The small red fruit is about the size and shape of a blueberry. Lingonberries should not be picked until fully ripe, or the flavor may be bitter. When ripe the fruit has a sweet, acidic flavor much like a cranberry. Some varieties produce fruit that is fairly tart in flavor, while other varieties are milder flavored. Often it is pleasant to blend two contrasting varieties when cooking. A frost or two is said to improve their flavor. In a pinch, berries can supposedly be left on the plant for early spring picking. However, the fruit will be soft from repeated freezing and thawing. It is best to pick berries when they are dry to avoid mold and rot development if they are not used right away.

When the fruit is fully red, it can be harvested in a manner similar to lowbush blueberries. For quick picking, the fruit is gently raked from the plant with a hand-held blueberry rake. Leaves and stems are separated out after raking. Care must be taken to avoid damaging the fragile branches or pulling the shallow rooted plant completely out of the ground. Raked fruit is usually used for cooking.

Fruit can also be picked individually. This is, of course, much slower, but less winnowing is usually needed. Fruit for fresh eating or home freezing will be of the best quality when hand picked.

Picked fruit is high in vitamin C and should be refrigerated immediately. Its shelf life is about three weeks when kept cool. The fruit can also be frozen, canned, or dried for later use.

17. Currants & Gooseberries

Currants, gooseberries, and jostaberries, a hybrid black currant-gooseberry cross, have been quite ignored as members of the fruit garden in recent years. However, *Ribes* (the genus to which currants and gooseberries belong) are making a come-back and regaining their popularity of generations past. They could well be one of the best choices for the novice fruit gardener. Hardy, productive, fairly disease resistant, and ornamental, these bush fruit are best known for their use in jams, jellies and juices. While the varieties of days past tended to be tart in flavor, some of the newer varieties are larger and sweeter - ideal for eating out of hand. Currants and gooseberries are praised by health conscious gardeners for being high in vitamins A, B, and C as well as several minerals.

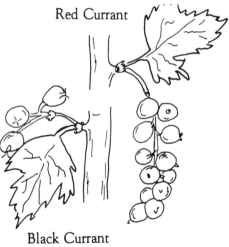

Red Currant

Black Currant

Figure 73. *Currant fruit*

Currants and gooseberries share many similarities, but each also has characteristics that are distinctly their own. Currant varieties are available with red, white, and black fruit. The red varieties are probably the most familiar, as they are commonly the source of the tart flavored currant jelly. Indeed they are ideal for this use since the fruit is high in pectin and the tart flavor remains pronounced in the jelly.

White (or pale yellow) currants are typically sweeter and less acid flavored than red currants. They are primarily eaten fresh. Some people may mistake them for the source of the light colored dried currants often found in baked goods, but the dried "currants" are actually grapes, not true white currants.

Black currants may be best known for the liqueurs made from them. They also make excellent juice and jam. A nutritious fruit, black currants are five times as high in vitamin C as oranges. One type of black currant, the clove currant, also known as the buffalo or Missouri currant, is an excellent landscape plant. It has very fragrant blossoms in addition to its edible fruit.

Gooseberries, like their relatives the currants, bear fruit of several colors - green, yellow, red, and pink. Unlike currants, however, most gooseberry bushes possess thorns and the fruit has tiny soft hairs. While red and white currants produce fruit in clusters (known as strigs) on smooth stemmed branches, gooseberries are borne individually or in pairs on thorny branches. Gooseberries also tend to be slightly more susceptible to the disease mildew. The flavor of gooseberries is an acquired taste for many, but those who enjoy this fruit, vow it is worth tangling with the thorny bushes. Fortunately today, plant breeding has also provided us with several relatively thornless gooseberry varieties. While currants are usually the size of a small blueberry, gooseberries range in size up to that of a good sized grape, depending on the variety.

Figure 74. Gooseberry fruit

As might be expected, eventually plant breeders went to work in search of a plant that would have the best attributes of both the currant and the gooseberry. The jostaberry, a cross between the black currant and the gooseberry, resulted. A thornless plant, bearing fruit high in vitamin C, the jostaberry is similar in most other ways to its parents. The fruit it produces is midway in size between the black currant and gooseberry and can be used in similar ways.

Site Requirements

Gooseberries and currants are native to cool climate areas and consequently grow best in the cooler regions of the United States - New England, the midwest, and the Pacific northwest - where they will also receive abundant summer rain. They do not grow well in the warm south and southwest. When temperatures exceed 86°F for an extended time, the bushes may even loose their leaves. If you are growing currants and gooseberries in the warmer reaches of their growing area it is advisable to mulch them well and plant them on a north slope or even provide some shading to keep them cool. Gooseberries will be the better choice of the two in warmer areas since they are somewhat more heat tolerant than currants.

Currants and gooseberries are quite winter hardy, generally thriving in USDA zones 3 thorough 5. They have no problem ripening fruit in areas with 120 to 140 day or longer growing seasons. The plants typically start growing and flowering quite early in the spring, so they do need to be planted in a location where the microclimate will protect them from spring frost damage. A planting site in full sun is preferred, but they will produce in partially shaded locations as well.

Considered to be rather undemanding in their soil requirements, currants and gooseberries will grow in a soil having at least one percent organic matter. Although they do need some moisture, they prefer a well drained soil where the water table is three to six feet below the surface. Currants and gooseberries will tolerate somewhat heavy soils, although, as with most fruit, truly wet sites should be avoided. Ideally, a fertile loam that has been enriched with compost or well rotted manure is their favored growing soil. They grow well in a fairly wide pH range from 5.5 to 7.0.

Pollination

Black currants are self sterile, so remember to plant two varieties close to each other. Other currants, gooseberries, and jostaberries are self-fruitful and can be planted alone as specimen plants or as a single variety hedgerow. Planting two different varieties of currant, gooseberry, or jostaberry for cross-pollination has been shown to increase yields slightly.

As mentioned earlier, currants are borne in clusters. Bloom on these clusters can occur over a fairly extended time. Often, up to twenty days may separate bloom of the terminal and the basal flowers. Keep this in mind when selecting varieties for cross pollination and choose those with overlapping bloom times.

Currant Varieties

Red Currant

Botanically, being of the same species (*R. sativum*), red and white currant varieties are similar in characteristics just different in color. Red and white currants are typically used for eating, jelly, or cooking. Numerous varieties are listed in catalogs, but some confusion exists over whether original sources were misnamed as many of the varieties very closely resemble each other.

Variety	Season	Comments
Cherry Red	Late-mid	For eating & preserves. Mildew resistant.
Jhonkeer Van Tets	Early	For eating & jelly. Large berry. Less heat tolerant than other varieties. Mildew and aphid resistant.
Perfection		Older variety. Extra large berries. Good overall quality and flavor. Productive bush.
Red Lake		Tart, but high quality berry is excellent for jelly. Hardy, easy to pick bush. Long ripening season. Somewhat susceptible to mildew.
Redstart	Late	Good for eating and jelly.
White Imperial	Early	White currant. Sweetest and richest flavored of the eating currants. Translucent berries are somewhat variable in size.

Black Currant

Black currants, are of a different species (*R. nigrum*), and distinct from the other currants not only in color, but also in flavor and growth characteristics. Black currants are richer bodied, less acid in flavor and are commonly used for making wine and liqueur, juice, and flavorings.

Variety	Season	Comments
Boskoop Giant	Early	Productive. Mildew resistant but rust susceptible. Easy to pick. Hardy to -30°F.
Brodtorp	Early	Large, sweet berry best for drying. Disease resistant.
Consort	Late	Resistant to White Pine Blister Rust, but susceptible to mildew and leaf spot.
Silver Gieter		Excellent flavor for eating.
Strata		Large, sweet berry for eating.

Buffalo or clove currant (*R. odoratum*) is the best known native currant. It grows ten feet tall with fragrant, yellow blossoms. Crandall is the most commonly available variety and best flavored of the native species. Tolerant to cold and heat, Crandall grows well as far north as the Dakotas and as far south as Texas. The fruit, which is rather tart for fresh eating, ripens gradually over a long season and is excellent for jelly, syrup, juice, and pie.

Gooseberry Varieties

Variety	Season	Comments
Colossal	Mid	Very large, egg shaped, green berry. Mild flavored with a tart skin. Fairly disease resistant.
Early Sulphur	Early	Smaller fruited, yellow variety, very similar to Hoenings Early.
Hinnomakis Yellow	Mid	Yellow fruited, very flavorful fruit with a hint of apricot taste. Mildew resistant.
Hoenings Early	Early	Considered the best flavored gooseberry. Sweet, juicy and plum-like. Golden colored fruit are somewhat hairy.
Poorman	Late	Large, berry is excellent for eating. Also good for pies and preserves. Mildew resistant. Grows well in the east, but doesn't do well in the west.
Whinham's Industry	Late	Sweet, productive red fruited all purpose variety.
Whitesmith	Mid	Very sweet, large fruit with a hint of grape flavor. One of the best green varieties.

Jostaberry

Jostaberry's black fruit is typically two to three times the size of most currant and American gooseberry varieties. Its flavor is not as strongly "foxy" as that of its black currant parent. The berry has an excellent shelf life and timely harvesting is not critical. Normally ripening in mid-July in the upper midwest, harvest often coincides with the end of the summer red raspberry crop.

The vigorous canes are resistant to powdery mildew, white pine blister rust, and imported currant worm. Very winter hardy, they have been able to withstand temperatures to -38°F. As self-sterile tetraploids, jostaberries need another jostaberry for pollination. Currants and gooseberries will not pollinate jostaberry.

There is currently some confusion in naming jostaberry varieties. It appears that recently imported nursery stock, brought in under various cultivar names, may all have originated from the same foundation stock. As of the date of publication of this book, that is assumed to be the case for the black fruited jostaberry, so no separate varieties will be listed here.

Planting

Red and white currant bushes typically grow from three to five feet in height with an equal spread. Black currants tend to be on the larger end, growing to five feet high and wide. Gooseberries range in size from two to five feet high and broad. The hybrid jostaberry is the most vigorous and typically reaches six to eight feet in height.

Currants and gooseberries can be incorporated into the garden in several ways, either planted as individual specimen plants or in hedgerows. Plant individual bushes in the landscape where needed, allowing sufficient room for their eventual mature size. If hedgerows are being planted, place red and white currants two to two and a half feet apart for a tight hedge or up to four feet apart for easier picking, disease control, and a loose row. Four feet between gooseberry bushes works well. Black currants are best planted five feet apart, with josta-berries spaced six feet between plants. If you are planting several parallel rows, leave from eight to twelve feet between rows.

Ribes plants are sold both bareroot and potted. However, unlike most other fruit plants, rather than being planted in spring, ribes are best planted in the fall. The bush leafs out and starts growth very early in the spring. Fall planting will allow better establishment of the roots and stronger shoot growth the following spring.

To plant the bushes, dig a hole large and deep enough to accommodate the root system. As a rule of thumb, a bushel basket sized hole often works well for a young bush. Set the plant in the hole so that it is just slightly deeper than the level at which it had been grown. (You will often be able to see the old soil line on the stems.) If you are transplanting older, large bushes plant them deep enough to cover the lower two or three buds. Fill the hole with compost enriched dirt. Remove any air pockets around the roots by firming the soil into place around the roots with the heel of your foot. Water thoroughly and spread a layer of mulch, several inches deep, around the base of the plant to retain moisture and control weeds.

For fall planted currants and gooseberries, in the spring following planting cut the branches back to five buds in length and allow four to six new branches to develop at the plant base each season. (For spring planted currants and gooseberries, cut them back immediately after planting.) Josta bushes become established more easily and do not need to be cut back at planting time. Once the bush has a dozen branches, you can annually remove the oldest ones and keep up to eight healthy younger branches to produce fruit.

If, as suggested, you planted your bushes in the fall, you may need to do very little supplemental watering. Natural rainfall will probably take care of most of the job for you, especially in the best suited northern growing areas. Spring planted bushes should be watered two or three times weekly during the first month. Currant and gooseberry are quite shallow rooted and will become better established if you help them along in this manner.

Pruning

To maintain the best production, like other bush fruit, currants and gooseberries need occasional pruning. The different types of ribes will be pruned somewhat differently based on their bearing habit. Pruning is most easily done during the dormant season.

Black currants bear fruit on one year old wood and spurs of two year old wood. Once the bush is established, one quarter to one third of all two year old wood should be removed. Any older or weak wood should also be removed. Poorly growing bushes can be rejuvenated by cutting old and weak growth off at ground level. The age of the shoots is easy to identify. New shoots are pale tan in color. Two year old branches are gray and older mature wood is black.

Red and white currants bear fruit on two and three year old wood. They should be pruned to remove any branches more than three years old. If many new shoots are originating at the base of the plant, prune most of them to the ground leaving the best six. Gooseberries bear their fruit on wood that is two to four years old. They are pruned much like red currants, except, in this case, wood that is removed should be older than four years of age. These branches are usually easy to recognize by the dark bark and multiple branching. Again, thin out newly arising shoots to the strongest six.

Fertilizer and Water

The plants of vegetatively propagated currants and gooseberries are fairly shallow rooted, with most of their roots located in the top eight to sixteen inches of the soil surface. They benefit greatly from a two to three inch layer of organic mulch that helps retain moisture, keeps the soil cool and reduces weed competition, especially in their early years. Plants propagated from seed, which is not the common method of propagating ribes, tend to have more of a tap root, but will also benefit from mulching.

Currants have a fairly strong need for nitrogen and potassium. A three year old currant bush will require about two ounces of nitrogen and by four years of age, the bush will utilize nitrogen at the rate of four ounces per bush. So, it is worthwhile to feed them with a complete fertilizer and additional compost annually. Liquid fertilizer with a weekly watering is one easy way to provide nitrogen and potassium. Blood meal and Sul-Po-Mag will also provide these nutrients over the long haul, but remember they are materials that are slow to break down to usable forms, so don't rely on them as the only fertilizer source for your currants.

Gooseberries' nitrogen requirements are slightly less than that of currants, but their potassium needs are similar. Feeding with one half cup 5-10-10 fertilizer (*ca.* 1/4 to 1/2 pound) annually per mature bush each spring will satisfy them. Do not use potassium chloride, however. Gooseberries are susceptible to chlorine toxicity.

During the first season after planting, it is helpful to provide a good watering two to three times a week. Currants and gooseberries seem to prefer having their roots kept cool. A good six inches of mulch will be very beneficial.

Diseases and Insect Pests

Currants and gooseberries are often touted as being plagued by very few diseases and insect pests. This is indeed true when they are grown as small, isolated plantings. However, they too fall victim to at least an occasional pest or disease.

The most infamous of these is **White Pine Blister Rust**. Misconceptions abound about this disease and the role that cultivated ribes species play in its spread. In recent years much of this misinformation has been cleared up and most states have lifted planting bans on ribes or are at least no longer enforcing the laws on their books. To the best of the author's knowledge, at the time of publication, Delaware, Maine, New Jersey, and North Carolina are the only states still prohibiting importation of ribes species. Massachusetts, New Hampshire, New York, Rhode Island, and Vermont still require written permission from their respective state department of agriculture before importing ribes into these states.

White Pine Blister Rust is a concern in certain areas because of its seriousness as a disease of native white pine and imported Swiss stone pine (five needled pines). These pine species played an important part in the lumber industry in much of this country in the early part of the century. At the time it was believed that all plants in the ribes genus contributed to the spread of the disease. Because the lumber industry was perceived to be at risk, laws were enacted in the early 1900s (and remained in effect until the 1960s) to ban planting of all currants and gooseberries as a means of controlling the disease.

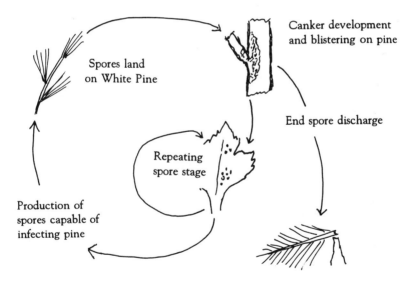

Figure 75. *White Pine Blister Rust disease cycle*

It was not fully understood at the time that cultivated species of ribes were not involved in furthering the disease cycle. The real culprits were the native wild currant and gooseberry species as well as the European black currant that was imported to North America and allowed to become wild years ago. These native wild ribes species are hosts for the rust during part of its life cycle. When the native species grow within 900 feet of the five needled pine species, the disease cycle can be completed and serious damage can result to the pines.

Today it is known that White Pine Blister Rust does not actually affect the red currant or gooseberry plant itself and that these cultivated species really play no part in the disease's life cycle. Many of the newer Canadian and European varieties of black currant are resistant to the disease and safe to plant. Also, most other pines such as red pine and Scotch pine are unaffected. This better understanding of the disease has lead to lifting most bans against planting ribes.

With the understanding of how the disease is transmitted, it is now also possible to interrupt its life cycle. Planting species or varieties that are resistant to White Pine Blister Rust is of course the best prevention. It is important to remember, however, that disease resistant does not mean that the plant has total immunity to the disease, only that it is much less likely to become a carrier. To insure that the rust fungus is not spread, it is recommended that ribes be planted at least 900 feet from any blister rust susceptible pine species.

Powdery mildew and **anthracnose**, as discussed in chapter 8, and **Leaf Spot** will occasionally plague currants and gooseberries. Powdery mildew is probably the most regular disease problem you will encounter. It appears as a white powdery growth on leaves, fruit, and branches. European gooseberry varieties are generally the most susceptible. Some American varieties are moderately susceptible while others are resistant. The best control is to choose resistant varieties. Keep the bushes pruned and don't crowd them. This allows air circulation that helps reduce the spread of the fungal spores. Anthracnose, which shows up as discolored leaves, and leaf spot, which, as its name suggests, appears as small spots on the leaves may also be an occasional problem. Controls are similar to those for mildew.

The only serious virus to affect currants is **Reversion Virus**. Black currant is most susceptible, with red currant less so. Gooseberry appears to be unaffected. Transmitted by the gall mite, this virus causes plants to stop fruiting and revert back to a wild growth state. Until a few years ago it had not been found in the United States, but was apparently brought in on contaminated stock recently. There is no cure for the virus other than totally destroying infected plants.

Insects

Aphids, scale, and **borers,** which were discussed in chapter 7, occasionally attack currants and gooseberries, but usually do not do serious damage to them. **Currant Fruit Fly** and **Gooseberry fruit worm** are the two pests likely to cause fruit damage to the respective fruit. In both cases, damage is done by larvae boring into the fruit after egg hatch. Damaged fruit will often show symptoms by coloring prematurely. *Bacillus thuringiensis* will control both of these insects.

Imported Currant Worm can defoliate plants in some years with its leaf feeding. Just as leaves reach full size, this pest appears. It may be overlooked because it starts feeding on the inside of the bush. A second generation may appear shortly before harvest. Black currant is most resistant to currant worm, followed by gooseberry, white currant, and red currant. Rotenone or pyrethrum can be used for control.

Harvest & Yield

Many ribes varieties will start producing fruit one to two years after planting. Full production however, is normally reached in the fourth or fifth year for currants and the sixth year for gooseberries. Jostaberries can take up to eight years to reach full production. Black currants easily produce for ten years or more and gooseberries as well as red or white currants will produce fruit for fifteen to twenty years.

Currant, gooseberry, and jostaberry fruit ripens over an extended period in mid-summer. Harvest can range from mid-May through August. Black currants usually ripen first, followed by red and white currants. Gooseberries are the last to ripen. Unlike most small fruit, it is not critical to pick currants and gooseberries as soon as they are ripe. Currants will hang well on the bush for up to a week or more after ripening. Gooseberries will do likewise unless exposed to rain or direct, hot sun, which can cause sunscald on the fruit.

Three to four year old bushes can produce from two to five quarts of fruit each. Mature red currant or gooseberry bushes yield five to ten quarts each. Black currant will produce even more. Usually two plants of each of the ribes species will provide for a family of four.

Currant berries are fairly soft and delicate when ripe. Although you can strip them from the bush individually, you will do less damage to them if you pick the full strig intact. Red or white varieties can be harvested in one picking. Black currants, which grow as individual berries, are best harvested in several pickings since their flavor changes over the course of several weeks as they reach maturity. Slightly underripe berries have the highest pectin content making them best for jelly. The most flavorful juice is produced from dead-ripe fruit.

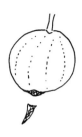

Figure 76. *Removing* "t.
from gooseberries

Gooseberries, which grow as individual fruit on the branch, can be harvested as they ripen. Slightly underripe berries are fine for cooking of preserves, but for full flavor and fresh eating, fruit should be allowed to ripen to full color. A somewhat sharp, pointed "tail" will be found on the end of the gooseberry fruit. Leave that in place while fruit is stored, but be sure to remove it when you are ready to use your fruit.

Section V.

Vine Fruit

18. General Principles of Grape Growing

Grapes are one of the oldest fruit to be included in the garden and one that offers many uses where the conditions are favorable for grape production. From juice and wine, jelly and preserves, to raisins or fresh eating, the grape can provide a bounty! The cultivated grapes of the garden and vineyard belong to the genus *Vitis*, which includes several species of bunch grapes as well as the muscadine grape, which bears individual berries.

The genus *Vitis* encompasses several native American grape species; *Vitis labrusca* - the fox grape, *Vitis riparia*, and *Vitis rupestris*. These grapes have all contributed parentage to today's cultivated bunch grape varieties. Genes of *Vitis vinifera* varieties of European origin predominate in many currently cultivated wine and raisin grape selections. Grapes in the genus *Vitis* share the characteristic of having a fairly concentrated harvest period. Their fruit also grows in fairly large clusters and so these grapes are often known collectively as bunch grapes. (In this book when American bunch grapes are referred to as a collective term, these will be taken to mean primarily those of *V. labrusca* parentage.)

Bunch grape species grow best where climatic conditions are not extreme, neither too cold nor too hot. They are generally winter hardy, but hardiness varies widely, depending on their parentage. With so many varieties to choose from, however, the gardener can find one suitable for all but the coldest locations. *Vinifera* grapes do not tolerate high heat or humidity well and, consequently, are not usually grown in the hot southeastern United States. This is where one finds the muscadine grape growing successfully.

Muscadine grapes (*Vitis rotundifolia*) make up the other major group of cultivated grapes. Also of American origin, the muscadine grape has characteristics quite different from those of the bunch grapes. Rather than bearing fruit in large bunches, much of the fruit is borne as individual berries or in small clusters. Native primarily to the southeastern United States and the Gulf coast, they are adapted to the heat of that climate. Yet, they require regular rainfall and do not grow well in the more arid regions of the west. Muscadine grapes are not winter hardy, so their growing region is limited largely to climates that stay above zero degrees F.

As distinctly different types of grapes, the *bunch grapes* and *muscadine* still share certain commonality that are discussed in the sections that follow. These are primarily site selection considerations, planting procedures, and pests and diseases. Other cultural requirements are as different as their classifications would imply and cannot be applied interchangeably. These differences in care and growth habits will be addressed in two respective chapters that follow.

Climatic Effects on Site Selection

Climate and the length of the growing season are the foremost limiting factors in selecting a site on which to grow grapes. Because their chilling requirement is extremely low, grapes, unlike other small fruit, do not have a clearly defined dormant period. Consequently they will grow at any time that moisture and temperature conditions are sufficient. Although grapes can indeed be grown in most parts of the United States, particularly careful selection must be made to match the type and variety of grape to the site's climate.

As already mentioned, muscadine grapes will only grow reliably where temperatures do not drop below zero degrees F. *Labrusca* and *vinifera* grapes will tolerate a wider temperature range, withstanding -15°F and -10°F respectively. In climates where temperatures often dip even lower, grapes can still be grown on a small scale if they are covered with dirt during the winter months.

Since grapes are typically a late ripening crop the length of the growing season in an area also becomes more important than with most other small fruit. The map on page 19 gave a general idea of what to expect for an average growing season length in various areas of the country.

Typically, muscadine grapes and the latest maturing European varieties require a minimum 200 frost free day season. The majority of the European varieties and French-American hybrids produce their best quality fruit with a 180 day or longer season, although many will produce acceptable fruit in a 170 day season. A season of 160 days will allow the growing of primarily early maturing European varieties. Only native American types are suitable if the growing season is less than 150 days.

When considering the length of the growing season in an area, it should be noted that the season length is important not only for maturing the best quality fruit, but also to provide a suitable period after harvest for the plant to gradually harden itself for the coming winter. Properly winter hardened vines have a much better chance of withstanding low winter temperatures than vines that defoliate right after harvest.

Site Selection and Soil

Grapes are more affected by various site factors than most small fruit. When selecting a site it is important to consider elevation, air drainage, and prevailing wind direction. Grapes, although not the earliest fruit of the season to bloom, are susceptible to crop losses from spring frosts when planted in low lying frost pockets. Higher elevations with adequate cold air drainage offer some frost protection by allowing cold air to drain to lower sites. Wind direction can also have an effect on the amount of air drainage a site will have.

Prevailing wind direction is important from another standpoint, too. Since grapes have such a large leaf surface area and are quite susceptible to numerous fungus diseases, air circulation is a significant tool in helping to minimize sprays for disease control. Planting parallel to prevailing winds will increase air circulation.

When locating a grape planting, exposure to sunlight needs to be considered since sunlight plays a major part in the development of the fruit sugars and ripening. This is so important in short growing season areas that some growers even remove the leaves immediately around the fruit clusters to better expose the fruit to sunlight in the later part of the growing season. Planting rows in a north/south direction offers maximum sun exposure. In areas with long growing seasons and high intensity sunlight, such as California, sunburn can pose a problem to the fruit clusters. Planting rows in a northeast to southwest direction helps reduce this problem somewhat.

Northern facing slopes will warm most slowly in spring, delaying bud burst and thereby providing some potential frost protection. At the same time, fruit planted on these slopes will be slower to ripen. The reverse is true for south facing slopes. They will warm more quickly in spring and also ripen fruit more reliably in cool climate, short season areas. In most areas, south facing slopes are usually the preferred planting sites.

Grapes are generally less demanding than other small fruit in the type of soil they require. They will grow in a fairly broad soil pH range from 6.0 to 7.5, with 6.5 being preferred. Highly fertile soil is not extremely critical nor recommended. Many of the world's most famous grape growing regions actually have fairly poor soils. When grown in soils high in nutrients (especially nitrogen) grapes develop excessive vegetative growth at the expense of fruit production and higher sugar content. These excessively vigorous grape vines are also late to ripen fruit and harden down at the end of the season. So, what would otherwise be considered marginal soils might be well suited for grapes. Sandy loam or even slightly gravelly soil conditions are favored by grapes. Like most small fruit, they do require a well drained site without standing water. Organic matter content of 4-5% is desirable for water retention.

Planting the Vine

When selecting planting stock, the gardener will need to consider both the variety of grape that will survive and produce well and the root system on which that variety is grown. Bunch grape varieties of American origin are most commonly propagated as cuttings that have been allowed to root directly. These are known as "own rooted" cuttings and can be easily propagated by the ambitious gardener.

Grape varieties of European origin are sold mostly as grafted vines. These vines are propagated by grafting a cutting of the desired variety (the scion) to a rootstock that is resistant to grape phylloxera, a plant louse that causes serious damage and eventual death to susceptible varieties. Although native American varieties have evolved to be largely unaffected by phylloxera, most of the European varieties are quite susceptible and should only be grown on resistant rootstocks. Other rootstocks are available that are nematode resistant or adapted to wet soils. Varieties grafted to these stocks should be used where these conditions present a problem. Grafted stock is also recommended where old grape sites are replanted with grapes.

Muscadine varieties are propagated by layering, due to low success rates with other propagation methods. Grapes are typically sold as one year old vines. Look for strong healthy vines on the appropriate root for your growing situation. Ideally, young planting stock should be at least the diameter of a pencil.

In cold climate growing areas of the United States, vines are normally planted in early spring once the ground has thawed and danger of major frosts is past. This is usually during April or early May. In warmer areas, fall or winter planting is sometimes possible. This applies mostly to California and the southeastern muscadine growing areas. Here, planting can be done from December through February. In all cases, the vines should be dormant when planted.

If you are not quite ready to plant when your shipment of vines arrives, the vines can be held temporarily at 36°F until planting. Keep the humidity high so that the vines are not allowed to dry out. If you do not have adequate refrigeration (and many home gardeners will not), the vines can be held by "heeling-in". In a cool, shaded location, dig a shallow trench. Place vine roots in the trench and cover them firmly with soil. Transplant them as soon as possible to their permanent location.

Just prior to planting, soak the roots in a bucket of water for no more than two to three hours. Only dead or broken roots should be pruned off. To plant, place vine roots in a ten to twelve inch deep furrow, allowing the roots to spread out fully. Adjust the vine depth so that it is the same as when the vine was planted in the nursery. This should be with the top roots about three inches below ground level. If the vines are on grafted rootstock, make sure that the graft union is above ground level once the vine is firmed in. Fill in the planting furrow and firm the soil around the roots with the heel of your hand. Do not shorten the roots to fit the planting hole. Doing so will permanently reduce the growth and productivity of the vine, since

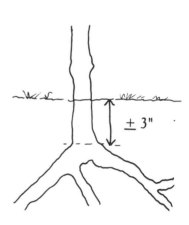

Figure 77. Proper planting height for grafted grape vine

these roots contain the stored carbohydrates needed for initial vine development. Instead, enlarge the furrow to accommodate the roots.

The space between vines in the row will be determined mostly by plant vigor and will vary more than with most other small fruit. Bunch grape varieties that do not grow very vigorously, can be planted with as little as three feet between them. Medium vigor

General Principles of Grape Growing 207

varieties should have four to five feet between them. For vigorous varieties allow six feet between plants. Muscadine varieties grow very vigorously and should be planted up to twenty feet apart in the row.

The space between rows will be determined primarily by what equipment, such as garden tractors, need to pass between the rows and which trellis system you have chosen to use (more on trellising later). Eight to nine feet between rows is often used in small home vineyards, but up to twelve feet between rows may be needed if larger equipment is to be used.

Once the vines have been planted, water them in well to insure that no large air spaces remain around the roots to dry them out. Trim the vine so that only two buds are left to send out new shoots.

Special Grape Growing Terms

Before details of trellis design, training and pruning of the various types of grapes is discussed in upcoming chapters, it is helpful to have an understanding of the related terminology. For some reason, grape growing, more than other fruit culture, has a vocabulary all its own. Once you understand these commonly used terms, you will find it easier to apply the cultural practices. These terms include:

Arms. Arms are the main branches of the trunk. Canes or spurs are borne on the arms.

Bud. A bud is a dormant, undeveloped, compressed shoot. It is formed in the axil of each leaf.

Cane. A mature, woody shoot containing buds after leaf fall. One year old fruiting wood.

Canopy. The canopy is the total leaf-shoot complex of the vine.

Cordon. Cordons are extensions of the trunk. Their growth is usually horizontal. They can bear arms, shoots, or canes.

Cluster. A group of flowers or fruit developing at certain nodes.

Curtain. The portion of the canopy which has had the shoots positioned according to a selected training system.

Fruiting Spur. The basal portion of a cane, usually pruned to less than six buds.

Head. The top of the trunk including the short upper arms.

Internode. The portion of the cane or shoot between nodes.

Lateral. A side shoot or cane.

Node. The thickened part of the shoot where the leaf and compound bud are located.

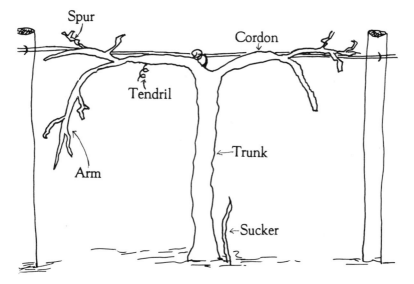

Figure 78. Parts of the grape vine

Renewal spur. A cane cut back to one or two buds meant to replace and renew an older spur or cordon.

Shoot. The green growth originating from a bud, arm, cane, spur, cordon or trunk in the spring. The shoot always bears leaves. It may also bear fruit.

Sucker. A shoot that develops from an underground bud.

Tendril. A twining, modified curly shoot that holds onto anything it touches. Occurs opposite a leaf.

Trunk. The trunk is a permanent, above-ground, vertically growing stem. Vines may have more than one trunk.

Vigor. The rate and amount of growth of the vine.

Vine size. The weight of the cane prunings.

Trellis Design Fundamentals

Healthy grape vines put out many feet of vegetative growth each season and as a result require some type of support to keep the vines and developing fruit off the ground. For the home gardener growing only a few grape vines, an arbor can be used as a support structure. However, if half a dozen or more vines are to be grown, it is likely they will be planted in rows as a mini-vineyard. This will call for the use of a trellis to support the vines.

Building a trellis for the home vineyard is a long-term investment which involves a commitment of both time and money. Constructing a sturdy trellis is well worth the initial effort to save many headaches later. The trellis should be strong enough to support heavy, fruit-laden vines with minimal sagging of support wires. All trellis systems include the major components of end posts, line posts that are spaced along the row, and one or more wires to support the vines.

The primary function of end posts is to provide an anchor for the trellis wires. They also provide a point from which the wires can be tightened when necessary. Since they are under considerable tension, end posts need to be heavy and well anchored. They should be at least nine feet long and five inches in diameter. Sometimes

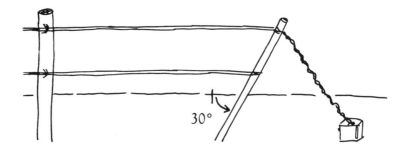

Figure 79. *Anchoring trellis end posts*

used utility poles are available and can be used. Treated posts will last the longest, but rot resistant cedar posts are an alternative for the gardener who does not want to use chemically treated materials.

End posts should be set three to four feet deep in the ground, anchored, and braced as shown in Figure 79. For maximum stability, the end post should be sunk into the ground angled away from the trellis at thirty degrees.

Line posts supporting the trellis wires should be sunk into the ground two to two and a half feet. They should be at least three inches in diameter and eight to nine feet long. In the past wooden posts have been used and are still popular today. In some systems metal posts (such as those used for livestock fencing) are being used. The metal posts are easier to handle, but more subject to bending once the trellis is fully weighted with fruit. Where metal posts are used, it is a good idea to still use wood for every third or fourth line post. Spacing between line posts will vary depending on the vine spacing chosen. Typically the posts are spaced twenty to twenty four feet apart. Three vines, eight feet apart, between posts twenty four feet apart works well. Posts should not be further than twenty four feet apart, however, or sagging of the cordon wires will occur.

The trellis wire supports the actual cordons. Wire is available in several gauges or weights. The lower the gauge number, the thicker the wire. Generally the top wire on most trellises should be number 9 wire. Number 10 or 11 wire is adequate for most lower wires. When possible, use galvanized wire. It causes less chafing on the vines and is more durable over time. A three wire trellis is versatile and easy for the home gardener to construct. Fence staples are used to position the wires on the windward side of the line posts. Staples should be tight enough to hold the wires in place but still allow the wires to be tightened. The wires should be placed so that the top wire is five and a half to six feet above the ground and the lowest wire is two and a half to three from the ground. The third wire is positioned midway between the top and bottom wires. The wires are fastened to the end post by wrapping them twice around the end post and twisting the end of the wire back around itself several times.

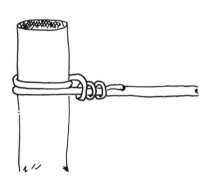

Figure 80. Anchoring wires to the end posts

Vine Training Systems

Numerous vine training systems have been developed, all with the goal of increasing sunlight exposure to the vines. This in turn encourages higher production of top quality grapes. Some of the training systems have also made picking and pruning easier and faster. Some systems are best suited to certain climates or vine growth habits. Those systems that promote vigorous renewal of bearing wood are generally most successful in northern climates. In warmer climates, where cold damage to the cordons is not a great risk, systems that don't require aggressive growth work well. Which system to use will vary with each garden's conditions and the varieties being grown. The most practical training systems for home gardens are discussed in this section.

General Principles of Grape Growing 211

Typically, the trellis is installed at the time of planting or within the first year of vineyard growth. Once the trellis hardware is in place, training of the vines can begin. One should differentiate at this point between training and pruning of the vine. Training is mainly the practice of positioning and selectively removing unnecessary vegetative growth in the early years of vine establishment. Through training, the vine becomes a strong supporting structure for the future production of fruit.

Pruning, on the other hand, is the annual removal of nonproductive and excess vegetative growth. Its purpose is to facilitate regular annual cropping by encouraging growth of new wood. Regular pruning also leads to maximum production of high quality fruit.

Figure 81. Four Arm Kniffen and Single Curtain Cordon systems

The **Four Arm Kniffen** system has traditionally been used in vineyards and is one that most people will recognize. In this system, the trellis has two wires. The cordons are trained parallel to the wires horizontally in both directions. This system works well for varieties of moderate vigor. Low vigor varieties are sometimes trained to a similar system using six arms on three wires. High vigor varieties grown on the four arm kniffen system tend to have poor production on the lower cordons due to excessive shading by the upper cordons.

The **Single Curtain Cordon** system is quickly becoming popular. A simple system to understand, it requires minimal labor. Cordons are trained in either direction along a single high wire. As shoots and spurs grow they are positioned to hang vertically. Many of the hybrid varieties produce well when trained to this system.

The **Fan** system is useful for growing tender varieties in colder climates. One or more trunks are grown to a foot in height. Once the head is formed, shoots grow upright to the upper wire. As they grow, the shoots are positioned, as the name suggests, to a fan shape. in a fan formation. This system allows for easier winter protection of the short trunk and good renewal of fruiting canes.

Finally, some grape varieties are **head trained**. This system involves no trellis. Rather, a strong stake is used to support each vine trunk. Four arms that develop at the head are allowed to cascade downward in an umbrella fashion. Each arm is pruned back to fruiting spurs of two to three buds each. The following season, four or five symmetrically placed canes are selected and also pruned back to become fruiting spurs. In subsequent seasons, additional spurs up to a maximum of a dozen on a vigorous vine, are developed. As old spurs become less productive, they are removed and new spurs developed to take their place. Head training is best adapted for use in long season, warm climate areas and varieties that fruit primarily from their basal buds.

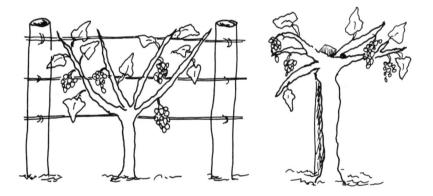

Figure 82. *Fan and Head-training grapes*

Pests and Diseases

Grapes are host to numerous insects and diseases. Not all of these pests are problems in all parts of the country, nor, fortunately do they all occur every season. It pays, however, for the gardener to be on the look-out for them before problems become severe.

General Principles of Grape Growing 213

Diseases

Powdery Mildew is one of the primary diseases affecting grapes. Its symptoms and control are discussed in chapter 6. It bears repeating however, that caution should be taken in applying sulfur to some varieties. Cultivars of American origin are particularly susceptible to sulfur burn. Particularly sensitive varieties include Chancellor, Concord, DeChaunac, Marechal Foch, and Ives. Other varieties may also show damage if sprayed when temperatures exceed 86°F.

Downy Mildew, although of minor consequence in California grape growing regions, thrives in the humid east coast growing regions. Symptoms show up first on the leaves as irregular greenish-yellow spots that turn to red-brown on the upper surface. Downy white spore patches are visible on the lower surface of the leaf. Eventually fruit is infected with a brown rot. *Vinifera* and its hybrids are particularly susceptible. Bordeaux sprays just before blossoms open and just as fruit sets are important for control of downy mildew. Additional sprays during the season may be needed when weather conditions favor disease development.

Black Rot is the third major fungus disease to affect grapes. It develops rapidly in conditions of moisture, heat, and still air. First infecting the leaves and canes, it appears as brown-black spots. Infected fruit will color prematurely, turn black, shrivel, and mummify. Black rot can be an elusive disease, causing very little damage in one season and very heavy damage the next. Fortunately controls are the same as for mildew. Sanitation and conditions that promote air circulation are helpful in preventing black rot.

Eutypa dieback, also known as dead arm, appears as black spots on infected tissue. In severe situations, it can kill canes, arms, and eventually the trunk. **Phomopsis cane and leaf spot** exhibits similar symptoms, but with less devastating results. Prompt removal of infected or dead canes is the major method of control for both diseases. Pruning tools should be properly sterilized to avoid further spread of the disease.

Crown Gall, primarily a problem on brambles, has been discussed in chapter 6. It is mentioned here only because it does occur regularly on grapes, especially in vineyard replant situations. In most cases it causes only minor problems on grapes.

Pierce's Disease can be a problem in mild climate areas that receive less than 700 hours of chilling. Believed to be caused by a bacteria-like mycoplasma, it is spread from grasses to grapes by leafhoppers. It looks much like water stress with marginal dieback and eventual decline of the vine. The only current control is planting resistant varieties (Lenoir, Champanel, and muscadine).

Botrytis Bunch Rot (Gray Mold), Bitter Rot, Ripe Rot, and **Macrophoma Rot** are all rots that damage the ripening berry. Macrophoma rot is a particular problem on muscadines. Fruit rots are usually viewed as detrimental, however, under the right circumstances, *botrytis* can be an asset. This rot desiccates the berries and changes the sugar content of the grapes in a way that is sometimes highly valued for wine production. Unfortunately in most home gardens, *botrytis* also becomes the avenue for less desirable rots to attack the berry and therefore is best controlled. All of the just mentioned rots can be controlled with the Bordeaux or sulfur sprays used on the mildews. Bordeaux sprays are the most effective of the two. Cultural techniques such as pruning for good air circulation and selective leaf removal offer partial control.

Insects

Grapes are preyed on by a large host of insects. In many cases their damage can be tolerated in the home vineyard. The listing that follows will only discuss those pests that do injury so severe that the vine dies or the fruit crop is badly disfigured or diminished.

Whenever grape growing is discussed, the name of **Grape phylloxera** comes up. An insect with a very complex life cycle, this plant louse causes major devastation in its root feeding stage. Affected roots soon be-

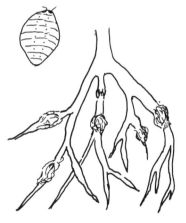

Figure 83. Grape phylloxera

come the site of secondary decay. Susceptible *vinifera* vines die rapidly. American native species are almost unaffected. This insect infests primarily heavy soils, hardly showing up in soils that are over 60% sand. The only practical control for phylloxera is to plant vines that are grafted on resistant rootstock. Experienced nursery professionals can advise you regarding their availability.

Grape flea beetle hibernates in ground litter. In May and June, as buds swell, the steel-blue beetle emerges to feed on the buds and young shoots. Eggs are laid on the canes and bark and hatching

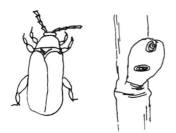

Figure 84. *Grape flea beetle*

larvae promptly seek out leaves to feed on. Sanitation offers partial control of this pest. In small backyard vineyards, satisfactory control can be achieved by knocking the adult beetles into a jar of kerosene before much egg laying has occurred.

Grape berry moth emerges from its pupal stage in early spring. It lays eggs that hatch into brown caterpillars that feed on the fruit stems. This brood pupates and hatches into a second generation of caterpillars that ravage the developing berry. Damage is usually severe enough to ruin the berry cluster. To avoid fruit damage, control must be aimed at stopping the first generation of caterpillars. Cultivation in late fall or early spring, to disrupt pupation offers some marginal control. In vineyards of several acres or more, mating disruption with pheromones is possible. In small scale backyard plantings, the insecticide Sevin offers the only truly effective control. A single application normally does an excellent job.

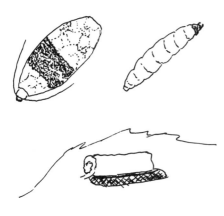

Figure 85. *Grape berry moth*

Climbing cutworm, Rose chafer, and **Japanese beetle** can all be severe nuisance pests on grapes. They are discussed in chapter 7. Birds are also a definite pest. They are discussed in chapter 9.

Weed Control

A note of warning is in order to all backyard vineyardists. Grape vines are extremely sensitive to certain weed killers. One herbicide in particular, 2,4-D, is often used on lawns for dandelion control. Any drift of this material from yours or a neighbors lawn onto any grape vines can cause dramatic symptoms. These include leaf curling, small and misshapen leaves, and vine death. Symptoms have been reported even where application was done up to two miles away from the vineyard.

19. Bunch Grapes

Bunch grapes represent the majority of grapes grown in the United States and will be the likely choice for most home vineyards. This chapter will discuss the differences in care required by the various types of bunch grapes. Varieties will also be discussed, but given that there are several thousand grape varieties, it will be impossible to examine even a fraction of them. So, one point to consider is that the grape grower may want to plant a small test vineyard with a vine or two of many varieties and continue to make selections from it based on personal taste and success.

Bunch grapes of native American background are the winter hardiest of all the grape types, generally surviving temperatures that consistently fall to - 15°F or below. Slightly less hardy, European varieties of bunch grapes should only be planted in areas where cold temperatures do not drop below -5°F if they are to be expected to produce reliably.

As previously mentioned, grapes of American origin actually fall into several species. The *Vitis labrusca* or "fox" grape gained its name primarily for its fairly strong aroma, which some people describe as "foxy". Its fruit is large, with fairly prominent seeds and "slip skins" that separate easily from the pulp inside. The *labrusca* types have been valued for their fruit size, vigor, and hardiness and their contribution of these characteristics to breeding efforts. They are the most frequently cultivated of the native species. Grape varieties of this background often make excellent juice or jelly and are also the most popular of the native species for eating fresh. Low in both acid and sugar content, few are used for wine making. Their foxy aroma also makes some varieties poorly suited to producing wine. Many commonly grown, hardy varieties belong to this species, including Concord and Niagara.

Vitis riparia has the broadest geographic distribution of the native grapes. It has been valued for its resistance to grape phylloxera, and is often used as the rootstock onto which susceptible varieties are grafted. The fruit has a higher sugar content and smaller seeds than

V. labrusca, making them desirable eating and wine grapes in their own right. Elvira is an old variety of this species that is still occasionally seen today.

Vitis rupestris has little to recommend it for crop production. The fruit, although pleasantly flavored, is very small and the vine quite unproductive. This species has achieved favor primarily for its use as a phylloxera resistant rootstock.

The *vinifera* grapes of European origin are prized first of all for the quality of the wines they produce. Many are also excellent table grapes. The fruit is either round or oval shaped. It has small seeds and a thin edible skin that adheres to the pulp. *Vinifera* varieties are generally sweeter and more delicately flavored than the American native species. Noted varieties of *vinifera* parentage include Cabernet Sauvignon, Chardonnay, Pinot Noir, Riesling, and Zinfandel. Some table grape varieties such as Tokay and Thompson seedless are members of this group, as are small fruited raisin types such as Black Corinth. Varieties of the *vinifera* type tend to be quite sensitive to winter cold, often not withstanding temperatures below -5°F, with some varieties only hardy to zero degrees F. They require a warm, but not hot, summer with low humidity and a long growing season to ripen fully. As a group, the *vinifera* are productive and easy to train, but not as resistant to pests and diseases as our native varieties.

As grape varieties were imported from one continent to another, breeding programs came about that attempted to achieve varieties with the hardiness and disease resistance of some of the American cultivars and the fruit quality of the European grapes. What resulted are known collectively as the French-American hybrids. Some of the more well known varieties include Beta, Freedom, and Einset as well as the popular wine grapes Baco Noir and Marechal Foch. Grapes in this group are typically hardy to -10°F with the most hardy of the group withstanding temperatures to -25°F or below. The novice will find the most success growing grapes of American parentage, followed in difficulty by the hybrids, and finally the *vinifera*.

Varieties

The grapes classified as table grapes in the lists that follow are chosen first for their high quality as eating grapes. In many cases, their use is not limited to eating alone. Many varieties are also excellent for juice or jelly and some also make good home wines.

Seedless Table Grapes

Variety	Use	Color	Season	Comments
Canadice	T,J	Red	Very Early	High quality. Moderately hardy.
Delight	T	Gold	Early	Muscat flavor. Excellent for raisins.
Einset	T	Red	Early	Strawberry flavor. Resistant to *botrytis*.
Flame	T	Red	Early	For zones 7-10. Needs hot summers. Good for drying.
Glenora	T	Blue	Early	Excellent quality berry. Hardiness can be problem.
Himrod	T	Yellow	Very Early	Very high quality berry. Good for home use.
Interlaken	T,J	Yellow	Very Early	High quality, cluster more attractive than Himrod. Less hardy than Himrod.
Lakemont	T	Yellow	Midseason	Hardier sister to Himrod & Interlaken. Top quality, resembles Thompson Seedless. Good for raisins. Tends to overbear.
Mars	T,J	Blue	Early	Dependable producer. Hardy. Mildew resistant. Similar to Concord.
Perlette	T	Green	Early	Crisp and juicy, quality of Thompson.
Reliance	T,J	Red	Midseason	High quality, productive. Good for home garden.
Remaily	T	White	Midseason	Good, but mild flavor. Only moderately hardy. Needs cluster thinning.
Saturn	T,W	Red	Early	Hardy. Large seed traces. Needs cluster thinning.
Thompson	T	Green	Late	The grocery store standard grape. Needs lots of heat. Thin for large berries.
Vanessa	T	Red	Early	Quality similar to Flame. Resists cracking. Good for west coast.
Venus	T,J	Black	Early	Fruit larger than Concord. Crack resistant. Disease resistant. May be only partially seedless

Use: T=table, J=juice, W=wine. *Season is relative to Concord. Early varieties ripen before Concord, midseason with Concord, and late after Concord.

Seeded Table Grapes

Variety	Use	Color	Season	Comments
Alden	T,W,J	Black	Midseason	European type grape with muscat flavor. Prune hard & cluster thinning to prevent overcropping.
Beta	J	Blue	Early	Extremely hardy. Not a table grape, except where no others are hardy.
Bluebell	T,J	Blue	Early	Concord flavor, earlier and hardier.
Buffalo	T,J	Black	Early	Highest quality early black.
Concord	T,J,W	Blue	Late September*	Standard for judging blue-black varieties. Used extensively for juice. Vigorous, hardy, but inconsistent in warm areas.
Edelweiss	T,W,J	White	Early	Very hardy, to -30°F.
Golden Muscat	T,J	Gold	Late	Excellent flavor. Subject to cracking. Mildew susceptible. Prune hard.
Kay Gray	T,J	White	Early	Very hardy to -40°F.
Niagara	T,J,W	White	Midseason	"White Concord". Most popular native American white. Hardy, ornamental vine. High quality juice.
Price	T,J	Blue	Early	Mild Concord flavor. Well suited to home garden. Hardy.
Seneca	T	Gold	Early	European character grape. Mildew susceptibility may make it difficult for home garden use.
Steuben	T,J,W	Black	Midseason	High quality, attractive, productive. Spicy flavor.
Swenson Red	T,W	Red	Early	Best quality red variety. Excellent hardiness.
Tokay	T,W	Red	Mid	Best where nights are cool and daytime temperatures are moderate. Well suited to the west coast.
Valiant	T,J	Blue	Early	Very hardy to -50°F. Similar to Concord, with smaller berry.

Wine Grapes

Varieties selected for the chart that follows are customarily used primarily for wine. Many have excellent flavor for eating as well, but due to small berry size, small clusters, or numerous large seeds they have not been widely grown for dessert use. The blue/black varieties make red wines. Ripeness or maturity of wine grapes is classified in two ways. Physical maturity is based on development processes within the plant. Industrial maturity is used by the wine industry and is based on picking the grape when it will produce the highest quality wine. Grapes can easily be (and usually are) physically mature before they are industrially mature. The chart below indicates relative industrial maturity. Keep in mind that areas with short growing seasons will not produce adequately mature fruit for top quality wines. Although all the varieties can be grown in hot, long season areas, some of the early maturing varieties may ripen too fast to produce to their best potential quality.

Variety	Use	Color	Season	Comments
Cabernet Sauvignon	W	Red	Late	Requires long season. Makes distinctive Bordeaux-type wine.
Catawba	W,T	Red	Late	Susceptible to mildew. Needs cluster thinning. Makes fruity American-type blush wine.
Chambourcin	W	Black	Late	Popular in France for Claret wines. Only moderate hardiness.
Chancellor	W	Blue	Midseason	Very productive. Adapted to short season areas. Needs good early mildew control.
Chardonnay	W	White	Midseason	Moderately hardy, good for cooler regions. Excellent dry white wine.
Chenin Blanc	W	White	Midseason	Produces its best quality wine in cool to moderate climate. Vigorous & productive.
DeChaunac	W,J	Blue	Midseason	Disease resistant. Very productive, needs cluster thinning.

Bunch Grapes 221

Delaware	W,J,T	Red	Midseason	High quality. Ornamental vine.
Marechal Foch (Kuhlman 188-2)	W,J	Blue	Early	Good in short season areas. Very hardy. Cherry flavored juice. Needs long pruning to be productive.
Merlot	W	Black	Mid-late	Produces rich red wine.
Pinot Gris	W	Gold	Midseason	Needs long, cool season.
Pinot Noir	W	Blue	Midseason	Susceptible to bunch rot. Does best in cool regions.
Riesling	W	Green	Late	Flowery semi-sweet wine. Grows best in cool regions. Hardy.
Sauvignon Blanc	W	Green	Mid-late	Moderately hardy. High quality white wine. Susceptible to *botrytis*.
Seyval Blanc	W	Yellow	Midseason	Needs cluster thinning. Widely adapted. Makes better than average wine.
St. Pepin	W,T	White		Riesling flavored wine. Female, use LaCrosse pollinator. Hardy to -20°F.
Vidal Blanc	W,T	White	Late	Resistant to Pierce's Disease. Excellent for zones 6-9 where humidity is low.
Vignoles	W	White	Early	Very hardy, but not highly productive. Distinctive high acid wine. Susceptible to *botrytis*.
Viognier	W	White	Late	Low productivity. Distinctive dry, white wine.
Zinfandel	W	Red	Mid-late	Productive. Grows best in areas with mild winter & cool summer.

Fertilizer and Water

Fertilizer requirements of bunch grapes vary widely depending on vine vigor and crop size, making it very difficult to give generalized recommendations. In most cases providing too much fertilizer to the vineyard causes more problems than erring on the side of too little.

The fruit crop itself removes relatively small amounts of actual nutrients from the soil. Most of its needs are met by water in the soil and atmospheric carbon dioxide. Soil nutrients are used primarily to maintain the vine. If the vine is supplied with an abundance of fertilizer, especially nitrogen, it may grow too vigorously. Rampantly growing vines produce succulent, late season growth susceptible to winter injury, fewer fruit clusters, and fruit that ripens slowly.

Plant growth and properly identified deficiency symptoms will give the gardener an idea of what fertilizers to provide. Young, immature vines often need no fertilizer at all in their first two or three years. As a general rule of thumb, for mature vines trained to the less intensive production systems, an annual application of two ounces of actual nitrogen per 100 square feet, applied three weeks before bud break is a sufficient maintenance dose. Vines trained to a double curtain may require as much as double these amounts. For more exact and accurate rates, however, a petiole sample is the only reliable diagnostic tool. (Details can be found in chapter 5.) The most significant nutrients that may need to be added to the soil on a regular basis are nitrogen, potassium, and magnesium. Iron, boron, and manganese need occasional supplementation in many east coast vineyards and high pH sites.

Care of the Young Vineyard

Immediately after planting, prune each newly planted cane back to two or three healthy, live buds. A shoot should soon grow from one of these buds. Once shoots start to grow from your newly planted vines, allow one or more active growing shoots to develop from the cane in the first growing season. These will form the trunk(s). Any excess shoots can be pruned off as they emerge. In areas with moderate winters, normally one trunk is retained. In cold climate areas, it is common practice to grow grape vines with two or more trunks. (In areas with very severe climates, three to six trunks may be retained on less hardy varieties.) This provides insurance against severe winters in which one trunk may be killed by cold. Very often the second one survives to continue production and a new growing shoot can then be trained up to develop into a second trunk again.

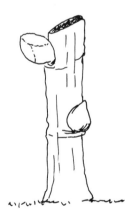

Figure 86. Newly planted and pruned grape vine

The basic general care of a young vineyard will be similar regardless of the type of grape grown. Fertilizer and water will be needed, weeds will need to be controlled, and the vines will need to be protected from insects and diseases. All of these activities are discussed in various sections of this book. When it comes to pruning and trellising of young grapes, however, one will find differences in how the vines may need to be handled in their early years. This is mainly due to the differences in growth and vigor between the various types of grapes. The following section is broken down accordingly, with grapes of similar growth habit grouped together. Early care and training of the young vines has a life-long effect on the productivity of the planting. The gardener who makes the extra effort to care for the developing vineyard in the early years will be well rewarded over time.

Training American and French Hybrid Varieties

The goal of vine training American and French hybrid varieties in the first year growth is the development of strong, healthy roots and a straight trunk. As shoots begin growth, select the best cane to begin forming the trunk. Tie the trunk to the lower trellis wire as it grows upward. A vertical guide wire or stake can also be installed to help the trunk grow straight up. When the selected cane reaches the top wire, rub off all but two to four of the best shoots to avoid excess side growth. These shoots will be trained to become the cordons. Remove any flower clusters as they develop the first season. Continue to tie canes to the trellis as needed and keep the ground around the vine weed free.

During the second growing season, most of the vine structure will be developed. If the vine trunk did not reach the top trellis wire in the first growing season, treat the vine as indicated during the first year. If the trunk reached its expected height, during the first season, retain an appropriate number of side shoots for the training system you have chosen. Remove any excess shoots as they develop. Also, continue to remove flower clusters. Although this will sacrifice the current season crop, it will help the vine concentrate growth in strong roots and shoots.

Before the third growing season begins, vines that have grown adequately should be dormant pruned. Those that have produced at least 3/4 of a pound of prunings should be allowed to produce a small crop. The gardener's goal during this season should be to guide the vine to a regular cropping habit. To prevent overcropping, thin flower clusters to a single cluster at each bud. If growth has not been adequate, treat the vine as a second year vine for an additional season. After the third season, the vine should begin cropping regularly and should be dormant pruned according to the balanced pruning methods outlined later in this chapter.

Training Vinifera Varieties

The *vinifera* grape varieties as a group tend to grow less vigorously than the hybrid or American varieties. Consequently, although the long term training goals are similar, they will be approached slightly differently.

During the first season, the goal will be strictly to develop a strong root system. Shoot growth will be moderate and no staking of the vines will be needed this first season. By the end of the summer, several shoots eight to fifteen inches long should have developed. Once the vine is dormant, remove all but the strongest cane and prune that cane back to two or three buds. This will allow additional energy to go toward increasing root mass. In cold areas cover the vine completely with dirt to protect it from winter damage.

The second growing season will be used to develop a strong, straight trunk. Uncover the vines before bud break in spring, if they were covered for winter protection. To stimulate growth, apply nitrogen ($\pm$ 1 oz./100 sq. ft.) if growth was weak the first season. If a trellis was not installed previously, that should be done now. To guide the trunk in straight vertical growth, tie a cord from the trellis to a peg in the ground and tie a single selected shoot (the future trunk) to it every nine inches. Remove any flower clusters that appear. Once the main shoot is a foot higher than the desired location for the cordon arms, shoot elongation will need to be curtailed and side branching encouraged. At about six inches below the wire, cut through the node immediately above where side branching is desired. Once buds break and side shoots develop, tie these side branches to the cordon wire, one to each side. To develop the cordons and first fruiting arms, cut the branches or cordon at a point where they are least 3/8 inch in diameter. Wrap the cordons one and a half times around the wire and tie the ends to it. Select spurs eight to twelve inches apart and prune the spurs to one or two buds each. Allow the vines to harden down for the winter.

Let the vine fruit with a light crop during the third season. As they develop from the spurs selected the previous season, tie the lateral shoots to the trellis according to the chosen training system. During the third winter, *vinifera* varieties can be dormant pruned for the first time.

Pruning

Pruning seems to be one of those garden chores that often leaves the gardener unsure of whether they have done "the right thing". This can be especially true with grapes, perhaps because grapes are one of the fruit where pruning can have such a distinct effect on the quantity and quality of the fruit.

Grape vines have a capacity to support and ripen only a limited number of fruit clusters. This capacity varies with variety. Pruning is done with the aim of balancing the vine's productive potential with its vigor. To help make the job easier - and it really is not as complicated as it might first seem - it helps to be systematic and to think about the reasons and objectives behind pruning. The objectives can be outlined as follows:

1. establish & maintain the vine's shape and form
2. evenly distribute bearing area over the vine
3. control crop size and produce top quality fruit
4. concentrate growth into permanent arms and bearing spurs
5. maintain adequate vine size, vigor, and fruiting wood for the following season

In order to balance the amount of wood removed against the vigor of the vine, pruning is best done during the dormant season. Often 70 to 90% of the previous season's growth is removed in pruning. When pruning grapes, one needs to pay attention to shaping the vine so that it can be properly positioned on the trellis and to selecting and distributing the buds with the best fruit production potential.

The canes with the best fruiting potential are those whose leaves received the most sun exposure the previous season. Typically these are the canes located at the top and outside of the vine canopy. These canes are usually dark in color and large in diameter, making them easy to identify visually. Canes with short to medium length internodes seem to have the highest quality buds, and pencil size diameter canes appear to be the most winter hardy.

Most grapes are pruned according to a system known as "balanced pruning". Under this system, the number of fruiting buds to leave on the vines is actually mathematically calculated based on the weight of the wood that was produced the previous growing season. This may sound very complicated, but with a little practice, you will soon find this a very systematic and easy way to know just how much wood to prune out and how much wood to leave.

To begin balance pruning, a visual estimate is made of how many pounds of one year old wood was produced. (Remember this is only the wood produced during the previous growing season. Older wood, two years old and up is not counted at all or pruned annually in this system.) Then, depending on the formula (which is listed at the end of this section) applicable to the variety you are pruning, enough wood is removed to leave slightly more buds than estimated on the vine. The prunings are cut up to manageable lengths, tied in a bundle, and weighed with a small hand scale. Based on the resulting weight, the number of buds to be left on the vine is calculated. A set number of buds is left for the first pound of prunings and an additional, lesser amount of buds is left for each additional pound of pruned one-year-old wood.

As an example, let's say that you are pruning the Niagara variety. Research has determined its balanced formula to be 25 + 10. You have estimated (let's assume fairly accurately) that three pounds of wood will be pruned off the vine. So you would aim to leave 45 buds on the vine. This was determined by leaving 25 buds for the first pound of prunings and 10 pounds each for the second and third pound (25+10+10=45). Now go back to your vine and actually count the number of buds remaining on the fruiting arms. If necessary, remove a little bit more wood to achieve the proper bud count. If you removed a bit too much wood, live and learn and remove slightly less wood on the next vine you prune. Don't fret too much, although your fruit yield may be slightly reduced for a season, the vine will still produce plenty of wood the coming season for you to have another chance at it next dormant season. As you become experienced at grape pruning, your estimates will become more and more accurate and eventually you will not need to weigh every bundle of prunings, just spot check yourself once in a while.

Most mature grape vines produce between 200 and 300 fruiting buds, but are only capable of properly maturing 80 to 100 clusters. If it seems like you are removing a lot of wood, keep this in mind.

If too much wood is left on the vine and it is forced to mature more fruit than it is capable of, fruit will be small and of poor quality. The vine will also be needlessly stressed and its life possibly shortened.

A special note about French-American hybrid varieties is also appropriate here. Many of these varieties tend to produce a higher number of fruit clusters per shoot (typically three to five) and also have secondary shoots that produce fruit. Balance pruning is a good place to start in controlling crop size for these varieties, but by itself, it is not enough, nor does heavier pruning solve this problem. Additional thinning of clusters is often needed.

Balance Pruning Formulas for Mature Vines

Variety	Formula	Maximum buds for vine at 8 ft. spacing
Concord	30 + 10	60
Fredonia	40 + 10	70
Niagara, Delaware, Catawba	25 + 10	60
Ives, Elvira, Dutchess	20 + 10	50
French Hybrids - small clustered varieties	20 + 10	50
Foch, Leon Millot, Baco Noir, medium cluster varieties	20 + 10	40
Vidal Blanc, Aurore, Cascade, Chelois, large cluster varieties	20 + 10	40
Seyval, Verdelet, Chancellor, Chambourcin, Villard Blanc, DeChaunac -- may need additional cluster thinning, Viniferas	20 + 20	40

Cluster Thinning

Just what is cluster thinning? Essentially, what it sounds like-- removing clusters of fruit in excess of what the vine has the capacity to reasonably support. Many grape varieties have the tendency to overcrop. In the long run this weakens the vine and leads to reduced production and poor quality fruit. To avoid these problems, excess fruit clusters need to be removed from the vine. This is most commonly done on large cluster varieties such as DeChaunac, Chancellor, Edelweiss, and Seyval. Cluster thinning has little effect on small cluster varieties.

As a rule of thumb, clusters should be thinned so that a three year old vine supports no more than a dozen clusters. At four years of age, the vine can support up to two dozen clusters. Once the vine is mature, from forty to eighty clusters can remain, cluster size and vine vigor determining whether the number of clusters retained should fall to the lower or higher end of this spread. When thinning clusters, it is preferable to thin so that only one cluster remains at each bud. Thinning should be done one week after bloom, with clusters closest to the shoot tip being removed first.

Growing in Containers

Bunch grapes adapt surprisingly well to growing in containers. Their ornamental quality makes them excellent candidates for landscaping an apartment balcony or patio. Grapes tend to restrain their cane growth and fruit production in accordance with the amount of space their roots are given. They can grow in something as small as a one gallon pot and still produce a few clusters of fruit. For most patio gardeners, a five gallon pot is the ideal size. It is not so big and heavy that it cannot be moved around. Yet, a yield of five pounds of grapes per vine is not an unreasonable expectation.

Large, unglazed clay pots are ideal containers for patio grapes. They allow slow, even warming and cooling of the roots, encourage proper oxygen exchange within the soil, and retain an even moisture in the soil. Rot resistant wooden planters also work well, as long as they have not been treated with toxic preservatives. The wood can be sealed with some of the nontoxic polymer varnishes. Copper or zinc based materials are less toxic than some of the other preservatives. A reputable garden center should have suitable wooden planters or can advise you how to properly treat them. Plastic pots, although popular because of their low cost, are not ideal containers in which to grow grapes. Their major drawback is that they heat-up rapidly when placed in full sun. This can be damaging to plant roots and growth. After several seasons of exposure to the sun's ultraviolet light, they can become brittle and crack, necessitating replacement.

One can plant a purchased grape vine or root a cutting for container culture. It is best to use sandy loam garden soil for planting rather than a commercial potting mix. Better adapted to flowering annuals, the potting mixes dry out to quickly and do not have the necessary nutrient balance for grape growing.

Grape vines grown in pots are most easily trained to a modified head pruning system. During the first two years, training is much the same as outlined for field planted vines. The exception is that once four shoots have been selected during the second year, the shoots are pruned back to spurs of two to three buds instead of being trained as longer arms. During the dormant period of the third growing season, remove the upper shoots that grew from each spur and prune the remaining shoot back to a two bud spur. Fruiting spurs should continue to be renewed annually using this procedure. Do not be surprised if you feel like you are removing a major portion of the vine when you prune. For mature container grown vines, annual pruning may mean removing up to 95% of their yearly growth.

During the first two years, flower clusters should be removed in order to funnel the plant's energy into vine establishment. In the third year, three or four fruit clusters can be allowed to fully develop. In subsequent years, an additional fruit cluster or two can be allowed to grow. Vines growing in a gallon container can support a maximum of about eight fruit clusters. A grape vine in a five gallon container will support between ten and fifteen fruit clusters maximum, depending on the variety. Excess clusters should be removed as outlined in the previous section.

Once the newly planted vine is six inches long, it should receive weekly doses of a low nitrogen fertilizer throughout the growing season. Fish emulsion works well. Once the vine is established, monthly fertilizer applications should be made during the growing season, until midsummer. Water the vine, so that the soil is sufficiently moist, but not soggy. In late summer, reduce the water to allow vines to harden. During the dormant season water only enough to keep the soil barely moist. Mineral buildup can be a problem for any container grown plant. A monthly flush with distilled water, will help prevent problems.

Due to differences in growth habit and productivity, some grape varieties are better suited to container culture than others. Of the seedless varieties, Canadice, Delight, and Interlaken are well adapted. Alden, Seyval, Swenson Red, and Valiant are seeded varieties that all grow well as containerized vines. All of these varieties can be found in the charts located earlier in this chapter. These are by no means the only choices available. You will have to experiment, but generally vines that produce fruit closer to the trunk, rather than nearer the cane tips work best for container growing.

Winter Protection

The easiest way to ensure a grape crop in cold northern climates is to select adapted, hardy varieties. In parts of the United States this is still a challenge, but with some effort grapes can be grown almost anywhere on a small scale. The following steps should be taken:

1) Train the vines to a system that will allow them to be easily removed from the trellis each fall.

2) Once leaves have dropped and the vines are fully dormant, prune the vines, leaving a few extra buds in case of some cold damage.

3) Release the vines from the trellis and gently bend them to lie on the ground.

4) Completely bury the vines with soil, straw, or shredded corn stalks. If rodents are a problem, soil is the best choice.

5) In early spring, before buds swell, remove the soil covering and return the vines to the trellis.

6) Tie the vines back onto the trellis. Uncovered vines left on the ground have shown bud damage from settling cold air.

Harvest

Harvest season for grapes usually begins in mid-July in the deep south, lasting into early September. In northern climates, grape harvest is typically a fall season activity. Most grapes require a long growing season to ripen. When to harvest the fruit also becomes a function of how the fruit will be used. Grapes to be eaten fresh will be picked at a different time than those of the same variety that are to be made into wine. In either case, however, the fruit must be allowed to ripen on the vine as it will not ripen further once picked.

What really determines a grape's ripeness is the amount of sugar it has developed. This sugar content is expressed in degrees brix. Typically wine grapes are harvested at a brix of 19-21% for white varieties and 20-24% for red varieties. Acid content of around .8% is preferred for wine making. Table grapes are normally left on the vine longer than grapes destined for wine. They are harvested at a point when sugar content is higher and acid is lower.

A comment on using grapes is suggested here, too. Although certain grape varieties have traditionally been considered "wine " grapes and others have been considered "table" grapes for eating, home gardeners certainly need not limit themselves to these narrow classifications. Many grapes that have been considered primarily as wine grapes were classified this way because they had small fruit, small clusters, or too many seeds to be marketed commercially as table grapes. If the flavor is to your liking, there is no reason why a wine grape cannot be eaten fresh, and many are excellent this way. Likewise, depending on your palate for wine, many table varieties make perfectly acceptable homemade wines.

An indicator that harvest is near, occurs when the seeds and cluster stems turn brown and woody. When harvesting, the grape cluster is cut from the vine as a complete cluster with a small "handle" of stem attached. Care should be taken to handle the cluster as little as possible to avoid rubbing off the powdery gray blush on the fruit. This will help maintain a longer storage life for the harvested fruit. Once harvested, grapes, like most fruit, should be refrigerated. Yields can be expected to range from five pounds per vine on the less productive varieties (such as Pinot Noir) to an average of twelve pounds per vine. In the best grow-

Figure 87. *Grape cluster with "handle" attached*

ing areas, under highly skilled management, top producing varieties can achieve yields of up to twenty four pounds per vine.

20. Muscadines

Muscadine grapes, also sometimes known as "Scuppernongs", are the home gardener's answer to grape growing in the deep south. Not hardy in northern climates, muscadine are native to the mild southeast and will only grow reliably in areas where winter temperatures remain above zero degrees F.

The muscadine has several characteristics that set it apart from the other grapes discussed in this book. First, rather than growing in large clusters, these grapes grow as individual berries on the vine or as small clusters of no more than a dozen grapes. Second, many muscadine grapes have the characteristic of tearing and leaving a wet scar on the fruit where the berry separates from the stem. Bunch grapes on the other hand typically have a dry scar where they abscise from the stem. Third, the fruit is round and quite large in size, with individual grapes ranging from the size of a quarter to that of a half dollar. Finally, muscadines have a thick tough skin, or hull as it is sometimes called. They are normally eaten by popping the pulp out of the hull, eating only the pulp, and discarding the skin.

The fruit ripens unevenly with individual berries being picked as they ripen. Muscadine fruit have a tendency to shatter, or drop from the vine, if they are not picked when ripe. Muscadine harvest, rather than being concentrated, is often spread over a period of three to four weeks. Depending on the variety, muscadine grapes will typically ripen from mid-August to November.

Muscadine grape flavor components are high in acid and low in sugar, producing a unique flavor that makes them excellent for cooking and preserves. They are used in pies, jelly, juice and to produce a sweet, semidry wine. Both the skin and pulp are rather tough and the skin adheres to the pulp. Although well suited for fresh eating from the home garden, commercial fresh sales are limited to local markets due to the juice bleeding from the scar and the fruit's short storage life compared to bunch grapes.

The long lived muscadine vine is well adapted to the sandy, acid soils found in its native growing region. It is very vigorous, productive, and able to withstand heavy rainfalls. Tolerant of the humid southern climate, the muscadine is quite resistant to disease and insect pests, making it an easy fruit to grow in the home garden.

Varieties

Variety	Color	Sex	Season	Comments
Carlos	Bronze	SF	Early	Very productive. Good for wine. Hardy.
Cowart	Black	SF	Midseason	Ripens unevenly, will shatter. Fair hardiness. Fry pollenizer. All uses.
Florida Fry	Bronze	SF	Mid-late	New variety for trial. Disease resistant. Hardiness not known.
Fry	Bronze	F	Early-mid	Excellent flavor. Variable fruit size. Some disease problems.
Golden Isle	Bronze	SF	Midseason	For wine use only. Non "musky" flavor.
Ison	Black	SF	Early	Dry scar. Productive.
Nesbitt	Black	SF	Mid-late	Good hardiness. May overcrop. Shows Pierce's Disease.
Noble	Black	SF	Early	For wine, juice, jelly. Good hardiness.
Summit	Pink Bronze	F	Midseason	High sugar content. Good hardiness. Disease resistant.
Supreme	Black	F	Mid-late	Dry scar, very large fruit. Will shatter.
Tara	Bronze	SF	Midseason	Productive. Some disease resistance. New variety for trial.
Triumph	Pink-Bronze	SF	Early	Non-slip skin. Good pollenizer. Poor hardiness.

Sex: F=Female, SF=Self-fertile

Pollination

When growing bunch grapes, the gardener does not need to worry about cross pollination as all the bunch grapes are self-fertile. This is not the case with muscadines. While many of the newer varieties are being selected for this characteristic, many of the old varieties are pistillate, or female. Consequently, they need to be planted together with a pollinating variety. For the best pollination, it is advisable to plant at least two self-fertile varieties within fifty feet of any pistillate variety. While self-fertile varieties do not require cross pollination, they do benefit from it, setting more and larger fruit as a result. Muscadine grapes typical blossom from mid-May to mid-June.

Training the Vine

Muscadine grapes are usually trained to a single cordon trellis. Since the vines are so vigorous, trellis posts should be set about twenty feet apart, with one vine centered between each set of posts. At planting time, the vines should have been cut back to no more than two or three buds. Once buds break after planting, select one shoot for the trunk. As the shoot grows, a small stake or wire can be used to guide it up to the trellis. Tendrils will usually hold the vine to this support. Otherwise, the gardener can gently wrap the developing shoot around the wire. If any tendrils become twined around the shoot itself, remove them, as they will constrict and kill the trunk. As lateral shoots develop, pinch them off. This will allow the vine's energy to go into trunk growth. Do not remove the leaves that grow directly from the main trunk at this time.

When the vine has reached the trellis wire, usually late in the first year or during the second growing season, pinch the shoot to encourage side branching. As they appear, select two lateral shoots that are growing in opposite directions, parallel to the trellis. These will be developed into the main arms. Preferably they should originate no more than six inches below the wire. Train these two arms to the trellis by spiralling them down the wire. Remove the original trunk supporting stake or wire. When the arms reach ten to twelve inches long, pinch their tips arms and continue pinching them each time the shoot tip grows an additional three inches. Train the arms to the cordon wire as they grow. Continue the pinching procedure until each side arm is ten feet long.

Pruning the Vine

Once the initial training of the vine is complete and a strong vine structure has been established, it is time to begin an annual dormant pruning program to maintain this framework. This usually happens when the vine is in its third growing season and starting to fruit. It is very important that muscadine grapes be pruned every year. If the vine is allowed to grow rampant, it may take several years to reestablish proper production.

Due to their great vigor and bearing habit, muscadine grapes are pruned differently than bunch grapes. Rather than fruiting on elongated canes, muscadine fruit is produced on short lateral canes or fruiting spurs. The technique used for pruning them is often referred to as spur pruning. Lateral canes are selected about every six inches along the main arms of less vigorous varieties and every ten to twelve inches along arms of vigorous varieties. Each selected cane is cut back to form a spur of two to three buds. In subsequent years, during the dormant season, growth originating from these spurs is also cut back to only two to three buds. This continuing spur development will determine the productivity of the vine.

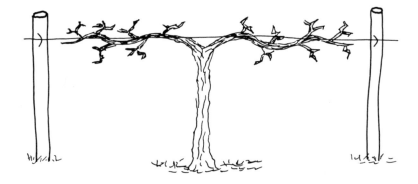

Figure 88. Spur pruned muscadine grape vine

Although training of the young vines involved shoot removal during the growing season, pruning of fruiting vines should always be done during the dormant season. It is highly advisable to wait until after the first of February to do any dormant pruning. This will help avoid winter injury to the vines. The gardener may notice that the vine "bleeds" sap at this time. This is of no serious consequence and does not harm the vine.

Fertilizer and Water

Getting vines off to a good start is critical to the long term production of muscadines. Vines stunted early in life never make up for the lost growth. In the first two years following planting, the vines should be fertilized lightly on a monthly basis. Once growth starts, applications of three ounces per vine of a complete fertilizer can be alternated with ammonium or calcium nitrate. Continue applying fertilizer monthly up to the first of August.

Once the vines have reached three years of age and started fruiting, a slightly different fertilizer regimen should be followed. A split application of complete fertilizer, two pounds in early spring and an additional pound after fruit set, is applied. Trace elements may be needed about every third year. Mature vines are given three to five pounds of complete fertilizer in early spring and another half pound of ammonium nitrate at fruit set. Healthy muscadine vines can be expected to add three to four feet of vertical growth each year and this should be used as a guide to the amount of fertilizer to apply. Rates should be adjusted according to the amount of growth the vine makes. Be aware that over fertilization sometimes causes muscadine grapes to drop their fruit prematurely.

Muscadines are well adapted to withstand the sometimes heavy rains that occur in their native southeast. At the same time, to support their extensive foliage, they have a need for more water than most small fruits. A minimum of three inches or thirty six gallons per plant is needed on a weekly basis. To reduce competition, weeds need to be removed by very shallow cultivation. Muscadine feeder roots grow mostly in the top 1/2 inch of soil, and are easily damaged by careless cultivation.

Fruit Drop

Muscadine berries are susceptible to a fruit drop that occurs for a number of reasons. First, female vines will drop fruit when blossoms have not been adequately pollinated. Severe drought or excess rainfall will also cause fruit drop. As mentioned earlier, over-application of fertilizer can cause fruit drop as well.

Winter Protection

Although southern winters are nowhere near as severe as those in the north, muscadine vines do need winter protection. Late in the fall, protect the lowest buds on the trunk from freezing by banking eight to twenty four inches of dirt around the base of each vine. In the event of severe damage to the exposed trunk, a new trunk can be established from these buds without completely replanting the vineyard. Do not use straw, bark, or other mulch materials as winter protection. They will not provide the level of protection that dirt will and they are an enormous invitation to rodents. Each spring remove the banked dirt. Vines that are ten to twenty five years old tend to be more susceptible to cold injury than younger vines. As a result, many muscadine growers start replacing old vines when they are around twelve years old.

Harvest

Muscadine grape harvest usually starts shortly before Labor Day for the earliest varieties and can last into mid-November for the latest ripening fruit. Those berries being harvested for wine are picked when brix levels of 16-17 degrees are reached. For fresh eating berries may be left on the vine until sugar levels have reached 20 degrees.

There are two methods used to harvest muscadine. The first is individual hand picking of the ripe fruit. This is preferred for fresh fruit to avoid bruising. For faster harvesting of large quantities of fruit, a catching frame of cloth can be held beneath the vine while it is tapped gently to encourage ripe fruit to fall off into the catching frame below. In both cases, several pickings will be required, since muscadine berries do not ripen uniformly.

Typical yields of a muscadine grape vine are as follows:

Age	Self fertile	Female
1	none	none
2	12 - 25 pounds	3 - 12 pounds
3 and beyond	50 - 75 pounds	25 - 50 pounds

21. Kiwifruit

As you begin kiwifruit cultivation, you are embarking on an adventure of sorts, into somewhat unknown territory. To date, relatively little has been done to study the most successful methods of producing "hardy" kiwifruit. Equally little, perhaps, is known about the individual varieties. In some cases, conflicting information makes matters truly confusing. If you are ready for some experimenting, this relative newcomer to the fruit garden can prove rewarding.

In essence, two types of kiwifruit exist, the "fuzzy" type, which can be found in grocery store produce departments and the lesser known smooth skinned types. The kiwifruit, sometimes called "Chinese gooseberry", is prized for its very high vitamin C content and unique sweet, tangy flavor.

The "fuzzy" kiwifruit, *Actinidia deliciosa*, typically has oblong fruit the diameter of a golf ball and can only be grown where it will not be exposed to severe winter cold. Some people may refer to this type of kiwifruit as a subtropical fruit. This is not correct, however. Like other temperate zone fruit, it also requires a period of chilling in order to grow and fruit properly. This is the kiwifruit most often grown commercially, with most of the United States production coming from Cali-

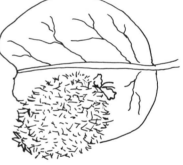

Figure 89. *Fuzzy kiwi fruit*

fornia. *Actinidia deliciosa* is generally hardy to 15°F. It requires a 225 to 240 day season to ripen fully.

The smooth skinned "hardy" kiwifruit, as it is sometimes called, is smaller in size, equal to that of a large grape. Numerous species of this type exist. The two most popular, generally available cultivated types are *Actinidia araguta* and *A. kolomikta*. *Actinidia chinensis* and *A. melanandra* are slowly becoming known and available as word of their superb taste gets around. Although none of the "hardy" kiwifruit are currently used for commercial production, they lend a unique crop to the home garden. Since they have a wider tolerance for low temperatures when fully dormant, they have the most potential to be grown over a wider portion of the United States. With the exception of climatic requirements, culture of the different species of kiwifruit is similar. One drawback of all the currently available kiwifruit types is that they tend to start growth very early in the spring and are often severely set back by a late spring frost. Once bud break occurs, even the hardy kiwifruit cannot withstand 31°F. This often catches the novice grower by surprise, especially when one has purchased a hardy kiwifruit, concentrating primarily on the word hardy.

Actinidia araguta was the first hardy kiwifruit to be introduced to the gardener. The smooth skinned, green fruit grows in a small

grape-like cluster. The fruit ripens on the vine and is quite fragile at harvest. Storage life of the fruit is approximately two months when refrigerated. The flavor is wonderfully sweet. *Actinidia araguta* is said to be hardy to a winter temperature of -25°F. A fairly long growing season of 150 days is required to ripen the fruit. The vigorous growing vine also makes an attractive landscape plant. Deep red petioles attach the glossy green leaves to the vine offering an interesting contrast of colors on an arbor or trellis.

Figure 90. *Actinidia araguta*

Actinidia kolomikta, an even hardier species, withstands winter temperatures between -30 and -40°F. It only requires a growing season of 130 days to mature its fruit. The fruit, like that of A. *araguta*, is smooth skinned and sweet, but slightly

smaller in size. It is very high in vitamin C content, containing up to fifteen times as much vitamin C per 100 grams of fruit as an orange. Watch the fruit carefully as they approach maturity. They have a habit of dropping from the vine when ripe. The vine itself is somewhat less vigorous than the other kiwifruit and even prefers to grow in partially shaded conditions. Prized as a landscape plant, it has striking variegated leaves of green, white and red. Because of its great winter hardiness, it is often known by the name Arctic Beauty.

Figure 91. *Actinidia kolomikta*

240 the Backyard Berry Book

Actinidia polygama, a more difficult-to-find species, is occasionally grown as a landscape plant. Sometimes known as Silver Vine, it has large heart shaped leaves. The fruit is small and rather bitter until fully ripe. Cats seem particularly attracted to this plant which seems to have the same effect on them that catnip does.

Site and Soil

Kiwifruit should be planted on as frost free a site as possible. They have a tendency to begin bud growth very early in the spring, but at that stage of development they are not at all tolerant to frost. Selecting a north facing slope for your planting site will help delay plant growth in the spring somewhat and may be the best choice if late spring frosts are typical in your area. The main disadvantage of a north slope is that, since plants are slower to bud out, they may also be slower to ripen (by several days at least). If you live in an area with a short growing season, you will have to balance the odds of a damaging late spring frost against that of an early fall frost damaging the not-yet-ripe fruit.

Although air circulation is helpful in reducing fungus diseases, truly windy sites should be avoided. High winds will easily break the long, heavy fruit laden vines and cause additional moisture transpiration as well. Wind breaks or buildings that will shelter your vines from wind should be taken into consideration when choosing a planting site, too.

Much debate still exists about whether the hardy kiwifruit species should be planted in full sun or partial shade. As native plants, they are forest understory plants, so it makes reasonable sense that they may need some shading. Some reports indicate that *A. aragula* needs 20 to 30% shade, while *A. kolomikta* requires as much as 75% shading. On the other hand, both species appear to require at least six hours of sunlight daily to produce sufficient fruit buds. Which side of the debate growers line up on appears to be somewhat influenced by their location. Not surprisingly, growers in warmer areas tend toward the shade, more temperate locations appear to have a greater need for a sunny site. So, at this time, it is up to each grower to experiment for themselves.

A light, well drained soil with plenty of organic matter is definitely best for growing kiwifruit. The vines are quite sensitive to crown rot, which is primarily a problem in heavy soils. Heavy water logged soils can cause rapid decline of the vine and extremely sandy soil will not hold enough moisture to satisfy their heavy demand for water. If your soil is not particularly well drained, planting your vines on a raised mound will help somewhat. Try to remedy the drainage problem by improving the soil structure as discussed in chapter 2.

Slightly acid soil conditions with pH of ranges from 5.0 to 6.5 are necessary for growing kiwifruit of the *deliciosa* and *araguta* species. In some cases, a pH of 6.0 is preferred. This is especially true for kiwifruit grown on calcareous soils, as lime chlorosis can become a problem. Some experience has shown that kiwifruit of the *kolomikta* species prefer an even higher pH in the range of 7.0.

Clearing the site of weed and other plant competition ahead of planting is essential when establishing kiwifruit. The young vines compete very poorly with weeds and other vegetation, so it is best to carefully follow all the site preparation steps from chapter 2 and to till the ground just prior to planting.

Pollination

Unlike most other cultivated fruit, kiwifruit have some plants that bear male flowers and other plants that bear female flowers. Although flowers on either type of plant will have both male and female reproductive parts, only one reproductive structure is functional in each case. The male, or staminate flowers, have poorly developed female structures but produce the viable male pollen. Female, or pistillate, flowers on the other hand have properly formed ovaries but produce nonviable pollen, even though they have the necessary pollen bearing structures. Normally the female flower is slightly larger in size than the male flower, making it possible to visually distinguish between the two.

Flowers are usually produced on vines at least three to four years old. Very little pollination of kiwifruit flowers occurs by wind. It is almost all accomplished by bees. Kiwifruit flowers have pollen but no nectar, so they are not the most attractive to bees. This makes it important to keep bloom of competing flowers, such as dandelions, mowed when kiwifruit is in bloom.

Bees seem to show a preference for visiting either male or female flowers based on the amount of competition from other bees and the availability of other pollen sources. In commercial situations, it is recommended that about 10% of the vines planted bear male flowers.

flowers. In the home garden, its is best to have a male flowering kiwifruit vine within twenty feet, and definitely no further than thirty five feet, away from any given female vine. As a rule of thumb, a ratio of one male per six female vines is recommended.

Cross pollination does occur between the different species of kiwifruit, so it is not necessary that you have vines all of the same type. The gardener may purposely want to try different varieties as a way of testing which will grow best in a particular locale.

Fruit size is in direct relation to the number of seeds in each fruit. The multiple ovary structure of the kiwifruit flower requires that it be visited by bees numerous times for pollination to be effective. The varieties must also bloom at the same time. To bear a sizeable crop, it is important that as many female flowers as possible are pollinated. In the home garden, where one most likely has only a few plants and not a large number of bees, it is possible to take a male flower and rub pollen from it on the female flower to ensure pollination. Female flowers are receptive for up to nine days after opening and male pollen is viable for up to three days after the bloom opens. One male flower can usually be used to pollinate as many as five females. Hand pollination should be done immediately after the male flower is picked. The fruit that results will have the characteristics of the female parent.

Varieties

Much confusion still needs to be sorted out regarding the parentage of numerous kiwifruit varieties. The listing below will attempt to provide a description of the varieties grouped by type that are both available through specialty nurseries and are most successfully grown in the home garden. Generally, named berry varieties can be reliably obtained from a wide number of sources, both mail order and local. When purchasing kiwifruit it is especially important to deal with a nursery that specializes in these plants as so few nurseries have as yet learned the peculiarities of raising or naming of these plants.

Actinidia deliciosa (Fuzzy kiwifruit)
> **Abbott** and **Allison** are two very similar, productive females. They have a moderate chilling requirement and produce good flavored, medium size fruit.
> **Blake** is female with low chilling requirements that produces

heavy crops of small early ripening fruit. Fruit thinning is needed to obtain reasonable fruit size and avoid plant stress.

Elmwood, a low chill female, is considered one of the best for producing large size fruit.

Hayward is the standard commercially grown female kiwifruit found on grocery store shelves. It has large fruit of excellent flavor although the core of the fruit tends to be hard. It has a chilling requirement of 700 hours which is sometimes difficult to satisfy in warm climates.

Saanichton 12 is a female very well suited to growing in the home garden. The fruit has excellent flavor and large size. It appears to be hardier than other *deliciosa* varieties.

Chico 3, also known as California, is a midseason blooming male with low chill requirements.

Matua is a vigorous male with a long bloom season. It tends to be cold tender.

Actinidia araguta (Hardy kiwifruit)

Ananasnaja or **Anna** is a pineapple scented female that produces fruit with a reddish blush when exposed to the sun. Said to be the hardiest *araguta*, some confusion still exists about its origin. It is sold under numerous variations of its name.

Cordifolia is reputed to be the sweetest female *araguta*.

Ken's Red is an intensely flavored female that is actually an *araguta* x *melanandra* cross. It produces the largest *araguta* type fruit. Ripe fruit has a deep red skin. Considered one of the best.

Issai, often sold as *the* hardy kiwifruit, is a bisexual plant that pollinates only itself. It is actually an *araguta* x *polygama* cross. As a garden grown plant it shows weak growth that is subject to some annual vine die-back. It is only hardy to -10°F. Its niche is as a container grown plant. Issai has a habit of dropping its fruit when ripe.

Male *araguta* vines are sold as unnamed varieties, all apparently suitable as pollinators.

Actinidia kolomikta (Arctic Beauty)

Krupnopladnaya is the most widely available female. It bears very large fruit (for the species) with excellent flavor. It does not have the variegated foliage that other A. *kolomikta* exhibit.

Numerous other male and female varieties, most with Russian names, are being sold. Many are still untested in the United States. Typically, male plants tend to have prominent variegation of the foliage. Variegation is less pronounced in the females. For the best *kolomikta* variety selection consult the nursery from which plants are being purchased.

Actinidia melanandra and *A. chinensis* are just becoming available. Where all kiwifruit have a flavor that can be described as various combinations of strawberry, banana, and pineapple. *A. melanandra* tends to have a somewhat tart fruit that leans heavily in the direction of the strawberry flavor component. *A. chinensis* has been described as having the typical sweet kiwifruit flavor with a dose of passion fruit thrown in as well.

Planting

Kiwifruit is normally planted in early spring after danger of serious frost is past. Plants should have a trunk diameter of about 1/2 inch and be three to six feet high before field planting. The crown should be set 1/4 to 1/2 inch above the soil surface to prevent crown rot.

The vines are typically planted anywhere from eight or ten feet apart in the row for the less vigorous *kolomikta* varieties. The more vigorous growing *deliciosa* and *araguta* varieties are planted fifteen feet and sometimes as much as eighteen to twenty feet apart in the row. Distance between rows is commonly about fifteen feet. You may need to experiment to find your best planting distance based on how vigorously kiwifruit grow in your climate, how much they are contained by spring frost damage, and what garden equipment needs to pass between the rows.

A T-trellis or single cordon, similar to those used for grapes, can be used for kiwifruit growing in a garden row. When possible, set the plants midway between two posts to better support their considerable weight. Decorative espalier, arbors, or pergolas can be another interesting way to support kiwifruit in the home garden and provide an unusual landscape accent as well.

The First Critical Years

Novice kiwifruit growers often give up after trying to start numerous vines that never survive beyond the first growing season. Once a few "secrets" are revealed, the plants can be given a proper start and prosper. Experienced kiwifruit growers will tell you that the vine needs a period of acclimation and a well developed root system before being set in its permanent site. This is most easily achieved by growing the new plant in a pot for the first year or two.

Kiwifruit also appear to grow best when they have "warm feet" (up to about 90°F.). Plants grown in pots will typically have warmer roots and develop more quickly. In extremely warm temperatures, care must be taken to avoid cooking the roots. Shading or mulching around the pot will help in these situations.

Due to their prolific vegetative growth, vine development often outstrips the young root system's ability to take up enough moisture. To counteract excessive transpiration, some growers find that by fashioning a mini-greenhouse around the young vine, they can maintain enough humidity to guard against the vine becoming stressed. A chicken wire cage is constructed around the vine. The cage is then wrapped in plastic, leaving the top and three inches at the bottom open. This allows air circulation and keeps temperatures from becoming too high inside the "greenhouse". Once the vine is two or three years old and well established, the plastic can be removed. The cage can remain as a deterrent against rodents, cats, and other wildlife.

Very often young vines die as a result of trunk splitting following a quick, hard frost on a sunny autumn day. This is caused by uneven freezing and thawing on the warmer and colder side of the trunk, similar to "southwest injury" on fruit trees. The remedy is similar, too. Trunks of the vines can be painted with white latex paint to deflect some of the sun's warming rays. Burlap or paper trunk wraps are also reported to work.

Growing in Containers

Vigorous kiwifruit vines would seem unlikely candidates for container growing. Surprisingly, several varieties lend themselves well to such restricted growth. A five to fifteen gallon pot filled with a 50/50 mix of potting soil and garden dirt works well. The soil level should be one to two inches below the rim of the pot to allow adequate area for sufficient watering of these very thirsty vines. A three foot ornamental trellis, available at most garden centers, is used to support the plant.

Plant the vine as outlined above, with the crown above soil level. Issai, which is self-fertile takes well to pot growing and appears to grow more consistently in a pot than in the garden. *Actinidia kolomikta* and *A. polygama*, being less rampant growers than A. *araguta*, also do well as container plants and are very attractive plants. Vines are kept in check by regularly pinching new growth, as one would with many house plants. During the growing season, plants can decorate a patio or terrace. Once cold weather arrives, move the plants to a protected location or mulch heavily around all sides of the pot to protect the roots from freezing and heaving. Do not bring the plant inside or its chilling requirements will not be satisfied. When spring arrives, repot in the next larger size pot.

Fertilizer and Water

Kiwifruit vines are especially sensitive to root burn from fertilizers when they are young. The best way to fertilize young kiwifruit vines is by small applications of a balanced, slow release organic fertilizer several times during the growing season. Generally .2 pounds of nitrogen is an adequate dose for a two year old plant. Rates double each year - .4 pounds at three years old, .8 pounds at four years, and one pound per plant at 5 years of age. No fertilizer should be applied later than early July, however, to avoid late succulent season growth.

Mature kiwifruit vines can be fed maintenance doses of fertilizer in split applications. Nitrogen is applied at the rate of one third pound per 100 square feet, with 2/3 being applied just as growth starts in the spring and the remaining 1/3 applied after flowering. Phosphorous is applied in late winter-early spring at rates of two ounces per 100 square feet. Kiwifruit vines use large amounts of potassium. A rate of one half to three quarter pounds per 100 square feet is normally applied in three equal applications. The first application can be made at the same time phosphorous is applied, the second and third applications can be made at the time that the nitrogen is applied.

Kiwifruit have a much higher need for magnesium than most other fruit. This is due to the fact that the bright green coloring of the fruit comes from the plant pigment chlorophyll. Magnesium is the central building block to the structure of the chlorophyll molecule. To satisfy the magnesium needs of the plant, magnesium at two ounces per 100 square feet, total should be applied along with the potassium.

The kiwifruit is a very vigorous growing vine with an extensive, spreading root system. Because the mature vine will often have four to five thousand leaves covering over four hundred square feet of area, moisture loss through transpiration can exceed twenty gallons a day during the hot summer months. If this is not replaced by natural rainfall, supplemental watering should be provided. Young vines should be watered three or four times per week and older vines, four years and up, at least twice a week. Fortunately, the root system is quite good at extracting soil moisture, going down as much as eight or more feet in sandy soils. On heavy soils, roots typically reach only three feet down. It is very important to keep kiwifruit vines well watered during the growing season. If the plants become water stressed, fruit growth will stop temporarily and will not completely recover even when water again becomes available. In extremely dry areas, irrigation may be the only assurance of a steady moisture supply.

Frost Protection

Kiwifruit's great sensitivity to spring frost has already been mentioned. In some cases, gardeners can take action to protect the vines. Overhead sprinkler irrigation, as discussed fully in the strawberry chapter can also effectively protect kiwifruit. When the vines are still small, in the first year or two, the heavier weight floating row covers can also be placed over the vine if frost is anticipated. Both of these methods will provide a few degrees of protection.

Pruning

The basic reasons for pruning a fruit bearing vine are outlined in chapter 19. Pruning mature kiwifruit is in many ways like pruning grapes. The principles can be systematically applied to kiwifruit in a similar manner. A T-trellis or arbor is required to support the rampant growing vine and heavy fruit load. If the trellis is about six feet tall, fruit will hang down from above, making picking fairly easy.

The trunk and main arms become the permanent structure of the vine. To begin establishing a young kiwifruit vine, a stake is set in the ground next to the vine and a strong shoot is trained up the stake to the central trellis wire. Additional shoots growing from ground level are removed as are shoots originating below the graft union (on grafted vines). In harsher climates, sometimes two shoots

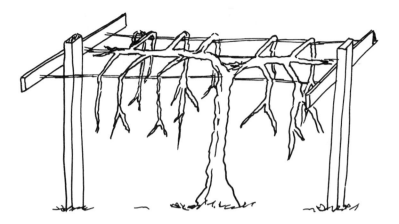

Figure 92. Kiwi fruit vine trained on a T-trellis

are maintained as potential main trunks. If one is killed by winter injury in the early years, the other can be substituted as the trunk. As the main shoot (or future trunk) reaches the trellis wire, it is tipped to encourage side branching. As two side branches develop, they are trained in opposite directions along the trellis to form the main branch canopy. These main side branches are sometimes known as the "leaders".

Over the years, secondary side branches will develop from this main structure. These are the branches that will bear the fruit. Buds closest to the main trunk, with short internodes of less than two inches, will be the most productive. During the dormant season, prune these lateral branches back to a length of eight to thirteen buds. This will stimulate the growth of fruit buds. The cane will then fruit for two years. During each dormant season, cut fruited canes back to a length of eight to thirteen buds to stimulate growth of additional new fruiting wood.

Every two to three years, fruiting wood is renewed by pruning off up to sixty percent of the existing side branch vegetation. This encourages vigorous new growth. Flowers, and consequently fruit, are produced only on shoots of current season growth originating from one-year-old wood.

Occasional summer pruning is also suggested. Many kiwifruit growers are unaware that the vine produces two types of vegetative growth. One type grows for several feet early in the growing season,

Kiwifruit 249

then stops growing, withers at the tip, and dies. This has been referred to as "terminating growth". The other type of growth, "nonterminating growth", continues growing until autumn frost. In late summer, nonterminating growth can be trimmed back a point where it is 1/4 inch in diameter. Terminating growth can be pruned off entirely. Do not summer-prune too early in the summer, or new shoot growth will result that is too tender to overwinter.

Similar terminating and nonterminating habits can be found on fruit spurs. Terminating fruit spurs produce normally the first year and then die back. They will set a few fruit buds at the tip of the remaining growth. These will bear a small quantity of fruit in their second year. Due to their minimal productivity, it is best to remove these spurs. Nonterminating fruit spurs are dormant-pruned as discussed above.

Pests and Diseases

Perhaps because they are a relatively new introduction to American gardens, kiwifruit do not have many native pest and disease problems. Omnivorous leafroller and scale occur as occasional problems on the west coast. *Phytophthora* root rot and crown rot are the primary disease problems for kiwifruit grown on poorly drained sites. Symptoms are the same as discussed in chapter 8.

Unlike most fruit, where insects are the major pests, cats and gophers pose the greatest pest problems to homegrown kiwifruit. Apparently, kiwifruit plants mimic the attraction of catnip. Consequently, our feline friends rub and claw at the vines and chew on the foliage. Oddly enough, some varieties seem to stimulate this feline reaction and other varieties remain relatively untouched.

Gophers have an affinity for the roots of kiwifruit. In both cases the simplest remedy seems to be chicken wire. In the case of cat damage, the vine can be protected for the first three or four years of life by a wire cage fashioned around it. Once the vine has reached this age, it is usually large enough to withstand a playful cat. To protect against gophers on the rampage, kiwifruit vines can be grown with their roots planted in a three foot deep basket fashioned of chicken wire. With luck, the basket will last long enough for the root system to reach adequate size to withstand most attacks. Smoking of gopher tunnels has also been suggested, but in most cases, the gopher just moves elsewhere, only to return at a later date.

Harvest

Harvest season for kiwifruit typically occurs from mid-September through early November, depending on location and variety. To assess ripeness, a refractometer can be used to measure soluble sugar level (or brix) of the fruit. Fuzzy kiwifruit are usually picked when their brix level reaches 6.5. Ripe hardy kiwifruit have a brix level that may exceed 20. Lacking a refractometer, the home gardener can observe the change in seed color from white to brown to black as an indicator of fruit maturity. The fruit will also begin to soften as it ripens. Fruit that is picked hard will be bitter and remain hard inside even after sitting at room temperature for several days. Properly ripe fruit will be sweet and soften all the way thorough when left out to ripen (much the way a pear will).

Kiwifruit are typically harvested in several pickings, with the ripe fruit being removed each time. The remaining fruit often continues to increase in size until picked. Fuzzy kiwifruit will pick clean from their stem when ripe. Hardy kiwifruit should be picked carefully with a portion of the stem attached (like sweet cherries), or rot is likely to occur at the torn scar. Fuzzy kiwifruit have a storage life of four to five months under refrigeration. Two months is the normal storage life for refrigerated hardy kiwifruit.

Kiwifruit vines take up to eight years to reach peak production. However, under ideal growing conditions, kiwifruit of the *kolomikta* type will start fruiting the first year after planting. By three years of age the other types of kiwifruit will also start to produce a small crop. At four years old *A. deliciosa* can yield thirty to fifty pounds of fruit per vine. A mature vine can yield as much as 200 pounds of fruit. Yields on mature hardy kiwifruit can range from fifty to one hundred pounds per vine.

Section VI.

Resources & References

Trouble Shooting Questions & Answers

Every once in a while, a situation will crop-up in the fruit garden that has even the more experienced gardener puzzled. This section is intended to address those occurrences that are so sporadic that one may not know where to seek an immediate solution. Problems with fairly predictable answers, such as most pest infestations or nutrient deficiencies will not be found here. For those problems, go directly to the respective chapters on those topics. Consulting the solutions below, should help you deal with the obscure and quickly become a seasoned green thumb.

Strawberry

???I had my frost protection sprinklers on my strawberries and waited until temperatures were above freezing to turn it off but I still got a lot of damaged buds, how come?

You may have turned the sprinkler off too early. All the ice should be melted from the plants before frost protection sprinklers are turned off. If temperatures fell into the low 20s, it may have been too cold for even the sprinklers to provide protection.

???My strawberry plants had lots of blossoms, but hardly any fruit.

This is most likely due to frost damage. Check the centers of the blossoms, if they are damaged they will be black.

???My strawberries are dying, but I don't see any insect attacking them. They have enough water and fertilizer.

Cut open the roots and crown lengthwise. If the crown is discolored - pink or brown, cold injury is probably to blame. Select a hardier variety the next time you plant. If the roots are red inside see red stele in the disease section of chapter 10.

???My strawberry plants looked healthy when I planted them, but they don't seem to be growing.

They may be planted too deep. Recheck the diagrams in chapter 10 for proper planting depth.

Brambles

???Why do my raspberries have hard seedy crumbly areas?

???I'm careful picking my raspberries, why do they still fall apart?

Virus diseases (Tomato ringspot virus, Raspberry leaf curl, Raspberry bush dwarf) are most likely to blame. No cures are available. Care should be taken with new plantings to buy certified virus free plants and to replant away from old existing brambles (or better yet, remove old brambles, which may be easier said than done).

???Some of my raspberries are turning white. They are also hard and shriveled.

The white coloring is likely to be sunburn, especially in the south. This is a common problem on Royalty.

???The margins of my plant's leaves are brown and somewhat dried out. My plants are watered enough. What could this be?

The most obvious causes might be potassium or calcium deficiency. Over-fertilizing with muriate of potash or herbicide injury are other possible causes. More obscure, but not uncommon, especially in suburban gardens planted near a street, is toxicity from winter road salt.

???Why are the tips of some of my bramble canes wilting and dying? I can't find any obvious disease and I've kept them watered.

Raspberry cane borer damage exhibits these symptoms (see page 141-142). The canes may have been damaged by strong winds and broken at the base. Hold the cane upright by the tip and wiggle it. If it feels loose, look for callusing at the base of the cane where the break may have occurred. This problem is most common on erect growing blackberries and black or purple raspberries that have not been trellised. Trellising or planting a windbreak will help some if this is a regular problem in your bramble patch.

Blueberry

???My plants are several years old, but still haven't grown much from the time I planted them. What is wrong?

Weed competition, lack of water, nematodes, restricted root growth due to hardpan or other soil conditions, root feeding by white grubs (scarab beetle), or stunt virus are all possible causes.

???The branch tips of my bushes are dried up and dying, why?

If it is early in the spring, winter damage is the first thought that comes to mind in cold climate areas, assuming nutrient deficiencies (potassium or boron), insects, and diseases (*Botrytis*, anthracnose, and mummy berry) have been ruled out. Insufficient water may be the cause in warm or dry seasons.

???The leaves on my bush are turning yellow (or red) even though it is only mid-summer.

After ruling out nutrient deficiencies or virus diseases, herbicide injury may be the culprit.

???My blueberries are always small, why?

Variety differences, poor pollination, lack of pruning, lack of water, or too heavy a crop can all be responsible for small fruit.

Currants

???My currants are losing their leaves in mid-summer. They don't look as though they have a disease or insect problem.

This may be a response to stress. Currants are not tolerant of hot climates or weather. When temperatures exceed 86°F, some currants drop many of their leaves. This varies from one variety to the next, but it is particularly prevalent with the Wilder and Victoria varieties.

Lingonberry

???My soil test says I have all the proper soil nutrients, but some of my lingonberry leaves are red not green. It's early summer; what's wrong with my plant?

There may indeed be nothing wrong with your plant, new growth on young lingonberry plants is often tinged red. This is normal.

Grapes

???It's July and my muscadine grape buds never opened. They look dead. What killed them?

Maybe nothing. Newly planted muscadines can be very slow to leaf out, sometimes not opening until August. Be patient.

???The leaves on my grapes are small and gnarled up when they leaf out. The vine isn't growing as strongly as I think it should.

This could very well be herbicide injury from 2,4-D. Grapes are extremely sensitive to this herbicide. It is very volatile and if applied on a breezy day can drift and affect grapes as much as two miles away. This herbicide is commonly used for dandelion control and so may even have been sprayed by a neighbor the previous fall without your being aware of it.

???Do I need to wait for a frost to harvest my grapes?

No, although some varieties used for making certain wines are purposely left on the vine late into the season. If your grapes are ripe and you like their flavor, a frost will not improve them.

Kiwifruit

???My kiwifruit plants always have plenty of flowers, but I never get any fruit. What's wrong?

Most likely you have either all female or all male plants. You need at least one of each (or at least one male for every eight female plants) for proper pollination.

???Fruit seems to be dropping off my kiwifruit vine for no reason. Why?

Some varieties have the characteristic of dropping fruit when it is ripe. To avoid this, pick fruit slightly immature or select another variety for your next planting that does not have this genetic characteristic. Severe water stress could also be a possible cause, although other symptoms are probably apparent then too.

???My kiwifruit vine suddenly lost its leaves during a hot spell even though I kept it well watered.

Chances are your plant was damaged by an earlier heat wave and had not fully recovered. This time it was too weak to transport enough water to the already damaged leaves.

???The leaf edges of my vine are browned and dry. What is this?

This could be from inadequate (too little) water or if you applied fertilizer recently, it could be fertilizer burn. Young plants are particularly sensitive.

???My plant practically falls out of the ground and has no roots. Why?

Gophers, got it and chewed off most of the roots. White grubs could be another culprit.

???My supposedly female plant never produces flowers. What's wrong?

The vine's chilling requirement may not be properly satisfied, especially if you are located in a mild climate. Hardy kiwifruit do not grow well in warmer areas due to this problem and even some fuzzy (A. deliciosa) kiwifruit, notably Hayward, suffer from it too. Replant with a variety better matched to your climate.

Annual Almanac

This calendar is meant to give a general sequence of activities as they might occur in a typical small fruit garden. The time frame is representative of what a gardener might expect in New England or the upper midwest. In the warmer climate of the southern or western United States, the sequence will remain the same, but events will occur several weeks earlier.

January
 Catch up on reading your gardening magazines

February
 Enjoy a good gardening book

March
 Prune grapes, blueberries, currants,and gooseberries
 Mow/prune primocane fruiting raspberries
 Tune up garden equipment, see that sprayer works properly

April
 Apply fertilizer to all fruit except strawberries
 Plant new berry plants & bushes
 Begin fungicide spray programs to prevent anthracnose
 Prune kiwifruit and blackberries

May
 Remove winter mulch from strawberries
 Watch for late frosts and be prepared to apply frost protection measures on strawberries
 Put additional compost and mulch around plants and bushes
 Be on the look-out for tarnished plant bug, strawberry clipper, and cutworm infestations
 Watch for mildew and be prepared to take preventive action
 Begin trickle irrigation if conditions warrant

June

Harvest strawberries and rhubarb
Start preparing site if new plantings are anticipated next year
Continue seasonal pest and disease control
Put bird netting or deterrents out, where needed

July

Harvest blueberries, raspberries, currants, gooseberries, lingon-
berries, and day neutral strawberries
Finish harvest of June bearing strawberry varieties
Renovate and fertilize June bearing strawberries
Start taking tissue samples for fertility analysis

August

Prune old, fruited floricanes out of raspberries
Plant winter cover crops on sites to be planted in the spring

September

Harvest primocane bearing raspberries, blackberries, kiwifruit,
and early grapes
Take soil samples for fertility analysis

October

Harvest blackberries and grapes
Plant currants & gooseberries
Bury grape vines for cold protection after vines have defoliated
Rake mulch back from plants to reduce rodent habitat

November

Harvest lingonberries
Mulch strawberries for winter protection if several hard freezes
have already occurred
Spread lime where needed

December

Mulch strawberries for winter protection
Share berry preserves as holiday gifts
Order plants for spring planting
Give a gift certificate for some berry plants and a copy of *the
Backyard Berry Book* as a holiday gift

Annual Almanac 261

Resources

Since many of the more uncommon fruit varieties are often difficult to find, this section of nurseries has been included to help you find just what you are looking for should it be unavailable locally. All of the nurseries below were surveyed prior to publication of this book and indicated their desire to be included here. Each carries a wide selection of different fruit and a number of standard varieties in their catalog. A listing does not necessarily constitute an endorsement of the business or the quality of their products. In the interest of keeping current, the publisher welcomes information about your experience with the businesses listed below or about other mail order nurseries that should be included in future editions.

Allen's Berry Book. PO Box 310, Fruitland, MD 21826-0310.
Vernon Barnes & Sons. PO Box 250, McMinnville, TN 37110. 615-668-8576.
Bay Laurel Nursery. 2500 El Camino Real, Atascadero, CA 93422. 805-466-3406.
Bear Creek Nursery. PO Box 411, Northport, WA 99157
The Blueberry Patch. 1201 Longview Dr., Rogers, AR 72756.
Boston Mountain Nursery. 20189 N Hwy 71, Mountainburg, AR 72946. 501-369-2007
Brittingham Plant Farms. PO Box 2538, Salisbury, MD 21802. 410-742-1594.
Bottoms Nursery. Rt. 1, Box 281, Concord, GA 30206. 706-495-5661
Boyer Nurseries. 405 Boyer Nursery Rd., Biglerville, PA 17307. 717-677-8558
Buckley Nursery & Garden Center. 646 N River Rd., Buckley, WA 98321. 206-829-1811
Burnt Ridge Nursery. 432 Burnt Ridge Rd., Onalaska, WA 98570. 206-985-2873
W. Atlee Burpee Co. 300 Park Ave., Warminster, PA 18991. 215-674-4915
Champlain Isle Agro., Isle La Motte, VT 05463.
Classical Fruits. 8831 AL Hwy. 157, Moulton, AL 35650. 205-974-8813
Cloud Mountain Farm. 6906 Goodwin Rd., Everson, WA 98247. 206-966-5859
Concord Nurseries. Mileblock Rd., North Collins, NY 14111.
Cooley's Strawberry Nursery. PO Box 472, Augusta, AR 72006.
Degrandchamp's Blueberry Farm. 15576 77th St., South Haven, MI 49090.
Dyke's Blueberry Farm. Rt 1, Box 251, Vincent, OH 45784.
Edible Landscaping. PO Box 77, Afton, VA 22920. 800-524-4156
Exotica Rare Fruit Nursery. PO Box 160, Vista, CA 92085. 619-724-9093

Fedco Trees. Box 50, Waterville, ME 04903. 207-873-7333
Fowler Garden Center & Nurseries, Inc. 525 Fowler Rd., Newcastle, CA 95658.
916-645-8191
Gurney's Seed & Nursery Co. 110 Capitol St., Yankton, SD 57079.
605-665-1671
Harmony Farm Supply. PO Box 450, Graton, CA 95444. 707-823-9125
Hartmann's Plantation. PO Box E, 310 60th St, Grand Junction, MI 49056.
616-252-4281
Henry Field Seed & Nursery Company. 415 N. Burnett, Shenandoah, IA 51602.
605-665-4491
Hidden Springs Nursery. Rt 14, Hidden Springs Ln., Cookeville, TN 38501.
615-268-9889
Highlander Nursery. PO Box 177, Pettigrew, AR 72752. 501-677-2300
Hollyridge. 1570 Compton, Cleveland Hts., OH 44118.
Indiana Berry & Plant Co. 5218 W 500 South, Dept. OT94, Huntingburg, IN
47542. 800-295-2226.
Ison's Nursery & Vineyards. Brooks, GA 30205. 800-733-0324
Johnson Nursery. Rt. 5, Box 29J, Ellijay, GA 30540. 706-276-3187
Just Fruit. Rt. 2, Box 4818, Crawfordville, FL 32327. 904-926-5644.
Kelly Nursery. 410 8th Ave. NW, Faribault, MN 55021.
Krohne Plant Farms. Rt 6, Box 586, Dowagiac, MI 49047.
Lawson's Nursery. Rt 1, Box 472, Ball Ground, GA 30107. 706-893-2141
Henry Leuthardt Nursery. Montauk Hwy., Box 666-BOG, E. Moriches, Long Island,
NY 11940. 516-878-1387
Lewis Strawberry Nursery. PO Box 24, Rocky Point, NC 28457.
Louisiana Nursery. Rt.7, Box 43, Opelousas, LA 70570. 318-948-3696.
Mellinger's. FGB West Range Rd., North Lima, OH 44452. 216-549-9861
J E Miller Nurseries, Inc. 5060 W Lake Rd., Canadaigua, NY 14424. 800-836-9630
North Star Gardens. 2124 University Ave, W., St. Paul, MN 55114-1838.
Northwind Nursery & Orchards. 7910 335th Ave., NW, Princeton, MN 55371.
612-389-4920
Northwoods Nursery. 27635 S. Oglesby Rd, Molalla, OR 97013. 503-226-5432
Nourse Farms, Inc.. RFD Box 485, South Deerfield, MA 01373. 413-665-2658
Oregon Exotic Rare Fruit Nursery. 1065 Messenger Rd., Grants Pass, OR 97527.
503-846-7578
Pense Nursery. Rt 2, Box 330-A, Mountainburg, AR 72946. 501-369-2494
Plumtree Nursery. 387 Springtown Rd, New Paltz, NY 12561.
Pony Creek Nursery. PO Box 16 Nursery Ln., Tilleada, WI 54978. 715-787-3889
Raintree Nursery. 391 Butts Rd., Morton, WA 98356. 360-496-6400
Southmeadow Fruit Gardens. Box SM, Lakeside, MI 49116. 616-469-2865
Stark Brothers. PO Box 10, Louisiana, MO 63353. 800-325-4180
Tripple Brook Farm. 37 Middle Rd., Southampton, MA 01073.
M. Worley Nursery. 98 Braggtown Rd., York Springs, PA 17372. 717-528-4519

Specialty Nurseries - The businesses below specialize in a particular fruit, but offer a wide selection of varieties (including some hard to find varieties). Some of these nurseries are smaller home-based businesses. To help defray printing and mailing costs, please include a long, self-addressed, stamped envelope and the payment indicated.

Currants and Gooseberries
Alexander Eppler Ltd.. PO Box 16513, Seattle, WA 98116-0513. Phone: 206-932-2211. $3.
Ed Mashburn. 707 Front St., Northumberland, PA 17857. Phone: 717-473-9910.
Whitman Farms. 3995 Gibson NW, Salem, OR 97304. 503-585-8728.

Grape
Boordy Vineyard. Box 38, Riverwood, MD 21139.
Lake Sylvia Vineyard Nursery. Rt. 1, Box 149, South Haven, MN 55382.
Lon Rombough. 13113 Ehlen Rd., Aurora, OR 97002-9746. Phone: 503-678-1440. Cuttings only. $1.
Ray Schneider Nursery. 2383 S Euclid Rd., Grandview, WA 98930.

Kiwifruit
Kiwis R Us. RD 1 Tippets Rd., Rt. 54, Nesquehoning, PA 18420. Phone: 717-645-3652
Living Tree Center. PO Box 10082, Berkley, CA 94709. Phone: 510-420-1440
Puget Sound Kiwi-scions. 1220 NE 90th, Seattle, WA 98115. Phone: 206-523-6403. Scionwood only.

Lingonberry
Barwacz Farm. 05146 59th Street, Grand Junction, MI 49056. Phone: 616-253-4419
Hartmann's Plantation. PO Box E, 310 60th St, Grand Junction, MI 49056. Phone: 616-252-4281

Organizations & Miscellaneous Resources

American Wine Society. 3006 Latta Rd., Rochester, NY 14612-3298.
This organization promotes the appreciation of wine. Publications include American Wine Society Journal, which comes out quarterly and a booklet on making fruit wines.

California Rare Fruit Growers. The Fullerton Arboretum, California State University, Fullerton, CA 92634.
A non-profit organization dedicated to the study and preservation of rare fruit varieties. Activities include local chapter meetings, a bi-monthly magazine The Fruit Gardener, and a "hotline" for answering horticultural questions.

Fruit Testing Association Nursery, Inc.
Geneva, NY 14456.
This non-profit cooperative, formed to introduce the most promising selections from the New York State Agricultural Experiment Station at Geneva, was listed in earlier printings of this book. Unfortunately due to budget cuts this well known source of plant material has closed, but is still noted here to save readers the frustration of trying to locate it.

Home Orchard Society
PO Box 230192, Tigard, OR 97281-0192
A non-profit educational organization assisting new and experienced fruit growers with fruit bearing trees, shrubs, and plants in the home landscape. Annual membership of $10.00 includes quarterly POME NEWS journal, branch and chapter events, and use of media library. Major events include a spring scionwood exchange and rootstock sale, summer orchard tours, and autumn All About Fruit Show.

The International Ribes Assn. (TIRA)
707 Front St., Northumberland, PA 17857
Edward Mashburn, President. 717-473-9910
TIRA is dedicated to furthering knowledge of currants, gooseberries, and jostaberries. The annual meeting features international speakers. TIRA works with USDA and Canadian researchers to test new varieties in the U.S. and maintains a database of all Ribes cultivars currently being grown in the U.S. Members receive the newsletter Ribes Reporter.

North American Bramble Growers (NABGA).
13006 Mason Rd. NE, Cumberland, MD 21502-9235
Richard Fagan, Exec. Sec. 301-724-4085
NBAGA *activities include local field days and an annual meeting. Proceedings are issued following the annual meeting. Members receive a newsletter twice a year and a subscription to Northland Berry News.*

North American Fruit Explorers
Rt. 1, Box 94, Chapin, IL 62628
NAFEX, *for short, is a network of over 3000 individuals interested in discovering, cultivating and furthering knowledge of superior fruit and nut varieties. Membership is $ 8.00 for one year or $ 15.00 for two. Membership benefits include the quarterly journal, POMONA, an 80 page collection of articles written by members; a lending library book list and borrowing privileges; a propagating stock exchange; special interest group participation; and an annual meeting.*

North American Strawberry Growers Assn. (NASGA)
PO Box 160, West Paducah, KY 42086
Dr. J.W. "Bill" & Treva Courter, Exec. Sec. 502-488-2116
NASGA *hosts an educational meeting that begins annually on the second Sunday in February. Various levels of membership are available and members can choose whether they would like to receive a quarterly newsletter, Proceedings of the annual meeting, and Advances in Strawberry Research (a peer review journal). NASGA donates approximately $25000 annually to universities for strawberry research and is in the process of establishing a foundation to fund larger on-going projects.*

Seed Savers Exchange
3076 North Winn Rd., Decorah, IA 52101
Seed Savers Exchange *is a non-profit organization dedicated to saving heirloom and endangered varieties of food plants. A small collection of extremely hardy grapes has been planted. Seed Savers Exchange publishes the Fruit, Nut, and Berry inventory; an extensive list of variety descriptions and nursery sources. Annual membership is $25.00 or send $1.00 (to help defray costs) for a full color brochure further outlining member benefits and projects.*

Master Gardener Program

The Master Gardener Program is an out-growth of an educational program originally developed by the cooperative extension service. It has two functions:

1. as an educational program providing current horticultural information to active gardeners, and

2. as a service program of volunteer activities provided by Master Gardeners.

Master Gardeners receive approximately 40 hours of classroom and field training in horticulture and participate in an equal amount of time providing community garden services. Approximately half of this time is spent working with cooperative extension in answering "garden hotline" questions or developing educational materials. The balance of volunteer time is spent on community beautification projects, providing horticultural therapy, staffing informational booths, or other community gardening activities.

Cooperative Extension Service (CES)

As a cooperative effort between federal, state, and local government, the extension service disseminates information based on the research conducted by the land grant colleges or universities in each state. The extension service has a number of services for the home gardener including informational bulletins, seminars, soil testing services, and the advice of a horticultural or agricultural agent. Most of these services are moderately priced and some are free of charge.

Most states have an extension office in each county. You may find the office listed under any of the following headings in your local phone book - agricultural agent; cooperative extension service; County, extension service; Federal or U.S. government, extension service; Land grant university name, extension service.

If you need the services of your extension office, most state programs are set up in such a way that you contact your local office. If they are unable to immediately answer your question, they will contact a specialist at the state land grant college and obtain the answer for you or refer you to that specialist.

Appropriate Technology Transfer for Rural Areas (ATTRA)
PO Box 3657
Fayetteville, AR 72702   Phone: 800-346-9140
This US Fish and Wildlife Service program provides free information on low input/sustainable agriculture. Several reports are available on raising fruit as well as more general soil fertility management and pest control.

Office of Small Scale Agriculture
USDA/CSRS, OSSA
Ste. 328-A, Aerospace Center
Washington, DC 20250-2200 Phone: 202-401-1805
Geared to providing a wide array of information to the small scale farm and specialty crop grower, this USDA office provides fact sheets and reports on a number of topics related to fruit. A free newsletter covering numerous agricultural/horticultural topics is also available.

Publications

The following is a random list of publications the author has found helpful in locating additional information, resources, or rare plant material that other fruit gardeners may also enjoy.

Fruit Nut & Berry Inventory
Seed Savers Exchange, 3076 North Winn Rd., Decorah, IA 52101
A descriptive index of over 5800 fruit and nut varieties with cross referencing on which of over 300 mail order nurseries carries each variety.

Garden Literature: An Index to Periodical Articles & Book Reviews
Garden Literature Press, 398 Columbus Ave, Ste. 181, Boston, MA 02116-6008
An annual index of over 100 English-language periodicals; some horticultural, some general interest; that include garden topics.

Gardener's Index
Compudex Press, PO Box 27041, Kansas City, MO 64110-7041
Annual comprehensive subject index of 6 major U.S. gardening magazines (Am. Horticulturist, Fine Gardening, Flower & Garden, Horticulture, National Gardening, and Organic Gardening).

Gardeners Source Guide
PO Box 206, Gowanda, NY 14070-0206
Listing of mail order nurseries, including fruit, that send free catalogs as well as associations, societies, and clubs.

Gardening By Mail by Barbara Barton
A comprehensive listing of plant sources, including many fruit tree and berry sources. Available at most bookstores.

Glossary of Terms for the Home Gardener by Robert Gough, PhD
Haworth Press, 10 Alice St., Binghamton, NY 13904
A handy pocket glossary of gardening terms. Not limited to fruit production, this is a ready reference for any gardener striving to better understand gardening and its terminology.

Further Reading

Magazines

Kiwifruit Enthusiasts Journal. Box 1466, Chelan, WA 98816.

Common Sense Pest Control Quarterly and The IPM Practioner. Bio-Integral Resource Center, PO Box 7417, Berkley, CA 94707.

Country Journal. 4 High Ridge Park, Stamford, CT 06905.

Great Lakes Fruit Grower News. PO Box 128, Sparta, MI 49345

Harrowsmith Country Life. The Creamery, Ferry Rd., Charlotte, VT 05445.

Horticluture. 98 N. Washington St., Boston, MA 02114-1913.

HortIdeas. 460 Black Lick Rd., Gravel Switch, KY 40328.

Journal of Small Fruit and Viticulture. The Haworth Press, 10 Alice St., Binghamton, NY 13904-1580

National Gardening. 180 Flynn Ave., Burlington, VT 05401.

Northland Berry News. 2124 University Ave W, St. Paul, MN 55114-1838. Phone 612-659-2418/612-659-2420 FAX

Organic Gardening. 152-180 E.Minor St., Emmaus, PA 18098.

National Agricultural Library, USDA, Room 111, Beltsville, MD 20705. Phone 301-504-5755.

The library houses primarily technical publications on all aspects of agriculture. Items may be requested through interlibrary loan from public and university libraries. It also offers AGRICOLA, an on-line computer data base, and an electronic bulletin board.

Books

General Fruit Growing/Specific Fruit

Creasy, Rosalind. *Organic Gardener's Edible Plants*. Van Patten Publishing, Portland, OR. 1993.

Reich, Lee. *Uncommon Fruits Worthy of Attention*. Addison-Wesley Publishing Company, Inc., Reading, MA. 1991

St. Pierre, Richard and Susan Campbell. *The Lingonberry, A Versatile Wild Cranberry*. Horticultural Research and Extension, Dept. of Horticulture, University of Saskatchewan (lists additional technical reading).

Regional Fruit Growing

Gordon, Donald. *Growing Fruit in the Upper Midwest*. University of Minnesota Press, Minneapolis, MN. 1991.

McEachern, George. *Growing Fruits, Berries & Nuts in the South*. Gulf Publishing Co. Houston, TX. 1989.

Walheim, Lance and Robert L. Stebbins. *Western Fruit, Berries, and Nuts: How to Select, Grow, and Enjoy*. H.P. Books, Tuscon, AZ, 1981.

Soil Fertility/Composting/Mulching

. *Backyard Composting*. Harmonious Technologies, Ojai, CA. 1992.

Campbell, Stu. *The Mulch Book*. Garden Way Publishing Co., Charlotte, VT. 1973.

_____. *Let It Rot! The Home Gardener's Guide to Composting*. Garden Way Publishing Co., Charlotte, VT. 1975.

Solomon, Steve. *Organic Gardener's Composting*. Van Patten Publishing, Portland, OR. 1993.

Willis, Harold. *The Coming Revolution in Agriculture*. Harold L. Willis, Wisconsin Dells, WI. 1985.

Lee, Andrew W. *Chicken Tractor: The Gardener's Guide to Happy Hens and Healthy Soil*. Good Earth Publications, Shelburne, VT. 1994.

Pest & Disease Identification and Control

Ellis, Barbara W. and Fern Marshal Bradley. *The Organic Gardener's Handbook of Natural Insect and Disease Controls*. Rodale Press, Emmaus, PA. 1992

Marketing/Truck Farming

Gibson, Eric. *Sell What You Sow: The Grower's Guide to Successful Produce Marketing*. New World Publishing, Carmichael, CA. 1994.

Lee, Andrew W. *Backyard Market Gardening: The Entrepreneur's Guide to Selling What You Grow*. Good Earth Publications, Shelburne, VT. 1993.

Videos

Kiwis R Us (in the nursery listing) has a 40 minute video on growing hardy kiwifruit. It shows aspects of caring for the vine in all four seasons, propagating, harvesting, and packing the fruit.

Glossary

Acid soil. Soil with a pH less than 7.0. An acid soil is usually low in lime. Also caused by application of high amounts of fertilizer. Most often found in rainy climates.

Achene. A single-celled indehiscent fruit.

Aerobic. Chemical reaction that occurs in the presence of oxygen.

Aggregate Fruit. Fruit developed from a flower with many pistils that ripen simultaneously.

Air drainage. Providing the ability for a cold air mass to move to a lower elevation.

Alkaline soil. Soil with a pH greater than 7.0. Most often found in arid or desert climates. Can be modified by the addition of sulfur.

Allelopathy. The ability of one plant to suppress growth of another by means of excreted toxic compounds.

Anaerobic. Chemical reaction that takes place in the absence of oxygen.

Annual. A plant that grows, bears fruit and dies within a single season.

Anther. Pollen bearing flower part.

Asexual. Reproduction other than by seed. Vegetative propagation; budding, grafting as example.

Axillary Bud. A bud arising at the axil or base of a node or leaf petiole.

Ball and burlap (B&B). Plant is dug, sold and transplanted with soil left around the roots. Burlap is commonly wrapped around the root ball to keep the soil in place. Used most commonly for bushes.

Bare root. Plants sold without their roots in soil. Roots are usually wrapped in wet sphagnum for shipping. Plants are usually dug, shipped, and planted while dormant.

Basal. Arising from the base of the stem or shoot.

Bearing age. Age at which blossoms and fruit are usually borne.

Biennial bearing. Production of a crop only every other year.

Berry. A simple fruit with a fleshy pericarp.

Biennial. A plant having a two year life cycle. The first year growth is typically vegetative. The second year the plant fruits and dies.

Biological control. Pest control using parasites, predators, or naturally occurring chemicals.

Bloom. Translucent waxiness found on the skin of blueberries, grapes, and blackberries.

Budding. Method of propagation in which a single scion bud is grafted to a rootstock piece.

Budding rubber. Small strip of rubber or plastic used to secure grafts.

Bud scale. Modified leaf or scale that serves as protective cover for an unopened bud.

Calcareous soil. A soil with a pH higher than 7 due to free carbonate content.

Callus. Plant cell tissue overgrowth that develops in response to a wound, cut, or graft. In a graft, the callus will eventually form the graft union.

Calyx. The cup between the flower

and its stem. The collective group of the sepals of an individual flower. End of the fruit opposite the stem.

Cambium. Thin layer of cell tissue between the bark and wood of a bush or vine that is the origin of new growth.

Canker. Decayed or diseased area of the branch or cane, usually exhibiting signs of gumming or oozing sap.

Canopy. The "umbrella" or above ground portion of a fruiting vine formed by the branches and leaves.

Carbohydrates. Starch, sugar, or cellulose formed by a plant.

Carpel. The portion of the pistil containing the ovule.

Cation exchange capacity (CEC). A measure of positively charged ions that can be held on the surface of soil particles and replaced by other cations.

Complete fertilizer. A fertilizer containing nitrogen, phosphorous, and potassium. It may also contain minor elements.

Chilling requirement. Number of hours required below 45°F in order for a fruit plant to break dormancy, grow, flower, and fruit properly.

Chlorophyll. Green pigment in the leaf, essential for photosynthesis.

Chlorosis. A lack or loss of chlorophyll in the foliage that appears as yellowing of the leaves. Common symptom of nitrogen or other nutrient deficiency. Can also be caused by herbicide misuse.

Clay. Soil of mineral particles less than 0.002 mm in size. Has high moisture holding capacity.

Clonal Propagation. Asexual form of reproduction resulting in clone offspring.

Clone. Offspring that is genetically identical to its parent.

Cordon. Horizontal extensions of the trunk of a grape or kiwifruit vine.

Cross-pollination. Transfer of pollen from one flower to another.

Cultivar. Plant variety.

Day-neutral. A plant that flowers independent of photoperiod.

Deciduous. Plant that sheds its leaves at the end of each growing season.

Defoliate. To loose leaves.

Degree Days. An accumulation of heat units based on average temperatures above a given threshold.

Differentiate. Act of becoming a fruiting or a vegetative bud.

Division. A form of vegetative propagation where the plant crown is split into multiple smaller plants capable of growing independently.

Domestic variety. Grape varieties having their origin in North America as opposed to Europe.

Dormancy. Period of being dormant.

Dormant. Period during which active growth is suspended, but plant is capable of growth given proper conditions.

Dormant prune. To prune while the plant is dormant or during the dormant season (typically during the winter or very early spring).

Drip line. Boundary of the area to which the shoot tips extend. Rain drips to the ground at this boundary and forms a drip line on the ground.

Drought tolerant. Able to withstand lack of water or moisture stress conditions.

Drupe. A fleshy fruit developed from a single carpel, made up of a hard stone surrounded by flesh and skin.

Dwarf. A plant of smaller size than a seedling would typically produce. Usually achieved by grafting to dwarfing rootstock, manipulative pruning, or plant breeding.

Emitters. The part of a trickle irrigation system through which water is deposited near the plant root system.

Erosion. Excessive washing or blowing away of soil particles.

Everbearing. Producing more than one fruit crop in a season, typically summer and fall.

Exoskeleton. Hard, external support covering of an insect.

Fertilization. The transfer of genetic material between male and female flower parts during pollination.

Field heat. Accumulated heat within a just harvest fruit.

Filament. Stalk that supports the anther. Male flower part.

Floricane. The second year cane of a bramble, capable of bearing fruit.

Flower. Specialized plant reproductive structure.

Flower bud. Bud containing flower parts rather than shoots.

Frass. Excrement of an insect larva.

Freeze damage. Damage to tissue by cold weather.

French-American hybrid. Grape varieties developed by crossing grapes of native American parentage with those of European parentage.

Frost pocket. Low lying area, prone to an accumulation of cold air.

Fruit. Seed bearing part of the plant containing the mature ovary and related reproductive tissue.

Fruiting habit. Manner of fruiting and location of fruit on the plant.

Fruit set. Proper completion of the fertilization process, exhibited by swelling of the ovary.

Fungus. Organism with no chlorophyll, leaves, or flowers that reproduces by spores. Often responsible for fruit diseases. (plural: fungi).

Fungicide. Chemical used to control fungi.

Germinate. Initial growth of a seed or pollen grain.

Girdling. 1. Chewing all the way around a branch or cane by rodents. 2. Accidental constriction of branch growth by a wire or tie.

Graft Union. Area where scion and rootstock tissue are joined and grow together.

Grafting. Uniting scion and rootstock tissue to produce additional plants. see Budding.

Green manure. Vegetative crop that is grown and plowed under to enhance soil.

Ground color. The base color of the fruit skin; normally green, signals harvest maturity by changing or lightening in color.

Growth habit. Natural tendency to grow in a certain shape or form (e.g. upright vs. spreading).

Harden down. Slowing of active growth in preparation to withstand cold temperature.

Hardiness. Degree to which a plant is hardy.

Hardy. Able to withstand severe cold temperatures or to winter over without protection.

Hardpan. Impervious layer of soil.

Hardwood cutting. Method of vegetative propagation in which mature, often dormant wood is rooted.

Heading back. To cut back a branch to a weakly growing lateral branch.

Hedgerow. Row of closely planted trees or bushes, grown for decorative purposes or as protection from wind.

Heel-in. To lay the plant at an angle and bury the roots to hold it temporarily if planting time is delayed.

Herbicide. Weed killer.

Host Plant. A plant where an insect or disease can live.

Hybrid. Genetic cross of two plant species or varieties.

Incompatibility. Inability of scion and rootstock to form a strong graft union. Inability of pollen grain and egg to successfully form a fertilized egg that can mature.

Instar. Insect life stage that occurs between two successive molts.

Integrated Pest Management. Pest and disease control system based on understanding of fruit production as a total, interrelated cycle. Incorporates timing of manmade controls with existing natural controls to be least damaging to the natural environment. Uses selective control rather than broad spectrum controls.

Internode. The shoot area between two nodes.

Juvenile stage. Vegetative growth phase early in a plant's life, during which it does not produce fruit.

King bloom. First (and strongest) bloom to open in a flower cluster.

Larva(e). Immature wingless insect life-form that follows egg hatch.

Lateral branch. Side branch growing off of a primary scaffold branch.

Lateral bud. A bud growing on the side rather than the end of a branch.

Leaching. Washing away of minerals in the soil due to percolating water.

Leader. The most vigorous upward growing branch.

Leeward. Side sheltered from the wind.

Lenticel. Pore in the fruit skin or on the woody stem through which gases are exchanged between air and plant tissue.

Lime. Ground limestone applied to the soil to raise pH.

Loam. Soil composed of varying amounts of sand, silt, and clay.

Low chill. Requiring minimal (generally less than 400 hours) exposure to temperatures below 40°F in order to break dormancy.

Maturity. Stage of development when fruit has achieved its highest eating or storage quality.

Metamorphosis. A marked change in physical form (as in change from a worm to a winged insect).

Microclimate. Localized area of uniform climate.

Moisture deficit. Condition where rainfall has not returned soil moisture to field capacity.

Molt. To periodically cast off an exoskeleton.

Muck soil. Dark, mineralized soil where the original organic matter is no longer recognizable.

Mulch. Organic material placed on the soil to conserve soil moisture, maintain even temperature, or control weeds.

Mycoplasma. A virus like organism that can cause plant diseases.

Necrosis. Death of plant tissue.

Nematode. Microscopic worm-like parasite that feeds on plant roots.

Nitrogen fixing. Ability of bacteria within legume roots to convert atmospheric nitrogen for use by the plant.

Node. Point where a leaf is attached to a shoot.

Nutrients. Elements necessary for plant growth.

Nymph. Immature insect stage differing mostly in size from the adult.

Organic. 1. Containing carbon. 2. Having a natural origin as opposed to a synthetic origin.

Organic matter. Decayed leaves, roots, or wood that are part of the soil.

Ovary. Female flower part. Enlarged base of the pistil that protects the ovules.

Overwinter. Survive cold winter temperatures in a dormant state.

Ovule. Female flower part. The "egg" containing the genetic nucleus.

Own-rooted cutting. A plant, propagated by rooting cuttings as opposed to grafting.

Pathogen. Disease causing organism.

Pericarp. The wall of a ripened ovary.

Perennial. Plant that grows for many years, with new growth each season.

Petal. Showy, colored portion of a flower that serves to attract insects.

Petiole. The leaf stalk.

pH. Logarithmic scale from 0 to 14 that is used to express the acidity or alkalinity of the soil.

Pheromone. Insect hormone.

Photosynthesis. Process of converting water and atmospheric carbon dioxide into carbohydrates, with the help of chlorophyll in the leaves and sunlight.

Pistil. Female reproductive structure within the flower, made up of stigma, style, and ovary.

Pistillate. A flower with female characteristics.

Pollen grain. Male carrier of genetic material.

Pollenizer. Organism that assists the pollination process, usually a bee.

Pollination. Necessary part of the reproductive process where pollen is transferred from the stamen to the pistil.

Prill. Spherical, pelletized fertilizer granule.

Primocane. A first year, vegetative bramble cane.

Prune. Removal of diseased, broken or improperly located branches to maintain or improve plant health.

Pubescent. Soft, hair-like covering on the underside of leaves.

Pupa(e). Dormant, immature life stage of an insect that undergoes complete metamorphosis.

Rootbound. Cramped growth of roots caused by growing in too small a container.

Rootstock. Root material onto which a productive and useful fruit variety is grafted.

Rootsucker. Shoot originating below ground from the roots or rootstock of a plant or vine.

Rosette. Small, tight cluster of leaves growing in a bunch due to poor shoot growth. Can be symptom of boron or zinc deficiency.

Runners. A modified stem that sends out new plants at its tip.

Sand. Coarse textured soil particle.

Scion. Plant tissue grafted to the root to eventually form the fruit bearing portion of the plant or vine.

Seedling. Plant produced by growing from seed rather than by grafting.

Self-fertile. A plant able to pollinate itself and successfully produce fruit.

Self-sterile. A plant requiring cross-pollination by another variety than itself in order to successfully produce fruit.

Self-unfruitful. Inability of a blossom to be pollinated by a blossom of its own variety. Self-sterile.

Sepal. Leaf-like structure surrounding a flower bud and eventually supporting an open flower.

Shatter. To drop from the vine when ripe.

Silt. A soil particle intermediate in size between sand and clay.

Skeletonize. To chew away leaf or bud tissue so that only the veins (or skeleton) remain.

Softwood cutting. Cutting of succulent growth that is propagated by rooting.

Soil Type. Composition of the soil. Sand, loam, or clay.

Soil Texture. Fineness of the particle size of the soil type.

Southwest Injury. Longitudinal splitting of the bark in winter, usually on the southwest side of the plant, caused by uneven expansion of tissue that is heated by sun reflecting off bright snow.

Split application. A full season dose of fertilizer applied in multiple smaller doses over several weeks time.

Spur. Modified, compactly growing branch that primarily bears fruit buds.

Stamen. Male flower part containing anther and filament.

Staminate. Have male flower characteristics.

Stigma. Female flower part that is sticky and receptive to pollen.

Strig. The stem bearing a cluster of currants.

Style. Female flower structure that supports the stigma.

Sucker. An underground shoot arising from the rootstock.

Summer annual. A crop or plant that germinates in summer and dies that same season.

Sunscald. see Southwest Injury.

Table grape. A grape used primarily for eating fresh rather than wine or juice production.

Temperate zone. Area between the Tropic of Cancer and the North Pole that experiences annual change of warm and cold seasons.

Terminal bud. Vegetative bud at the end of a branch.

Thinning. 1. Removal of excess fruit from the plant. 2. Removal of excess vegetative growth to allow sunlight into the interior of the plant.

Tip layer. Propagation technique that produces new plants by rooting the tip of existing canes or vines.

Tipping. Pinching or pruning the growing tip of a shoot.

Tissue culture. Clonal propagation technique where new plants are produced from meristem tissue at the shoot tip.

Topography. Variations in elevation of a parcel of land.

Toxicity. Poisoning of the plant by an overdose of fertilizer or sensitivity to a pesticide.

Training. To spread and position shoots so that they develop a strong, well balanced plant or vine structure.

Triple mix. A fertilizer containing nitrogen, phosphorous, and potassium.

Triploid. Having three times the monoploid number of chromosomes. Fruit varieties that are triploid have sterile pollen.

Variety. Group of closely related plants within the same species. A species subgroup that shares traits common to the species, but has its own individual characteristics. see cultivar.

Vector. An insect or nematode that aids in the transmission of a virus from one plant to another.

Vegetative growth. Shoot growth.

Water logged. Soil with poor drainage, standing water, and insufficient oxygen for root growth.

Water table. The natural level of water in a given geographical area.

Winter annual. Crop that germinates in late winter/early spring and dies at the end of the growing season.

Winnow. To separate leaves, branches, and other debris from harvested fruit.

Index

Index 279

Index 283